AF564693

# FRESHWATER ECOSYSTEM AND XENOBIOTICS

# FRESHWATER ECOSYSTEM AND XENOBIOTICS


***Edited by***

**Dr. Pawan Kumar 'Bharti'**

*Environmental Scientist*

*Centre for Agro-Rural Technologies (CART-India)*

*20, Jamaalpur Maan, Raja Ka Tajpur, Bijnore (UP) - 246 735 (India)*

**Prof. (Dr.) Mona Saad Ali Zaki**

*Professor*

*Department of Hydrobiology*

*National Research Center, Cairo, Egypt*

**&**

**Dr. Avnish Chauhan**

*Assistant Professor*

*Department of Applied Science, College of Engineering*

*Teerthanker Mahaveer University, Bagarpur*

*Moradabad (UP) - 244 001*

**DISCOVERY PUBLISHING HOUSE PVT. LTD.**

**NEW DELHI-110 002**

*Published by:*
**Tilak Wasan**

**DISCOVERY PUBLISHING HOUSE PVT. LTD.**
4383/4B, Ansari Road, Darya Ganj
New Delhi-110 002 (India)
*Phone* : +91-11-23279245, 43596064-65
*Fax* : +91-11-23253475
*E-mail* : discoverypublishinghouse@gmail.com
sales@discoverypublishinggroup.com
parul.wasan@gmail.com
*web* : www.discoverypublishinggroup.com

*First Edition:* **2013**

**ISBN: 978-93-5056-299-4**

**Freshwater Ecosystem and Xenobiotics**



*Printed at:*
Aditi Fine Art Press
Delhi

# Preface

Freshwater ecosystems are important because they recycle nutrients, attenuate floods, purify water, recharge ground water and provide habitats for wildlife. The health of an aquatic ecosystem is degraded when the ecosystem's ability to absorb a stress has been exceeded. A stress on an aquatic ecosystem can be a result of physical, chemical or biological alterations of the environment.

Aquatic systems reflect perturbations in the environment. So, fish and invertebrates can often be used to indicate the health of an aquatic system because Xenobiotics (toxic chemicals) can accumulate in invertebrates from the water and sediment and in fish from water, sediment, and the food chain. The monitoring of these effects is extremely important to regulate and remediate pollution. To test the toxicity, they can apply biomarkers to detect low-level pollution in aquatic systems.

Xenobiotics are the toxic chemicals and their study is known as toxicology. Toxicology is the study of the effects of manufactured chemicals and other anthropogenic and natural materials and activities on aquatic organisms at various levels of organization, from sub-cellular through individual organisms to communities and ecosystems.

The effects of xenobiotics on the entire organism can be considered as neuro-physiological, reproductive and behavioural effects. These effects can often be inter-related. The effects always depend on the concentration of the xenobiotics and the time of exposure. These effects eventually can be either acute or chronic. The harmful effects that xenobiotics have upon individual organisms depend on many different factors. Not only the difference between the freshwater species, but also the form in which pollutants occur, and if the pollutant shows up in lotic or lentic systems. To measure the toxicity there has to get done some toxicity tests.

The effects of pollution on freshwater species are registered in the loss of some species, with maybe some profits for some of them. Because of the complexity of pollution, the effects of take-up in the aquatic life are also depended on the pollutants characteristic feature. If two or more xenobiotics are present together in an effluent they may exert a combined effect to an organism, which can be additive, antagonistic or synergistic.

The present book provides comprehensive coverage of the fundamental principles and current practices and trends in the field of aquatic environment and toxic chemicals. This book updates the subject matter, illustrations and problems to incorporate new concepts and issues related to aquatic ecosystem and environmental toxicology.

Particularly thanks are due to all contributors from Egypt, India; and publisher also for their contribution and assistance.

I hope this book will be of benefit to both present and future colleagues, who teach, study and working in the field of limnology, freshwater ecology, aquatic ecosystem, environmental pollution, fisheries and aquatic toxicology.

**Dr. Pawan Kumar 'Bharti'**

E-mail: *gurupawanbharti@rediffmail.com*

# Contents

# List of Contributors

**Abdel Razek Y. Desouky,** Fac. of Vet. Medicine Kafrelsheikh University, Kafrelsheikh, Egypt.

**Ahmed Hassan Osman,** Department of Pathology, Faculty of Vet. Med, Cairo University, Egypt.

**Ankur Jamwal,** Ph.D. Scholar, Fish Nutrition, Biochemistry and Physiology Division, CIFE, ICAR- Mumbai – 400 061, India.

**Attia A. Abou Zaid,** Animal Health Research Institute Kafrelsheikh, Kafrelsheikh, Egypt.

**A.K. Prusty*,** Scientist, Project Directorate for Farming System Research, Modipuram, Meerut, 250 110 (UP), India.

**A.P. Muralidhar,** Scientist, Fish Nutrition, Biochemistry and Physiology Division, CIFE, ICAR- Mumbai - 400 061, India.

**Barde R.D.,** S.G.B.S. Mahavidyalaya, Purna, Dist. Parbhani, Maharashtra, India.

**Eglal, A. Omar,** Department of Animal and Fish production, Fac. of Agriculture, Alexandria, University, Alexandria, Egypt.

**Faisal Abbas,** Department of Zoology & Environmental science, Gurukula Kangri University, Hardwar (Uttarakhand), India.

**Habeeba Ahmad Kabir,** Limnology Research Laboratory, Department of Zoology, Aligarh Muslim University, Aligarh, India.

**Hossam H. Abbas,** Hydrobiology Department, National Research Center, Cairo, Egypt.

**Isis M Awad,** Dept. of Biochemistry, National Research Centre, Egypt.

**Jagtap A.R.*,** P.G. & Research Dept. of Zoology, Yeshwant Mahavidyalaya, Nanded, (MH), India.

**Kapil Sunar,** Department of Biotechnology and Life Science, Adarsh Institute of Management and Science, (M.P.), India.

**Mahmoud A. El-Seify,** Fac. of Vet. Medicine Kafrelsheikh University, Kafrelsheikh, Egypt.

**Mali R.P.,** P.G. & Research Dept. of Zoology, Yeshwant Mahavidyalaya, Nanded, (MH), India.

**Mansour, T.A.,** Department of Animal and Fish production, Fac. of Agriculture, Alexandria, University, Alexandria, Egypt.

**Medhat Khafagy,** National Cancer Institute, Cairo University, Cairo, Egypt.

**Mona Saad Zaki*,** Department of Aquaculture, Vet. Division National Research Centre, Giza, Egypt.

**Mona S. Zaki*,** Dept. of Hydrobiology, National Research Centre, Egypt.

**Nagwa S. Ata,** Dept. of Microbiology, National Research Centre, Egypt.

**Neha Saxena**, Ph.D. Scholar, Department of Aquaculture, CIFE, ICAR-Mumbai - 400 061, India.

**Noor El Deen A I,** Dept. of Hydrobiology, National Research Centre, Egypt.

**N.K. Chadha,** Principal Scientist, Dept. of Aquaculture, CIFE, ICAR- Mumbai - 400 061, India.

**Olfat Mohamed Fawzi,** Department of Biochemistry, National Research Centre, Giza, Egypt.

**Osman K. Abdel Hady**, Hydrobiology Department, National Research Center, Cairo, Egypt.

**Pawan Kumar 'Bharti',** Centre for Agro-Rural Technologies (CART-India), 20, Jamaalpur Maan, Raja Ka Tajpur, Bijnore (UP) - 246 735, India.

**Rashmi Yadav,** 418, Yadav Sadan, Ramnagar, Near Tahseel, Jwalapur, Haridwar (UK), India.

**Safinaz G.M. Ismail,** Inst. of Oceanography and Fisheries, Alex. Branch, Egypt.

**Safinaz, G.Mohamed,** National Institute of Oceanography and Fisheries, Alexandria Branch, Alexandria, Egypt.

**Saltanat Parveen,** Limnology Research Laboratory, Department of Zoology, Aligarh Muslim University, Aligarh, India.

**Shahinaz, M.H. Hassan,** Animal Research Institute, Alexandria Lab. Alexandria, Egypt.

**Shailendra Sharma,** Department of Biotechnology and Life Science, Adarsh Institute of Management and Science, (M.P.), India.

**Soad Nasr,** Dept. of Parasitology, National Research Centre, Egypt.

**Soliman, M.K,** Department of Poultry and Fish Diseases, Fac. of Veterinary Medicine, Damanhour University, ElBostan, Egypt.

**Srour, T.M.,** Department of Animal and Fish Production, Fac. of Agriculture, Alexandria, University, Alexandria, Egypt.

**Susan O. Mostafa,** Dept. of Biochemistry, National Research Centre, Egypt.

**Suzan Omar Mostafa,** Department of Biochemistry, National Research Centre, Giza, Egypt.

**S.I. Shalaby,** Department of animal Reproductive, National Research Center, Cairo, Egypt.

**Taniya Sengupta*,** Department of Biotechnology and Life Science, Adarsh Institute of Management and Science, (M.P.), India.

**W.D.Saleh**, Dept. of Microbiology , Fac. of Agriculture, Cairo University, Egypt.

**Vikas Phulia,** Ph.D. Scholar, Fish Nutrition, Biochemistry and Physiology Division, CIFE, ICAR- Mumbai - 400 061, India.

Suzan Omar Mostafa, Department of Biochemistry, National Research Centre, Cairo, Egypt.

S.I. Shalaby, Department of Animal Reproduction, National Research Center, Cairo, Egypt.

Tanaya Sengupta, Department of Biotechnology and Life Science, Adesh Institute of Management and Science, M.P., India.

W.D. Saleh, [illegible] of Microbiology, [illegible] of Agriculture, Cairo University, Egypt.

Vikas Bhalla, Ph.D. Scholar, Dept. [illegible] Chemistry and [illegible] Division, [illegible] Mumbai - 400 [illegible], India.

1

# Freshwater Ecosystem and Xenobiotics

**Pawan Kumar 'Bharti'**, ***India***

## INTRODUCTION

Animals and plants can't live without freshwater, because all organisms are made up mostly by water. A tree for example is about 60 per cent water by weight and most animals are about 50-65 per cent water. Also each of us needs huge amounts of water. Only a tiny fraction of the planet's abundant water is available to us as freshwater. About 97.4 per cent by volume is found in the oceans and is too salty for drinking, irrigation, or industry. Most of the remaining 2.6 per cent water is freshwater and locked up in ice layers or glaciers or it's too deep underground to be reached or too salty to be used. Thus, only about 0.014 per cent of the earth's total volume of water is easily available to us as soil moisture, usable groundwater, water vapor, and lakes and streams.

Science of Aquatic ecosystem is the multidisciplinary study of aquatic systems, encompassing both marine and freshwater systems. Scientific investigations within this field often examine the human impact on and interaction with aquatic systems and range in scale from the molecular level of contaminants to the stresses on entire ecosystems. Some of the major fields of study within aquatic sciences include: biogeochemistry; aquatic ecology; oceanography; marine biology; hydrology and the study of lakes, rivers, groundwater and wetlands (limnology).

Freshwater life zones occur where water with a dissolved salt concentration of less than 1 per cent by volume accumulates on or flows through the surfaces of terrestrial biomes. Examples are lentic bodies of freshwater like ponds, lakes, and inland wetlands, and lotic systems like streams and rivers. The major components of a freshwater ecosystem are producers (plants with roots and phytoplankton), consumers (zooplankton, turtles and fish), and decomposers (fungi and bacteria). Their interaction with abiotic components (light penetration, water currents, dissolved nutrients, and suspended solids) forms an aquatic ecosystem. The producers supply $O_2$ to the aquatic systems through photosynthesis. This $O_2$ is then used by the producers, consumers and decomposers through aerobic respiration. The $CO_2$ enters an aquatic system from the atmosphere and through aerobic respiration by producers, consumers, and decomposers and it's removed by photosynthesizing producers. The concentrations of $CO_2$ and dissolved $O_2$ in water vary greatly with depth because of differences in the photosynthesis and aerobic respiration rates.

Broadly, aquatic ecosystems of the entire earth can be divided in to two types of ecosystems:

1. Marine Ecosystem
2. Freshwater Ecosystem

## MARINE ENVIRONMENT

Marine ecosystems cover approximately 71 per cent of the Earth's surface and contain approximately 97 per cent of the planet's water. They generate 32 per cent of the world's net primary production (Alexander, 1999). They are distinguished from freshwater ecosystems by the presence of dissolved compounds, especially salts, in the water. Approximately 85 per cent of the dissolved materials in seawater are sodium and chlorine. Seawater has an average salinity of 35 parts per thousand (ppt) of water. Actual salinity varies among different marine ecosystems (USEPA, 2006). Marine ecosystems can be divided into the following zones: oceanic (the open part of the ocean where animals such as whales, sharks, and tuna live); profundal (bottom or deep water); benthic (bottom substrates); intertidal (the area between high and low tides); estuaries; salt marshes; coral reefs; and hydrothermal vents (where chemosynthetic sulfur bacteria form the food base) (Alexander, 1999). Classes of organisms found in marine ecosystems include brown algae, dinoflagellates, corals, cephalopods, echinoderms, and sharks. Fish caught in marine ecosystems are the biggest source of commercial foods obtained from wild populations. Environmental problems concerning marine ecosystems include unsustainable exploitation of marine resources, marine pollution, climate change, and building on coastal areas (Bharti, 2013).

## FRESHWATER ENVIRONMENT

Upland habitats are cold, clear, rocky, fast flowing rivers in mountainous areas; lowland habitats are warm, slow flowing rivers found in relatively flat lowland areas, with water that is frequently coloured by sediment and organic matter. These classifications overlap with the geological definitions of "upland" and "lowland". An "upland" is generally considered to be a land that is at a higher elevation than the alluvial plain or stream terrace, which are considered to be "lowlands". The term "bottomland" refers to low-lying alluvial land near a river.

Many freshwater fish and invertebrate communities around the world show a pattern of specialisation into upland or lowland river habitats. Classifying rivers and streams as upland or lowland is important in freshwater ecology as the two types of river habitat are very different, and usually support very different populations of fish and invertebrate species.

Freshwater ecosystems cover 0.80 per cent of the Earth's surface and inhabit 0.009 per cent of its total water. They generate nearly 3 per cent of its net primary production. Freshwater ecosystems contain 41 per cent of the world's known fish species (Daily, 1997).

There are three basic types of freshwater ecosystems:

- Lentic: slow-moving water, including pools, ponds, and lakes.
- Lotic: rapidly-moving water, for example streams and rivers.
- Wetlands: areas where the soil is saturated or inundated for at least part of the time (Vaccari, 2005).

## LAKE ECOSYSTEM

Lake ecosystems can be divided into zones:

- Pelagic (open offshore waters);
- Profundal;
- Littoral (nearshore shallow waters); and
- Riparian (the area of land bordering a body of water).

Two important subclasses of lakes are ponds, which typically are small lakes that intergrade with wetlands, and water reservoirs. Many lakes, or bays within them, gradually become enriched by nutrients and fill in with organic sediments, a process called eutrophication. Eutrophication is accelerated by human activity within the water catchment area of the lake (Alexander, 1999).

## RIVER ECOSYSTEM

The major zones in river ecosystems are determined by the river bed's gradient or by the velocity of the current. Faster moving turbulent water typically contains greater concentrations of dissolved oxygen, which supports greater biodiversity than the slow moving water of pools. These distinctions form the basis for the division of rivers into upland and lowland rivers. The food base of streams within riparian forests is mostly derived from the trees, but wider streams and those that lack a canopy derive the majority of their food base from algae. Anadromous fish are also an important source of nutrients. Environmental threats to rivers include loss of water, dams, chemical pollution and introduced species (Alexander, 1999).

## WETLANDS

Wetlands are dominated by vascular plants that have adapted to saturated soil. Wetlands are the most productive natural ecosystems because of the proximity of water and soil. Due to their productivity, wetlands are often converted into dry land with dykes and drains and used for agricultural purposes. Their closeness to lakes and rivers means that they are often developed for human settlement (Alexander, 1999).

## PONDS

These are a specific type of freshwater ecosystems that are largely based on the autotroph algae which provide the base trophic level for all life in the area. The largest predator in a pond ecosystem will normally be a fish and in-between range smaller insects and microorganisms. It may have a scale of organisms from small bacteria to big creatures like water snakes, beetles, water bugs, frogs, tadpoles, and turtles. This is important for the environment.

## ABIOTIC CHARACTERISTICS

An aquatic ecosystem is composed of biotic communities and abiotic environmental factors, which form a self-regulating and self-sustaining unit. Abiotic environmental factors of aquatic ecosystems include temperature, salinity, and flow (Loeb, 1994).

The amount of dissolved oxygen in a water body is frequently the key substance in determining the extent and kinds of organic life in the water body. Fish need dissolved oxygen to survive. Conversely, oxygen is fatal to many kinds of anaerobic bacteria (Manahan, 2005).

The salinity of the water body is also a determining factor in the kinds of species found in the water body. Organisms in marine ecosystems tolerate salinity, while many freshwater organisms are intolerant of salt. Freshwater used for irrigation purposes often absorb levels of salt that are harmful to freshwater organisms. Though some salt can be good for aquatic organisms.

## BIOTIC CHARACTERISTICS

The organisms (also called biota) found in aquatic ecosystems are either autotrophic or heterotrophic. These may be:

- Producer
- Primary Consumer
- Secondary Consumer
- Ultimate Consumer
- Decomposers

## AUTOTROPHIC ORGANISMS

Autotrophic organisms are producers that generate organic compounds from inorganic material. Algae use solar energy to generate biomass from carbon dioxide and are the most important autotrophic organisms in aquatic environments (Manahan, 2005). Chemosynthetic bacteria are found in benthic marine ecosystems. These organisms are able to feed on hydrogen sulfide in water that comes from volcanic vents. Great concentrations of animals that feed on these bacteria are found around volcanic vents. For example, there are giant tube worms (Riftia pachyptila) 1.5m in length and clams (Calyptogena magnifica) 30cm long (Chapman and Reiss, 1998).

## HETEROTROPHIC ORGANISMS

Heterotrophic organisms consume autotrophic organisms and use the organic compounds in their bodies as energy sources and as raw materials to create their own biomass (Manahan, 2005). Euryhaline organisms are salt tolerant and can survive in marine ecosystems, while stenohaline or salt intolerant species can only live in freshwater environments (USEPA, 2006).

## FRESHWATER ECOSYSTEMS AND POLLUTION

The dissolved $O_2$ concentration highly depends also on the amount of pollutants, because most water pollutants cause low oxygen levels in freshwater. These pollutants make it difficult for species to live, and many aquatic organisms, especially fish, die when dissolved oxygen levels fall below 4 or 5 ppm. There are a few natural sources of pollutants present in aquatic ecosystems. But mostly, freshwater ecosystems may become unbalanced by factors due to human activities. Human activities affect the bioavailability of chemicals to organisms, cause temperature fluctuations, and modify rainfall, pH and salinity.

Water plays a key role in diluting pollutants and because of that superiority as a solvent, it also means that water-soluble wastes pollute water easily. For instance, runoff from nearby land provides freshwater life zones with an almost constant input of organic material, inorganic nutrients, and other pollutants. Some 1500 substances have been listed as pollutants in freshwater ecosystems.

## FRESHWATER BIOTA

The types of species that could become affected by water pollution in freshwater ecosystems are:

- Insects
- Crustaceans
- Fish
- Amphibians
- Arthropods
- Aquatic plants
- Fungi
- Bacteria
- Algae
- Viruses, etc.

Insects are usually the most sensitive group, followed by crustaceans, fish and amphibians. Any changes could have harmful or disastrous effects for them. Adverse effects, such as the presence of toxic substances in industrial effluents, may affect many components of the aquatic ecosystem. The extent of which will depend on both biotic and abiotic site-specific characteristics.

## AQUATIC POLLUTANTS

Around 1500 substances have been listed as pollutants in freshwater ecosystems, and each of them occurs in the following types of freshwater pollutants. The major pollutants are: Acids & alkalis; Anions; Domestic sewage and farm manures; Detergents; Gases (e.g. chlorine, ammonia); Oil and oil dispersants; Organic toxic wastes (e.g. formaldehyde, phenols); Heat; Metals (e.g. cadmium, lead, mercury); Food processing wastes (including processes taking place on the farm); Nutrients (especially phosphates, nitrates); Pesticides; Polychlorinated biphenyls; Pathogens; Radionuclides; etc.

The different pollutants put forth different problems to different freshwater ecosystem (Bharti, 2013). Mostly, expressed in the amount of oxygen that is available for fish and other species. This sometimes results in habitat destruction and extinction of local populations.

## LENTIC ECOSYSTEM

A lentic ecosystem is the ecosystem of a lake, pond or swamp. Included in the environment are the biotic interactions (amongst plants, animals and micro-organisms) and the abiotic interactions (physical and chemical). Lentic refers to standing or still water. It is derived from the Latin lentus, which means sluggish. Lentic ecosystems can be compared with lotic ecosystems, which involve flowing terrestrial waters such as rivers and streams. Together, these two fields form the more general study area of freshwater or aquatic ecology.

Lentic systems are diverse, ranging from a small, temporary rainwater pool a few inches deep to Lake Baikal, which has a maximum depth of 1740 m (Brönmark and Hansson, 2005). The general distinction between pools/ ponds and lakes is vague, but Brown (1987) states that ponds and pools have their entire bottom surfaces exposed to light, while lakes do not. In addition, some lakes become seasonally stratified (discussed in more detail below.) Ponds and pools have two regions: the pelagic open water zone, and the benthic zone, which comprises the bottom and shore regions. Since lakes have deep bottom regions not exposed to light, these systems have an additional zone, the profundal. These three areas can have very different abiotic conditions and, hence, host species that are specifically adapted to live there (Brown, 1987).

## PRODUCER

Aquatic plants are more buoyant than their terrestrial counterparts because freshwater has a higher density than air. This makes structural rigidity unimportant in lakes and ponds (except in the aerial stems and leaves). Thus, the leaves and stems of most aquatic plants use less energy to construct and maintain woody tissue, investing that energy into fast growth instead. In order to contend with stresses induced by wind and waves, plants must be both flexible and tough (Reynolds 2004). Light is the most important factor controlling the distribution of submerged aquatic plants. Macrophytes are sources of food, oxygen, and habitat structure in the benthic zone, but cannot penetrate the depths of the euphotic zone and hence are not found there.

Algae, including both phytoplankton and periphyton are the principle photosynthesizers in a aquatic ecosystem like ponds and lakes. Phytoplankton are found drifting in the water column of the pelagic zone. Many species have a higher density than water which should make them sink and end up in the benthos. To combat this, phytoplankton have developed density changing mechanisms, by forming vacuoles and gas vesicles or by changing their shapes to induce drag, slowing their descent. A very sophisticated adaptation utilized by a small number of species is tail-like flagella that can adjust vertical position and allow movement in any direction. Phytoplankton can also maintain their presence in the water column by being circulated in Langmuir rotations (Kalff, 2002). Periphytic algae, on the other hand, are attached to a substrate. In lakes and ponds, they can cover all benthic surfaces. Both types of plankton are important as food sources and as oxygen providers (Brönmark and Hansson, 2005).

## CONSUMER

### Invertebrates

Zooplankton are tiny animals suspended in the water column. Like phytoplankton, these species have developed mechanisms that keep them from sinking to deeper waters, including drag-inducing body forms and the active flicking of appendages such as antennae or spines (Brown, 1987). Remaining in the water column may have its advantages in terms of feeding, but this zone's lack of refugia leaves zooplankton vulnerable to predation. In response, some species, especially Daphnia sp., make daily vertical migrations in the water column by passively sinking to the darker lower depths during the day and actively moving towards the surface during the night.

Also, because conditions in a lentic system can be quite variable across seasons, zooplankton have the ability to switch from laying regular eggs to resting eggs when there is a lack of food, temperatures fall below 2 °C, or if predator abundance is high. These resting eggs have a diapause, or dormancy period that should allow the zooplankton to encounter conditions that are more favorable to survival when they finally hatch (Gliwicz, 2004). The invertebrates that inhabit the benthic zone are numerically dominated by small species and are species rich compared to the zooplankton of the open water. They include Crustaceans (e.g. crabs, crayfish, and shrimp), molluscs (e.g. clams and snails), and numerous types of insects (Brönmark and Hansson, 2005). These organisms are mostly found in the areas of macrophyte growth, where the richest resources, highly oxygenated water, and warmest portion of the ecosystem are found.

The structurally diverse macrophyte beds are important sites for the accumulation of organic matter, and provide an ideal area for colonization. The sediments and plants also offer a great deal of protection from predatory fishes (Kalff, 2002).

Very few invertebrates are able to inhabit the cold, dark, and oxygen poor profundal zone. Those that can are often red in colour due to the presence of large amounts of hemoglobin, which greatly increases the amount of oxygen carried to cells (Brown, 1987). Because the concentration of oxygen within this zone is low, most species construct tunnels or borrows in which they can hide and make the minimum movements necessary to circulate water through, drawing oxygen to them without expending much energy.

### Vertebrate

Fishes have a range of physiological tolerances that are dependent upon which species they belong to. They have different lethal temperatures, dissolved oxygen requirements, and spawning needs that are based on their activity levels and behaviours. Because fishes are highly mobile, they are able to deal with unsuitable abiotic factors in one zone by simply moving to another. A detrital feeder in the profundal zone, for example, that finds the oxygen concentration has dropped too low may feed closer to the benthic zone. A fish might also alter its residence during different parts of its life history: hatching in a sediment nest, then moving to the weedy benthic zone to develop in a protected environment with food resources, and finally into the pelagic zone as an adult.

Other vertebrate taxa inhabit lentic systems as well. These include amphibians (e.g. salamanders and frogs), reptiles (e.g. snakes, turtles, and alligators), and a large number of waterfowl species (Moss, 1998). Most of these vertebrates spend part of their time in terrestrial habitats and thus are not directly affected by abiotic factors in the lake or pond. Many fish species are important as consumers and as prey species to thc larger vertebrates mentioned above.

Fish size, mobility, and sensory capabilities allow them to exploit a broad prey base, covering multiple zonation regions. Like invertebrates, fish feeding habits can be categorized into guilds. In the pelagic zone, herbivores graze on periphyton and macrophytes or pick phytoplankton out of the water column. Carnivores include fishes that feed on zooplankton in the water column (zooplanktivores), insects at the water's surface, on benthic structures, or in the sediment (insectivores), and those that feed on other fish (piscivores).

Fish that consume detritus and gain energy by processing its organic material are called detritivores. Omnivores ingest a wide variety of prey, encompassing floral, faunal, and detrital material. Finally, members of the parasitic guild acquire nutrition from a host species, usually another fish or large vertebrate (Brönmark and Hansson, 2005). Fish taxa are flexible in their feeding roles, varying their diets with environmental conditions and prey availability. Many species also undergo a diet shift as they develop. Therefore, it is likely that any single fish occupies multiple feeding guilds within its lifetime.

## MICROORGANISM

Bacteria are present in all regions of lentic waters. Free-living forms are associated with decomposing organic material, biofilm on the surfaces of rocks and plants, suspended in the water column, and in the sediments of the benthic and profundal zones. Other forms are also associated with the guts of lentic animals as parasites or in commensal relationships. Bacteria play an important role in system metabolism through nutrient recycling (Brönmark and Hansson, 2005).

The vast majority of bacteria in lakes and ponds obtain their energy by decomposing vegetation and animal matter. In the pelagic zone, dead fish and the occasional allochthonous input of litterfall are examples of coarse particulate organic matter (CPOM>1 mm). Bacteria degrade these into fine particulate organic matter (FPOM<1 mm) and then further into usable nutrients. Small organisms such as plankton are also characterized as FPOM. Very low concentrations of nutrients are released during decomposition because the bacteria are utilizing them to build their own biomass. Bacteria, however, are consumed by protozoa, which are in turn consumed by zooplankton, and then further up the trophic levels. Nutrients, including those that contain carbon and phosphorus, are reintroduced into the water column at any number of points along this food chain via excretion or organism death, making them available again for bacteria. This regeneration cycle is known as the microbial loop and is a key component of lentic food webs (Brönmark and Hansson, 2005).

The decomposition of organic materials can continue in the benthic and profundal zones if the matter falls through the water column before being completely digested by the pelagic bacteria. Bacteria are found in the greatest abundance here in sediments, where they are typically 2-1000 times more prevalent than in the water column (Gliwicz, 2004).

## BENTHOS

Benthic invertebrates, due to their high level of species richness, have many methods of prey capture. Filter feeders create currents via siphons or beating cilia, to pull water and its nutritional contents, towards themselves for straining. Grazers use scraping, rasping, and shredding adaptations to feed on periphytic algae and macrophytes. Members of the collector guild browse the sediments, picking out specific particles with raptorial appendages. Deposit feeding invertebrates indiscriminately consume sediment, digesting any organic material it contains. Finally, some invertebrates belong to the predator guild, capturing and consuming living animals (Brönmark and Hansson, 2005). The profundal zone is home to a unique group of filter feeders that use small body movements to draw a current through burrows that they have created in the sediment. This mode of feeding requires the least amount of motion, allowing these species to conserve energy. A small number of invertebrate taxa are predators in the profundal zone. These species are likely from other regions and only come to these depths to feed. The vast majority of invertebrates in this zone are deposit feeders, getting their energy from the surrounding sediments (Jónasson, 2003).

## FOOD WEB

The biota of lentic habitat is linked in complex web of trophic relationships. These organisms can be considered to loosely be associated with specific trophic groups (e.g. primary producers, herbivores, primary carnivores, secondary carnivores, etc.). Scientists have developed several theories in order to understand the mechanisms that control the abundance and diversity within these groups. Very generally, top-down processes dictate that the abundance of prey taxa is dependent upon the actions of consumers from higher trophic levels. Typically, these processes operate only between two trophic levels, with no effect on the others. In some cases, however, aquatic systems experience a trophic cascade; for example, this might occur if primary producers experience less grazing by herbivores because these herbivores are suppressed by carnivores. Bottom-up processes are functioning when the abundance or diversity of members of higher trophic levels is dependent upon the availability or quality of resources from lower levels. Finally, a combined regulating theory, bottom-up: top-down, combines the predicted influences of consumers and resource availability. It predicts that trophic levels close to the lowest trophic levels will be most influenced by bottom-up forces, while top-down effects should be strongest at top levels (Brönmark and Hansson, 2005).

## AQUATIC TOXICITY

The harmful effects that chemicals have upon individual organisms depend on many different factors. Not only the difference between the freshwater species, but also the form in which pollutants occur, and if the pollutant shows up in lotic or lentic systems. To measure the toxicity there has to get done some toxicity tests. Then there is clarity what the dose is of a chemical that a type of specie will die, which will be expressed in a LC50 or LD50.

## XENOBIOTICS AND TOXICITY

The effects of xenobiotics on the whole organism are considered under three main headings, namely neuro-physiological, reproductive and behavioural effects. These effects can often be inter-related: neurological changes can affect behaviour; changes in behaviour can affect reproduction and so on. A compound doesn't always put forth an effect on a target organism or a community. It always depends on the concentration of that compound and the time of exposure to it. These effects eventually can be either acute or chronic. Acute toxicity occurs rapidly, are clearly defined, often fatal and rarely reversible. Chronic effects develop after long exposure to low doses or long after exposure and may ultimately cause death.

A xenobiotics is lethal when it causes death, or sufficient to cause it, by direct action. And it is sub lethal when the poison is below the level that directly causes death. Then it results in the regression of the physiological or behavioural processes of the organism, and its overall fitness is reduced. Only in the case of radioactive pollution, it is likely that it will cause irreversible effects at the ecosystem (www.lenntech.com).

The effects of pollution on freshwater species are registered in the loss of some species, with maybe some profits for some of them. There normally is a reduction in diversity but not necessarily numbers of individual species, and a change in the balance of such processes as predation, competition and materials cycling. Because of the complexity of pollution, the effects of take-up in the aquatic life are also depended on the pollutants characteristic feature. If two or more poisons are present together in an effluent they may exert a combined effect to an organism, which can be additive, antagonistic or synergistic.

An example of an additive interaction is the combined toxicity of zinc and cadmium to fish. Calcium in antagonistic to lead, zinc and aluminium. Copper is more than additive with chlorine, zinc, cadmium and mercury, while its decreases the toxicity of cyanide. The toxicity to the mayfly Baetis rhodani of phenol and ammonia at low concentrations is additive, but at higher concentrations the effect is more than additive.

## TOXICITY TESTING

Aquatic systems reflect perturbations in the environment. So fish and invertebrates can often be used to indicate the health of an aquatic system because chemicals can accumulate in invertebrates from the water and sediment and in fish from water, sediment, and the food chain. The monitoring of these effects is extremely important to regulate and remediate pollution. To test the toxicity, they can apply biomarkers to detect low-level pollution in aquatic systems. First there has to be developed the right biomarkers, and then they can be applied in the Daphnia magna to detect pollution in contaminated groundwater with an aim to develop measures of toxic hazard and risk.

Aquatic toxicology is the study of the effects of manufactured chemicals and other anthropogenic and natural materials and activities on aquatic organisms at various levels of organisation, from sub-cellular through individual organisms to communities and ecosystems (Rand and Petrocelli, 1985). In addition to analytical testing for known pollutants, aquatic, whole effluent toxicity tests have been standardized and are performed routinely as a tool for evaluating the potential harmful effects of effluents discharged into surface waters (USEPA, 2007).

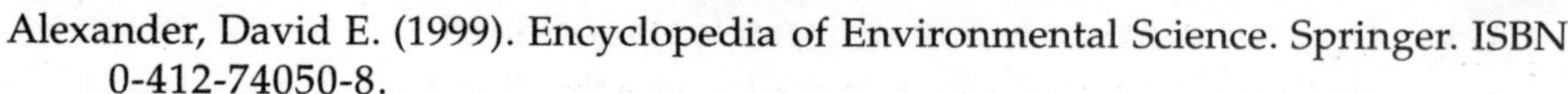

## REFERENCES

Alexander, David E. (1999). Encyclopedia of Environmental Science. Springer. ISBN 0-412-74050-8.

Bharti, P.K. (2013): Aquatic Environment and Toxicology, *Discovery Publishing House, Delhi*, pp. 284.

Brönmark, C. and L. A. Hansson (2005). The Biology of Lakes and Ponds. Oxford University Press, Oxford. p. 285.

Brown, A. L. (1987). Freshwater Ecology. Heinimann Educational Books, London. p. 163.

Browne, R.A. (1981). Lakes as Islands: Bio-geographic Distribution, Turnover Rates, and Species Composition in the Lakes of Central New York. *Journal of Biogeography*, 8 (1): 75–83. doi:10.2307/2844594. JSTOR 2844594.

Chapman, J.L. and Reiss, M.J. (1998). Ecology. Cambridge University Press. ISBN 0-521-58802-2.

Daily, Gretchen C. (1997). Nature's Services. Island Press. ISBN 1-559-63476-6.

Giller, S. and B. Malmqvist (1998). The Biology of Streams and Rivers. Oxford University Press, Oxford. p. 296.

Gliwicz, Z. M. (2004). Zooplankton (In: The Lakes Handbook). P. E. O'Sullivan and C.S. Reynolds. pp. 461-516.

Hillebrand, H. (2004). On the Generality of the Latitudinal Diversity Gradient. *American Naturalist*, 163 (2): 192-211. doi:10.1086/381004. PMID 14970922.

Hillebrand, H.; A. I. Azovsky (2001). Body Size Determines the Strength of the Latitudinal Diversity Gradient. *Ecography*, 24: 251-256. doi:10.1034/j.1600-0587.2001.240302.x.

http://www.lenntech.com/aquatic/toxicity-response.htm#ixzz1gFAF6vpf

http://www.lenntech.com/aquatic/introduction.htm#ixzz1gF18fUrE

http://www.lenntech.com/aquatic/types-pollution.htm#ixzz1gF2nHfNq

http://www.lenntech.com/aquatic/nutrients.htm#ixzz1gFB2Q623

Jónasson, P.M. (2003). Benthic Invertebrates (In: The Lakes Handbook). P.E. O'Sullivan and C.S. Reynolds. pp. 341-416.

Kalff, J. (2002). Limnology. Prentice Hall, Upper Saddle, NJ. p. 592.

Loeb, Stanford L. (1994). Biological Monitoring of Aquatic Systems. CRC Press. ISBN 0-873-71910-7.

Manahan, Stanley E. (2005). Environmental Chemistry. CRC Press. ISBN 1-56670-633-5.

Moss, B. (1998). Ecology of Freshwaters: Man and Medium, Past to Future. Blackwell Science, London. p. 557.

Rand, Gary M. and Petrocelli, Sam R. (1985). Fundamentals of Aquatic Toxicology: Methods and Applications. Washington: Hemisphere Publishing. ISBN 0-89116-382-4.

Sommer, U.; Z. M. Gliwicz, W. Lampert and A. Duncan (1986). The PEG-model of Seasonal Succession of Planktonic Events in Freshwaters. *Archiv für Hydrobiologie,* 106: 433-471.

USEPA (2007). Whole Effluent Toxicity, an Overview of the U.S. Federal Bio-monitoring Publications, U.S. Environmental Protection Agency.

USEPA (2006). Marine Ecosystems. United States Environmental Protection Agency, Retrieved 2006-08-25.

Vaccari, David A. (2005). Environmental Biology for Engineers and Scientists. Wiley-Interscience. ISBN 0-471-74178-7.

Winfield, I. J. (2003). Fish Population Ecology (In: The Lakes Handbook). P.E. Sullivan and C.S. Reynolds. pp. 517-537.

2

# Respiratory Metabolism in Snakeheaded Fish *Channa punctatus* Under Influence of Copper Sulphate from Godavari River, Nanded (Maharashtra), India

**Jagtap A.R.,** *India*; **Mali R.P.,** *India*; **Barde R.D.,** *India*

**ABSTRACT**

The fresh water fish *Channa punctatus* was selected for experimentation. Toxic influence of metals leads to respiratory changes in the animal. The animals were collected and brought to the laboratory to acclimatize them with laboratory conditions. The total oxygen consumption and the rate of oxygen consumption per unit body weight were studied by modified Winkler's Method (Welsh and Smith, 1959). The animals were subjected to sub-lethal concentration on $CuSO_4$ and oxygen consumption was studied at 0, 24, 48, 72 and 96 hr. and the rate of oxygen consumption in cc/gm/hr was calculated. The total oxygen consumption was increased initially later on declined up to 96 hr.

*Keywords: Channa punctatus*, Copper Sulphate, Oxygen Consumption.

## INTRODUCTION

Pollution of water is responsible for a very large number of mortalities and in capacitations in the world. Polluted state of water resources has led to a steady decline in fisheries. Today impact of pollutants in aquatic ecosystem show levels above the expected background. The chemical nature of most pesticides and fertilizers results in their accumulation and retention in nature. This will occur in the plants and animals as well as environment itself. The increasing population density, faster urbanization and industrial growth has increased the complexity of pollution and led to deterioration of environment (Ahmad, et.al, 2000, Radha Krishnan et. al, 1991).

The primary source of pollution is waste waters having toxicants in the form of pesticide residue, heavy metal salts, oils. Modern civilization with its rapidly growing industrial units and an increase in the population, leads to an increase in degradation of the freshwater resources. The water bodies are subjected to a wide variety of human activities such as washing, swimming, bathing and waste disposal, disposal of industrial effluents etc. These pollutants are likely to affect the biological systems in different ways according to their chemical properties. The sum of physiological changes created particular pollutants is likely to be characteristics of these pollutants. Thus by observing the effects of polluted water and a set of physiological parameters. It might be possible to establish specific responses of that pollutant. From this it is easy to identify a pollutant on the basis of its physiological effect pattern (Sastry *et al.*, 1979).

Now a days the development of industries in last few decades leads to increased concentration of copper in the aquatic resources such as river, lake etc. This affects the normal metabolic activities in aquatic organisms including fresh water fishes and depletes natural resources. Heavy metals have become major environmental hazards, although they have great biological significance as micronutrients. The major sources for copper in aquatic resources are industrial discharges and sewages. The study of copper toxicity on aquatic biota have been studied by various workers viz., Eriksen et al., 2001; Wepener et al., 2001; Paquin et al., 2002; Dhanapakiam et al., 2006. Copper sulphate is widely used as an algaecide to control phytoplankton in fish ponds. It is also used as an herbicide, for aquatic weed control (Carbonell and Tarazona, 1993). In industrial level Copper sulphate has applications to prepare Bordeaux mixture which act as a fungicide and for manufacture of other copper compounds.

Pesticides mixed into the aquatic resources through runoff from treated land, washing of the equipments in water resources or through the control of aquatic weed. Some of the copper sulphate containing pesticides which are commonly used when treated wrongly leads to the death of living organisms living it (Oti, 2002; Olusoji et. al., 2003; Ayuba et. al., 2002; Dupree et. al., 1984). In living beings copper is a trace metal which is essential for cellular metabolism. The concentration of copper content is found to increase of this metal in estuarine and marine environments around the world. At equilibrium, there are few free copper ions in natural waters since most copper is associated with inorganic ions or organic substances which is harmful for living beings in water resources (Niencheski et. al., 2000; Morillo et. al., 2005; Velisek et. al., 2009; Mukke and Chinte, 2012; Andhale and Zambare, 2012).

Respiration is the sign of life and index of all biochemical activities taking place in the body. It is an essential physiological activity of all living organisms by which they obtain energy for carrying out all other metabolic activities of the body. All living organisms and plants depend on the oxygen to carry out their metabolic activities. Thus respiration is the energy producing physiological activity in living organisms and plants. The metabolic activity of organisms can be measured in terms of oxygen uptake, heat produced and carbon dioxide liberated. The rate of oxygen consumption in animal exposed to various experimental conditions is a good index of metabolic capacity of an organism to face environmental factors. The metabolic activities of freshwater fishes measured by estimating the oxygen consumption is a complex physiological process. The fishes subjected to various stresses shows variations in the metabolic activities.

The total chemical energy utilized by an organism is known as its energy metabolism. Metabolic rate means that the energy utilized by organism in a unit time (Schmidt-Nielson, 1975). The energy utilized by organisms is firstly by the energy expenditure required to carry out various physiological functions to supply oxygen to the various body tissues. The second category termed the energy utilized for 'cellular maintenance functions' which includes the energy requirements for the synthesis and turnover of cellular constituent's viz. lipids and proteins and for the basic cell processes such as ion transport. The main processes in organisms for consuming the energy are maintenance of the activities of $Na^+$ $K^+$ ATPases and protein synthesis (Jobling, 1993).

Several researchers studied on the effect of pesticides on aquatic animals is an important aspect of chemical contamination of the aquatic environment by pollutants. These polluntats discharged directly into water resources leads hazardous effects on aquatic life (Kaviraj, 1983 a and b). The pollutants have been extensively used which are utilized in agricultural operations. Among the heavy metals, mercury, cadmium, copper, zinc are potent toxicants. These metals are known to have various physiological effects due to bioaccumulation as well as inhibitory effects on growth, food intake, metabolism and general development of animal (Tungare and Sawant, 2000).

Copper Sulphate is a chemical compound used as an herbicide, fungicide, pesticide. It act as pollutant for the organism and are received easily from the industrial discharge. The present research is undertaken to study the toxicity of commonly used copper sulphate on the freshwater crab which is important part and parcel of aquatic ecosystem. To evaluate the toxic impact of copper sulphate on the eco-bio-system the fresh water male crab, *Barytelphusa guerini* is used as a biological indicator for the present work. Hence the present study is designed to determine the effect of this pollutant ($CuSO_4$) on cardiac physiology of the crab.

To overcome from this recent burning problem the present investigation is trying to fulfill the gap on the study of toxicity of commonly used copper sulphate on snakeheaded fish, as a parcel of aquatic ecosystem. To evaluate the toxic impact of copper sulphate on the eco-bio-system, the fresh water fish, *Channa punctatus* is selected for the toxicological studies. The investigation deals with the effect of copper sulphate on respiratory metabolism of the fresh water fish, *Channa punctatus*.

## MATERIALS AND METHODS

The freshwater fish, *Channa punctatus* was collected from the Godavari River, Nanded (Maharashtra) with the help of local fisherman for the present investigation. They were brought to the laboratory and kept in glass aquarium with continuously aerated tap water. The physico-chemical parameters of water were maintained and determined by standard methods (A.P.H.A, A.W.W.A., W.P.C.P., 1992). ($P^H$-7.0–7.2, Dissolved Oxygen-7.6 – 8.0 ppm, Carbondioxide-2.02 mg/L, Salinity 0.186 gms/L, Chlorinity - 0.112 gms/L). The fishes were acclimated at room temperature for 8-10 days prior to experimentation. Fishes were feed with the small pieces of earthworms to avoid the effect of starvation.

The water in the aquarium was replaced daily with fresh tap water. The feeding was stopped one day before the starting of experiment to eliminate the effects of differential diet. Only healthy fishes were selected for the experimentation to avoid the effect of sex and size (Ambore, 1976). The snake headed fish, *Channa punctatus* were subjected to various concentrations to carry out experiment. The experimental set was designed to investigate respiratory metabolism including estimation of total oxygen consumption and rate of oxygen consumption of freshwater fish, *Channa punctatus*.

## STUDY AREA

### Collection Sites Godavari River, Nanded (Maharashtra)

Nanded is one of the historical places in Marathwada region of Maharashtra State located in the southeastern part of Maharashtra, Bordering Andhra Pradhesh. The Nanded city is situated on the north bank of Godavari River. Nanded is a town of great antiquity. It is said that during the Puranic days, Pandavas travelled through Nanded district. Nandas ruled over Nanded through generations. The mention of Nanded is found in the Lilacharitra, a treatise written by Mahimbhatta. It gives the description of the idol of Narasimha in the town. Nanded is widely believed to have originated from "NANDI" the Vahan of Lord Shiva, who performed penance on the banks (TAT) of River Godavari. This "NANDI TAT" became NANDED. Today, Nanded gains prominence from the Sikh Gurudwara which is erected at the place where Shri Guru Govindsinghji Maharaj, the last Sikh Guru, passed away in 1708.

The District of Nanded lies between 18° 15′ to 19° 55′ North latitudes and 77° to 78°25′ East longitudes. It covers area of above 10,332 per Sq. Kms. It is located in the south eastern part of the state. It is bounded on the North by Yavatmal District, on the South West by Latur District, on the North West by Parbhani Distirct of Maharashtra State, on the East and South East by Adilabad and Nizamabad Districts of Andhra Pradesh and on the South by Bidar District of Karnataka State. The area presents undulating topography with uneven hills, plateau, gentle slopes and valley planes.

The Godavari is considered to be one of the big river basins in India. With a length of 1465 km, it is the second longest river in India (only after the Ganges), that runs within the country and also the longest river in South India. It originates near Trimbakashewar in Nashik District of Maharashtra state in India. It is a major waterway in central India, originating from Trimbakashewar to southern Maharashtra and reaches to Nanded. It is known as dakshin Ganga (Southern Ganges). It enters Andhra Pradesh and again touches eastern Maharashtra state border and drain into Bay of Bengal.

**Fig. 2.1: Map Shows the Collection Site of Fishes from Godavari River, Nanded**

Collection Site 1- *Govardhan Ghat*

Collection Site 2- *Nagina Ghat*

Collection Site 3- *Kautha*

Selection and Biology of the test species, *Channa punctatus*

The common name of *Channa punctatus* (Bloch, 1794) is 'Dhoke'. The fishes of channidae family are known as spotted snakehead because of their snake like appearance near the mouth region.

**Fig. 2.2: Channa punctatus**

*Channa punctatus* measures a total length of head of about 3.2 to 3.5 cm and 2.7 cm of standard length (Rahman, 1989). Commonly referred as snake headed fish. Body is elongated, cylindrical differentiated into head, trunk and tail. Head and body covered with cycloid scale. Eyes are located on the anterior of the head. Lower jaw is slightly protruding. Teeth on lower jaw are conical. Scales are large possesses irregular on head region. Supra branchial organ present for breathing Pectoral fin position is slightly above in position than pelvic fin and caudal fin is long and rounded. The color of the body is brown on the back side fading to lighter beneath. Lateral line is slightly curved; Air bladder long. The fish attains the maximum length up to 30 cm (Bhuiyan, 1964). Rahman (1989) reported that the length attains over 240 mm in length. The freshwater fish *Channa punctaus* prefers stagnant and muddy to running waters. It burrows in mud. The *Channa punctaus* is carnivorous. It constructs a nest of floating weeds, moves over ground from pool to pool. It is voracious feeding on small fishes and fries (Bhatti, 1934). The fish has great economic importance for its consuming value as a food. The flesh is good and good commercial value. The raw flesh of the *Channa punctaus* is used to cure ulcers.

## ESTIMATION OF OXYGEN CONSUMPTION

The oxygen consumption in freshwater fish, *Channa punctatus* was measured by using the Standard Winkler's Method (Welsh & Smith, 1960) modified by Saroja, (1959). The control set was designed to compare with the experimental set. The apparatus mainly consist of a black colored respiratory chamber and a reservoir so as to avoid any acceleration in metabolic activity of the animal due to light.

An initial sample of water was collected from respiratory chamber soon after the fish was placed inside the chamber, while after one hour, the final sample collected in BOD bottles. The amount of dissolved oxygen content of the water samples were estimated by the Standard Winkler's Iodometric Method. The difference between initial and final sample gives the oxygen consumed by fish. The total oxygen consumption and rate of oxygen consumption were calculated by considering the wet weight of fish. The experiment was carried out for 24, 48, 72 & 96 hours (experimental set) along with 0 hours (control set). To avoid the possible variations of diurnal rhythms, the experiment was conducted daily at a particular time only such as 11.00 am (Ramamurthi & Sainath Janak, 1973). To maintain the constancy all repeated experiments were carried out at same period of the day. The animals were subjected to sub-lethal concentration 0.9 mg/lit of $CuSO_4$ and the rate of oxygen consumption was estimated at 0, 24, 48, 72, and 96 hr.

## RESULTS

The total oxygen consumption was slightly increased at 48 hr. but later on there was steep decrease up to 96 hr. The results were compared with control set. The oxygen consumption per unit body weight in exposed and control animals showed parallel effects such as gradual increase at 48 while a sharp decrease at 96 hr. The results are represented in the following table and graphically (Table 1.1; Graph 1.1 a & 1.1 b):

**Table 1.1: I - Effect of Copper Sulphate on Total Oxygen Consumption in *Channa punctatus***

| CONTROL | | TREATED | |
|---|---|---|---|
| Exposure Periodin hr. | Oxygen Consumption | Exposure Period in hr. | Oxygen Consumption |
| 0 | 1.7231 ± 0.21 | 0 | 1.7233 ± 0.26 |
| 24 | 1.7233 ± 0.22 | 24 | 1.8218 ± 0.23 |
| 48 | 1.7242 ± 0.38 | 48 | 1.8660 ± 0.48 |
| 72 | 1.7244 ± 0.38 | 72 | 1.0219 ± 0.52 |
| 96 | 1.7231 ± 1.56 | 96 | 1.0122 ± 1.26 |

**(Each value represents mean of six readings ± S.D.)**

**II - Rate of Oxygen Consumption Per unit Body Weight**

| CONTROL | | TREATED | |
|---|---|---|---|
| Exposure Period in hr. | Rate of Oxygen Consumption | Exposure Period in hr. | Rate of Oxygen Consumption |
| 0 | 0.0284 ± 0.38 | 0 | 0.0284 ± 0.37 |
| 24 | 0.0283 ± 0.26 | 24 | 0.0292 ± 0.26 |
| 48 | 0.0281 ± 0.36 | 48 | 0.0298 ± 0.46 |
| 72 | 0.0282 ± 0.38 | 72 | 0.0124 ± 0.48 |
| 96 | 0.0281 ± 0.28 | 96 | 0.0118 ± 0.48 |

**(Each value represents mean of S.D.) six readings ±**

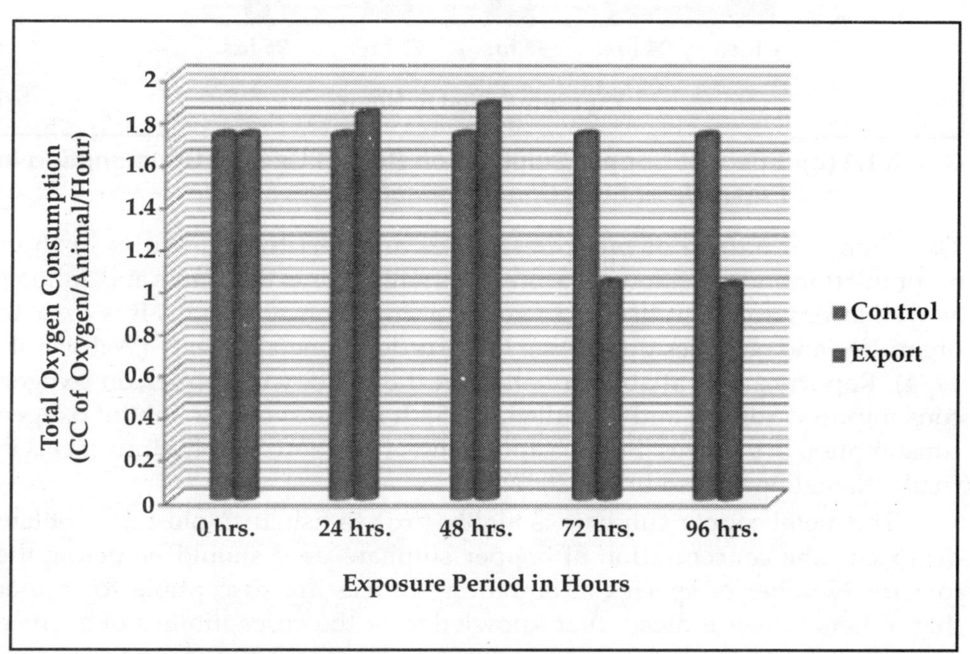


**Graph 1.1 (a): Effect of Copper Sulphate on Total Oxygen Consumption in Fresh Water Fish, *Channa punctatus***

## DISCUSSION

Industrial effluents contributing to aquatic pollution contain a vast array of toxic substances which include heavy metals. Indiscriminate discharges of these wastes alter the quality of water and cause hazards to flora and fauna. Copper is a micronutrient and is present as a metal ion in certain enzymes and plays an important role in the transfer of electrons in electron transport chain.

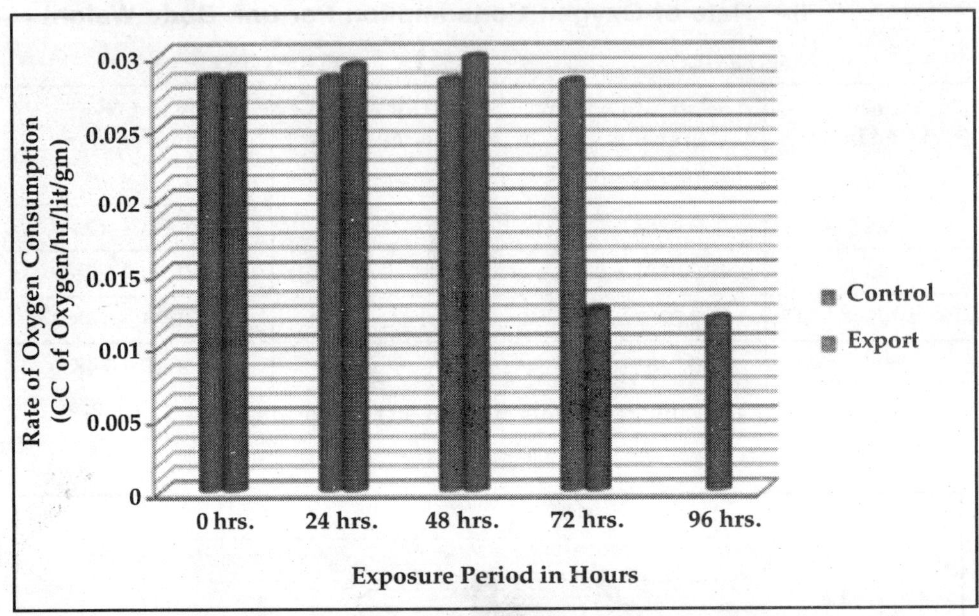


**Graph 1.1 (b): Effect of Copper Sulphate on Rate of Oxygen Consumption in Fresh Water Fish, *Channa punctatus***

The chemical nature of most pesticides and fertilizers results in their accumulation and retention in nature. This will occur in the plants and animals as well as environment itself. However, at high concentrations it is toxic to organisms and occupies third place in the order of metal toxicity (Waldichuk, 1974). Reports are available in fishes on the toxicity of copper on oxygen consumption (Sultana and Umadevi, 1995). It is also shown to inhibit oxygen consumption in bivalves (Sultana and Lomte, 1998) and carbohydrate levels in snails (Ramalingam and Indra, 2002).

The metal copper sulphate is highly toxic to fish, to avoid this problem of toxicity the concentration of copper sulphate used should be below the toxicity. Number of species in aquatic resources are susceptible to copper than others which indicate that knowledge of the susceptibility of a given cultured fish species before using copper sulphate. The experiment reveals that copper accumulate in fish if it is present in above the normal level in the water (Grosell, et. al., 2003).

As concerns to the freshwater fishes are economically important as they are used as a food source of man and it fulfill the human need of food to some extent in our country. But since last decade, their natural environment is being disturbed due to the pollution. The increasing population density, faster urbanization and industrial growth has increased the complexity of pollution and led to deterioration of environment. The study of the impact of pesticides on aquatic animals is an important aspect of chemical contamination of the aquatic environment by some of the heavy metals. Heavy metals discharged into water resources cause hazardous effects on aquatic life (Kaviraj, 1983 a and b). In many pesticides, heavy metals have been extensively used and they are vigorously utilized in agricultural operation now a days. Among the heavy metals, mercury, cadmium, copper, zinc are potent toxicants. These metals are known to have various physiological effects such as enzyme inhibition due to bioaccumulation as well as inhibitory effects on growth, food intake, metabolism and general development of animal (Tungare and Sawant, 2000). Present work deals with the toxicity of copper on respiratory metabolism in fresh water fish, *Channa punctatus*.

The supply of oxygen is essential to provide energy for living processes for carrying out all other metabolic activities. The changes in rate of oxygen consumption are a good index of the metabolic capacity of an organism to face environment stress. It is clear from the present observation that copper sulphate exerts its influence affecting oxygen consumption. The changes observed in the normal respiratory metabolism in freshwater fish may be due to its intimate contact with polluted water containing copper sulphate which decreases the oxygen diffusing capacity of the gills. (Nilkanth et. al., 1993; Khan et. al., 2000; S. S. Jadhav et. al., 2011)

Respiration is an essential physiological activity in all living organisms as oxygen is necessary to provide energy for life processes and for carrying out all other metabolic activities. The change in rate of oxygen consumption is a good index of the metabolic capacity of an organism to face environment stresses. It is evident from the result of present study that the metallic pollutants exert influence by affecting the rate of oxygen consumption. The interpretation of metal induced changes in a respiration is complicated and varies from metal to metal and from species to species and from one experimental condition to other.

Baby et.al, 1986 have observed that mercury, cadmium, and Zinc act as a respiratory depressant in brown mussel, *Perna indica*. The mortality rate of animals in toxic media including copper sulphate is attributed to the asphyxiation which ultimately leads to the failure of respiratory metabolism, which may be caused in the brain through respiratory surface. Some water born metals can bind to gills of fresh water fish and disrupt the ion regulatory and respiratory functions of the gills. Thus the biochemical responses to heavy metals such as Cd, Cu and Zn may vary greatly and Metal effects can be described as alterations of the biochemistry of the different sub cellular organelles (Varengo, 1985).

## CONCLUSION

Thus, from this it was clear that various pollutants affect the fish life directly or indirectly. Freshwaters are highly vulnerable to pollution since they act as immediate sinks for the consequences of human activity always associated with the danger of accidental discharges or criminal negligence (Vutukuru, 2005). Some water born metals can bind to gills of fresh water fish and disrupt the ion regulatory and respiratory functions of the gills. Thus the biochemical responses to heavy metals such as Cd, Cu and Zn may vary greatly. The extent of damage depends on the quality and quantity of the pollutants and the species of fish. The decreased rate of oxygen consumption when exposed to pollutant is due to depletion of dissolved oxygen content of water and increase in BOD. The decrement may be due to the respiratory distress as a consequence of the impairment of oxidative metabolism (Prashanth *et al.*, 2003). The pollutants also cause the damage of mucus membrane of the gill which directly affects the rate of respiration in freshwater fishes.

## REFERENCES

A.V. Andhale and S.P. Zambare (2012): Effect of Nickel Induced Respiratory Alterations in Fresh Water Bivalve, *Lammellidens marginalis*, International Multidisciplinary Research Journal 2(3): 01-03.

A.P.H.A., A.W.W.A. and W.P.C.P. (1992): Standard Methods for Examination of Water 18[th] Edition, American Public Health Associated, Washington.

Ahmad, I., Hamid, T., Fatima, M., Chand, H. S., Jain, S. K., Athar, M., Raisuddin, S. (2000). Induction of Hepatic Antioxidants in Fresh Water Fish (*Channa punctatus* Bloch.) is a Biomarker of Paper Mill Effluent Exposure. Biochem. Biophys. Acta., 1523: 37-48.

Ambore, N.E. (1976): Studies on Some Aspects of Physiology in Fresh Water Crab, Barytelphusa Guerini with Special Reference to Sex and Size. Ph.D. Thesis Submitted to Marathwada University, Aurangabad.

Ayuba, V.O. and P.C. Ofojekwu (2002): Acute Toxicity of the Junsons Weed (Datura Innoxia) to Clarias gariepinus, AJOL, Journal of Aquatic Science.

Baby K.V. and N.R. Menon (1986): Oxygen Uptake in Brown Mussel P. Indica Under Sublethal Stress of Mercury, Cadmium and Zinc. Indian. J. Mar. Sci 15 (2) 127-130.

Bello-Olusoji, O.A., O.T. Adebayo and T.O. Adebola (2003): Toxicity of Copper Sulphate and Aldrin on Rocky Freshwater Prawn, Caridina Africana, In Poisons et Peches Africains Africa Fish and Fisheries, Cotonou, du 10-14 November, 2003.

Bhatti, (1934): Habit and Habitats of the Food Fishes of the Punjab, *Journal of Bombay, National Historical Society, Bombay,* Vol. 37 (3), pp. 657-662.

Bhuiyan, A.L. (1964): Fishes of Daeca. Asiatic Society of Pakistan, Dacca pp. 148.

Bloch, (1794): National Ausland Fische, Vol. 7, pp. 141.

Carbonell, G. and J.V. Tarazona (1993): A Proposed Method to Diagnose Acute Copper Poisoning in Cultured Rainbow Trout (Oncorhynchus mykiss). Sci. Total Environ., 2, 1329-1334.

D'Adamo, R., M. Di Stasio, A. Fabbrocini, F.Petitto, L.Roselli and M.G. Volpe (2008): Migratory Crustaceans as Biomonitors of Metal Pollution in Their Nursery Areas, The Lesina Lagoon (SE Italy) as a Case Study. Environmental Monitoring and Assessment, 143: 15-24.

Dhanapakiam, P., V.R. Ramasamy and J. Mini Joseph (2006): Changes in the Level of Transaminases in Indian Corp, Labeo Rohita Exposed to Sublethal Concentration of Tannery and Distillery Effluent. J. Environ. Biol., 27, 567-570.

Dupree, K. Harray and Hunner V. Jay (1984): Propagating of Aquatic Animals Other than Fish, Prawns, Bullfrogs and Alligators. In the 3rd Report to the Fish Farmers: U.S. Dept. of the Interior Fish & Wildlife Service, pp: 206-293.

Eriksen, R.S., D.J. Mackey, R. Van Dam and B. Nowak (2001): Copper Speciation and Toxicity in Macquarie Harbour, Tasmania an Investigation Using a Copper ion Selective Electrode. Mar. Chem., 74, 99-113.

Grosell, M., C.M. Wood and P.J. Walsh (2003): Copper Homeostasis and Toxicity in the Elasmobranch *Raja erinacea* and the Teleost *Myoxocephalus octodecemspinosus* during Exposure to Elevated Water Borne Copper. Comparative Biochemistry and Physiology, part C: Toxicology. Pharmacology, 135: 179-190.

Jobling M. (1993): Bioenergetics: Feed Intake and Energy Partitioning. In: Rankin JC, Jensen FB (eds.) Fish Ecophysiology. Chapman and Hall, London, pp 1-44.

Kaviraj, A. 1983 (a & b): Effect of Mercury on Behaviour Survival Growth and Reproduction of Fish and on Aquatic Ecosystem. Envior. and Ecol. 1: pp. 4-9.

Khan, A.K., R.T. Patel, and F.I. Shaikh (2000): Effect of Mercuric Chloride on the Gills of the Fresh Water Crab, *Barytelphusa guerini*. Int. Conf. Biol. System pp. 134.

Morillo, J., J. Usero and I. Gracia (2005): Biomonitoring of Trace Metals in a mine Polluted Estuarine System (Spain). Chemosphere, 58: 1421-1430.

Niencheski, L.F. and M.G.Z. Baumgarten (2000): Distribution of Particulate Trace Metal in the Southern Part of the Patos Lagoon estuary. Aquatic Ecosystem Health and Management Society, 3: 515-520.

Niencheski,, L.F.H., B. Baraj, H.L. Windom and A.R.G. Franc (2006): Natural Background Assessment and its Anthropogenic Contamination of Cd, Pb, Cu, Cr, Zn, Al and Fe in the Sediments of the Southern Area of Patos Lagoon. Journal of Coastal Research, 39: 1040-1043.

Nilkanth, G.V. and K.B. Savant (1993): Studies on Accumulation and Histopathology of Gills Agter Exposure to Sublethal Concentration of Hexavalent Chromium and Effect of Oxygen Consumption, *Scylla serrata*. Pollut. Re. 12(1):11-18.

Oti, E.E. (2002): Acute Toxicity of Cassavamill Effluent to the African Catfish Fingerlings, AJOL: Journal of Aquatic Science.

Paquin, P.R., J.W. Gorsuch, S. Apte, G.E. Batley, K.C. Bowles and P.G. Campbell (2002): The Biotic Ligand Model: A Historical Overview. Comp. Biochem. Physiol., 33, 3-35.

Patil, H.S. and D.L. Koti (2000): Accumulation of Cu, Zn and Ni in Gambusia Offinis Exposed to Lethal and Sublethal Concentration. International Conference In Mumbai Feb. 2000.

Prashant, M. S. M David and Riveendra C Kuri (2003): Effect of Cypermethrin on Toxixity and Oxygen Consumption in the Freshwater Fish, *Cirrhinus mrigala*. *J. Ecotoxicology*. *Envron.Monit.*, 13 (4) : 271-277.

R. Ramamurthi and A.T. Sainath Janak (1973): Metabolism of Freshwater Crab, *paratelphusa hydrodromous* (Herbst) in Relation to Size, Sex, Season and Diurnal Rhythm, *Journal of Biomedical and Life Sciences*, Proceedings : Plant Sciences, Vol. 78, No. 06, pp. 275-281.

Radha Krishnan, K., Suresh, A., Urmila, B., Sivarama Krishnan, B. (1991): Effect of Mercury on Lipid Metabolic Profiles in the Organs of *Cyprinus carpio* (Linn.). J. Mendal., 8: 125-135.

Rahman, A.K.A. (1989): Freshwater Fishes of Bangladesh, The Zoological Society of Bangladesh, Department of Zoology, University of Dhaka, Dhaka 1000, pp. 364.

Ramalingam, K. and Indra, D. (2002): Copper Sulphate ($CuSO_4$) Toxicity on Tissue Phosphatases and Carbohydrate Turnover in *Achatina fulcia*. *J. Environ. Biol.,* 23 (2): 181-188.

S.S. Jadhav, V.D. Shinde, D. Sirsat, B.P. Katore, N.E. Ambore (2011): Impact of Mercuric Nitrate on the Oxygen Consumption of Fresh Water Crab. *Barytelphusa guerini, Recent Research in Science and Technology 2011,* 3(8): 50-51.

Saroja, K. (1959): Studies on Oxygen Consumption in Tropical Poikilotherms Oxygen Consumption in Relation to Body Size and Temp. in the Earthworm, *Megascolex mautithi* when kept in Water. Proc. India Acad. Sci. (B): 49, 183-193.

Sastry, K.V., Gupta, P.K. and Malik, P.V. (1979): A Comparative Study of Effect of Acute and Chronic Treatment of $HgCl_2$ on a Teleost Fish, *Channa punctata. Bull. Environ. Contam & Toxicol.,* 22 28-34.

Schmidt-Nielsen K. (1975): Animal Physiology Adaptation and Environment. Cambridge University Press, New York, pp. 699.

Sultana, M. and Lomte V.S. (1998): Metabolic Depression in the Freshwater Bivalve *(Lamellidens marginalis)* Exposed to Mercuric Chloride and Copper Sulphate. *Indian J. Comp. Anim. Physiol.,* 16: 28-30.

Sultana, R. and Uma Devi, V. (1995): Oxygen Consumption in a Cat Fish, *Mystus gulio* (Ham.) Exposed to Heavy Metals. *J. Environ Biol.,* 16 (3): 207-210.

Tungare, S.M. and A.D. Sawant (2000): Physiological Effects of Heavy Metals on Prawns.International Confer. on Probing in Biological System in Mumbai Feb. 2000 pp. 139.

Tungare, S.M. and A.D. Sawant (2000): Physiological Effects of Heavy Metals on Prawns. International Confer. on Probing in Biological System in Mumbai Feb. 2000 pp. 139.

V.K. Mukke and D.N. Chinte (2012): Effect of Sub Lethal Concentration of Mercury and Copper on Oxygen Consumption of Fresh Water Crab, *Barytelphusa guerini,* Recent Research in Science and Technology 2012, 4(5): 15-17.

Varengo, A. (1985): Biochemical Effect of Trace Metals. Mar. Pollu. Bull. 1985 Vol. 16-4 pp. 153-158.

Velisek, J., Z. Svobodova, V. Piackova and E. Sudova (2009): Effects of Acute Exposure to Metribuzin on some Hematological, Biochemical and Histopathological Para Meters of Common Carp, *Cyprinus carpio*. Bulletin of Environmental Contamination and Toxicology, 82: 492-495.

Vutukur, S.S. (2005): Acute Effects of Hexavalent Chromium on Survival, Oxygen Consumption, Hematological Parameters and Some Biochemical Profiles of the Indian Major Carp, *Labeo rohita. Int. J. Environ.. Res. Public Health*. Vol. 2 (3), 456-462.

Waldichuk, M. (1974): Some Biological Concerns in Heavy Metal Pollution. In: *Pollution and physiology of marine organisms*. Academic Press, New York. pp. 1-57.

Welsh J.H. and R.I. Smith (1959): The Laboratory Exerise in Invertebrate Physiology Minneapolis, Burgess, Publication Company.

Wepener, V., J.H.J. van Vuren and H.H. du Preez (2001): Utake and Distribution of a Copper, Iron and Zinc Mixture in Gill, Liver and Plasma of Freshwater Teleosts, Tilapia sparrmanii. Water SA, 27, 99-108.

3

# Biochemical, Clinicophathlogical and Microbial Changes in *Clarias gariepinus* Exposed to Pesticide Malathion

**Mona S. Zaki,** ***Egypt*****; Susan O. Mostafa,** ***Egypt*****; Soad Nasr,** ***Egypt***
**Noor El Deen A I,** ***Egypt*****; Nagwa S. Ata,** ***Egypt*****; Isis M Awad,** ***Egypt***

***ABSTRACT***

The effect of Malathion on Biochemical changes in catfish (Clarias gariepinus) after exposure to Malathion 4.5 mg/l for 98 hours and high temperature 30°. The obtained results showed significant increase in cooper, sodium, cortisol, urea as well as ALT and AST. It was concluded that Malathion produces metabolic stress, cell damage with malfunction of haemopoeitic system. The microbiological examination revealed presence of E-coli, Acromonas Sp, Vibrio. We can conclude that in fish reared on low CHO diet there was hyperglycemia due to increase in insulin and cortisol hormone. (Macrocytic hypochromic anemia was observed in fish in 38H and 98H treatment of Malathion. The hemogram shows increase in MCV and decrease of HB per cent, PCV and RBC's count. There is decrease in IgM. There was petichial haemorage in some part of skin, ascites and erosion due to complications of bacterial infections and there is vertebral column curvature syndrome.

*Key words:* Malathion Biochemical changes, Haematological changes, Microbial changes, IgM.

## INTRODUCTION

The organophosphorous insecticide malathion is used to control pests, which attack many economic crops, (Anderson,1990). In Egypt, the Ministry of Agriculture recommended the use of malathion against pests which attack vegetable crops, ornamental plants, medicinal and aromatic plants and for protection of stored grains. Malathion is also used to control different mosquito and fly species, household insects, animal ectoparasites and human head and body lice (Roberts, 1989). The wide use of malathion is attributed to its relatively low mammalian toxicity. But like DDT and other pesticides that have been found to cause irreparable damage to human and environmental health, malathion may pose a greater risk than the product label would lead one to believe.

Shown to be mutagenic, a possible carcinogen, implicated in vision loss, causing myriad negative health effects in human and animal studies, damaging to nontarget organisms, and containing highly toxic impurities, malathion has a legacy of serious problems (Cabello *et, al.* 2001).

According to a report by the Washington, D.C. based group, *World Resources Institute* (WRI), many pesticides appear to be increasing the incidence of infections, pneumonia, ear infections, and tuberculosis. The three pesticides listed as causing this problem were DDT, malathion, and the pesticide aldicarb (Breener, 1992).

The environmental protection agency (EPA) has been stating for years that they would require more detailed tests for chemical effects upon the immune and nervous system. However, to date, these requirements have not been implemented. Perhaps the biggest unknown risk from malathion is its potential to increase risk of contracting bacteria or viral infections such as encephalitis, this paradoxical situation arises since exposure to malathion can weaken a person's immune system (Giri *et, al.* 2001).

Other effects of malathion for which there is no research, but seriously needed include its ability to cause: Learning disabilities, short term memory damage, increase risk of allergies (Cabello *et, al.* 2001).

Research has accumulated which indicates that nutritional factors can significantly modify the host response to environmental toxicants. Correction of malnutrition can clearly mitigate the effects of many toxicants; however, evidence is mounting that supraphysiologic doses of nutrients (nutritional supplements) can further lessen toxicity. The possibility that nutrition could be implemented as a secondary prevention strategy on a public health scale raises important ethical and policy issues. Nutritional strategies can lessen, but not abolish, toxic effects; moreover, they require dissemination and compliance, which are unlikely to be fully effective (Hu *et, al.*1995).

Malathion accumulate in fish mainly in the visceral fat, where as the gills and muscles retain a lower amount subsequently, with an increase in fat consumption. For example, at the time of migration and hibernation, pesticides may enter the more sensitive organs and induce poisoning (Bruno and Stamps, 1987), (Barton and Iwama, 1991), (Bennett and Wolke, 1987) (Pickering and Duston, 1983). It has been presumed for decades that environmental pollutants especially pesticides can affect one or more of the immunological functions in the fish. It is almost common knowledge cat fish frequently then become more susceptible to various diseases given the extreme variety of pesticides used (Vergut and Studnicka, 1994), (Areechon and Plumb, 2000). Andreson, 1990 suggested a decreased disease resistance in fish exposed to various pesticides. There is so little is known about how pesticides affect the immune systems of fishes (Cabello *et, al.* 2001).

About: "Malathion":

Structure -

$CH_3O$ P - S – CH – $CO_2$– $C_2H_5$

$CH_3O$ $CH_2$ – $CO_2$ – $C_2H_5$

The chemical name is : S-1 2 bis (ethoxycaronyl) ethyl 0,0-dimethyl-phoshordithioate (IUPAC).

Trade names: Malathion, Cythion, Fyfanon and Calmathion (Royal Society of Chemistry, 1993).

The present study discusses the effect of low CHO diet on cat fish, which also exposed to Malathion (4.5 mg/l) as pesticide for 98H. Some microbiological and clincopathological parameters were interpreted.

## MATERIAL AND METHODS

### Experimental Condition

Catfish (50-60 gram/each) were obtained from River Nile Rashid branch, El-Kanater El-Khyria. Fish were acclimatized to laboratory conditions one week before infection in 115 L. glass aquaria with a flow system and dechlorinated tap water. Two groups of fishes were used.

The 1st group (15 fishes) was maintained kept on low carbohydrate diet but free from any toxicants, and kept on a balanced diet that meets its requirements from nutrients as described by (Robberts, 1989).

The 2nd group (15 fishes) were kept under the low CHO diet but were exposed to Malathion (4.5 mg/l) during 98 H hours (Areechon and plumb 1990). The diet ingredient is shown in (Table 3.1).

Copper, dissolved oxygen, temperature, pH, ammonia and nitrites were analyzed daily, while water alkalinity, hardness carbon dioxide, sodium, potassium and chlorides were analyzed before and after each water renewal using commercial kits of Bohringer, France, as shown in (Table 3.2). Malathion was obtained from National Institute of Pesticide, Dokki, Cairo. The 98h LC50 of Malathion for channel cat fish determined in separate study was 9.65 mg (Areechon and Plumb, 1990).

**Table (3.1) A: Ingredients and Proximate Chemical Composition of Diets Used in Experiments**

| Ingredients | Diets I (Control) | Diets 2 |
|---|---|---|
| Fish meal | 30 | 30 |
| Meat meal | 8 | 10 |
| Bone meal | 1 | 3 |
| Skimmed milk | 3 | 4 |
| Soybean | 5 | 7 |
| Wheat bran | 20 | 20 |
| Wheat flour | 20 | 5 |
| Yeast | 10 | 15 |
| God liver oil | 1 | 4 |
| Minenral & Vitamin* premix | 2 | 2 |

**Table (3.1) B: Proximate Chemical Composition**

| | | |
|---|---|---|
| Crude protein (CP) % | 35.87 | 38.89 |
| Metabolizable energy/kg | 2297.21 | 2415.4 |
| Ether extract (EE) % | 2.78 | 2.86 |
| Grude fiber (CF) % | 3.91 | 4.27 |
| Ash % | 8.735 | 10.25 |
| Calcium (Ca) % | 3.094 | 3.99 |
| Phosphorous (Ph) % | 2.069 | 2.53 |
| Lysine % | 2.105 | 2.29 |
| Methionine % | 0.562 | 0.613 |

* **Mineral and vitamin premix per/kg of pelleted food**

Vit.A, 8000 U; Vit. D, 9001, Vit. E 21 U, vit. K, 4 mg; Vit. B2 3.6 mg; niacin 20 mg choline chloride, 160 mg; pantothenic acid, 7 mg; pyridoxine, 0.2 mg; Vit. B 12, 5 ug; Mn, 70 mg, Zn 60 mg, Fe 20 mg, Cu 2 mg, I 1 mg, Co 0.2 mg.

## Blood Sampling

Blood samples were taken after 24h, 38h, 98h. The fish were anaesthetized by 1/1000 aqueous solution of Ms 222 and bled from the caudal vein. Blood samples were taken with heparinized microhaematocrit tube. The tubes were centrifuged at 3000 r.p.m. for 10 min. Serum was separated and stored at 20°C until used.

**Table 3.2: Water Quality Characteristics in Tanks. (Initial Conditions Values are Mean ± SE)**

| | |
|---|---|
| pH | 5.40 ± 0.1 |
| Temperature °C | 18°C ± 0.904 |
| Nitrates mg/l | 0.020 ± 0.04 |
| Un ionized ammonia (mg/l) | 0.0014 ± 0.004 |
| Carbonic dioxide (mg/l) | 4.1 ± 0.5 |
| Alkalinity (mg/l) | 31.8 ± 2.8 |
| Permanganate oxidabole matter (mg/l) | 3.54 ± 0.53 |
| Hardness (mg/l) | 34.6 ± 0.1 |
| Chlorides (mg) | 8.4 ± 0.6 |
| Potassium (mg/l) | 0.12 ± 0.007 |
| Sodium (mg/l) | 5.68 ± 0.01 |

Tested kits supplied form biomerieux (France) were used for determination of the activity of serum glutamic pyruvic transaminase (ALT) and glutamic oxaloacetic transaminase (AST) as described by (Reitman and Frankel, 1957).Serum glucose was assessed according to (Trinder, 1969). Haematocrit value was carried out by using micro-haematocrite capillary tubes centrifuged at 1200 r.p.m. for 5 min. mean corpuscular volume (MCV). Reticulocytis count according to (Drabkin, 1946). Serum cortisol level was determined using radioimmunoassay technique according to the method of (Pickering and Pottinger, 1983). Serum iron were determined using atomic absorption according to (Barham *et al.*, 1972). Values of sodium and potassium in serum were determined by flame photometer according to method described by (Silversmit, 1965). Serum creatinine was measured according to (Bartels *et al.*, 1972). Enzymatic determination of urea was done according to (Patton and Crouch, 1988). Insulin was estimated by radioimmunoassay method using oat. A Cout insulin Kits obtained from Diagnostic Corporation (DPC) west 96th street, Los Ageles U.S.A. (Pickering and Duston, 1983).

## Bacterial Isolation

Aseptic swabs from the skingills, base of fins and blood of tested fish were cultivated on blood agar, MacConky agar, Nutrient agar, TSA, Nutrient broth, and peptone water (Oxoid and Difco).

Inoculated media were incubated at 37°C for 48 hours. Bacterial isolates were identified by examination of the colony morphology and biochemical characteristic described by (Nagae *et al.*, 1993). Bacteria were detected by accounting colonies using surface spread plate technique according to quantitative method described by (Bruno & Stamps 1987).

**Measurement of serum immunoglobulin M (IgM)**

***IgM determination***

The serum IgM was measured according to (Fuda *et al.* 1991).

**Preparation of antisera**

Antisera of cat fish was prepared by immunizing rabbits as described by (Hara, 1976).

**(Cat fish) IgM antibody**

The procedure for labeling antibody of fragment with enzyme was performed according to the method of (Nagae *et al.*, 1993).

**Elisa assay procedure**

Assays were carried out in 96 well polystyrene ELISA microtiter plates (Titertex, Horsham, PA).

**Antibody coating**

The micortiter plates were coated with rabbit Anticat fish IgM which was fractionated by DE-52 at a concentration of 40 ug/ml in 0.01 M PBS. A volume of 150 µl was dispensed into each well and incubated for 4 hr at 4°.

**Blocking**

After one washing with 200 µl of 0.01 M PBS + 0.1 per cent Tween 20 per well and two washings with 200 µl of PBS + 1 per cent thimerosol was added to each well and included for 2hr at room temperature.

**Incubation of samples and standards**

After washing as described above 100 µl of sample and standard were placed into the appropriate wells in the microtiterplates and incubated at room temperature.

**Incubation with peroxidase labeled antibody**

After washings as described above, each well received 150 µl of peroxidase labeled antibody 1:1600 in PBS-BSA, followed by incubation 12 hr at room temperature.

**Enzymatic colour reaction**

The plates were washed as described above and 150 µl 0-phenylenediamine (3 mg/ml 0.1 M citric acid-phosphate buffer (pH 5.0) containing 0.02 per cent H2O2 were added to each well for enzymatic color reaction. The reaction was stopped after 30 min at room temperature by adding 100 µl of 4NHCI. The absorbance at 492 nm was 2250 (Richmond, CA).

Double antibody sandwish Elisa according to the method of (Matsubara *et al.* 1985) for determination of IgM described. After one washing with 200 µl of 0.01 M PBS + 0.1 per cent Tween 20 per well.

## STATISTICAL ANALYSIS

The obtained data were statistically subjected to the students't-test (Gad and Weil, 1983).

## RESULTS

Experimental exposure to Malathion (4.5 mg/l) revealed that there was a significant increase in the level of serum creatinine ALT, AST, urea, potassium and insulin, were increased in the 24 hours and 38 h and 98 h non-significantly. There was a significantly increase of cortisol, glucose, copper during all times of experiments. Concerning iron there was a significant decrease of iron level (Table 3.3).

Hematological results in the present work revealed anemia indicated by a significant reduction in RBCs count, HB concentration PCV per cent, MCV and increase in reticulocyte count especially in 38 h, (Table 3.4).

Concerning microbiological examination, the results showed that the isolated microorganisms from internal organs (liver and kidneys), gills, and fins were Aeromonas Vibrio Sp and E. coli. (Table 3.5). With regard to IgM, a significant decrease was observed by exposing cat fish to the pesticide. (Table 3.3).

There was petichial haemorhage in some part of skin and erosion due to complications of bacterial infection and vertebral column curvature syndrome.

## DISCUSSION

It was evident that decrease in the level of CHO with Malathion 4.5 mg/l in fish diet caused a significant increase in glucose level during the experimental period, also insulin level was slightly increased. It is well known that any stress factor such as handling, incubation, anaestesia etc. has been shown to cause hyperglycemia followed by hyperinsulinemia (Yallow and Bawman, 1983).

Low CHO diet with Malathion causes a significant increase of cortisol level which may be due to the activation of hypothalamus, pituitary internal axis. Induced a significant increase in cortisol level, these results coincide with those observed by (Barton and Iwama, 1991), who observed that serum cortisol increased linearly in salminid fish fed on 5 per cent CHO diet.

One consistent effect of cortisol was the reduction in the hemoglobin, PCV per cent and iron levels, as a result of decrease in appetite in the rainbow trout, or more likely to be the direct result of a catabolic effect, or cortisol of the fish tissues.

This present study revealed that, sodium and potassium concentrations were significantly increased. This retention may be attributable to kidney impairment where the kidney is the normal pass way for Na and K this may explain the main cause for elevation of the serum creatinine and urea in the treated groups.

Marked elevation was noticed in the activity of Asparate Amino Transferase (AST) and Alanine Amino Transferase (ALT). The liver is the primary organ of detoxification as well as a major site for detoxification reaction. Therefore, significant increase in the liver enzymes suggests explanation Malathion affected the liver cells or may be attributed to secondary bacterial infection.

**Table 3.3: Effect of Low CHO Diet on some Biochemical and Hormonal Parameters in Cat Fish Exposed to Malathion (4.5 mg/l)**

| Parameters | Control | 24 Hours | 38 Hours | 98 Hours |
|---|---|---|---|---|
| AST (U/I) | 77.0 ±0.53 | 80.7 ±0.60 | 83 ± 0.51 | 100±0.85** |
| ALT (U/I) | 15.3 ± 0.33 | 17.4 ±0.24 | 18.9 ±0.83 | 23.0±0.83* |
| Urea (mg/dl) | 4.3 ± 0.51 | 4.9 ± 0.76 | 4.9 ± 0.83 | 5.1±0.83* |
| Creatinine (mg/dl) | 0.67 ± 0.62 | 0.69 ± 0.72 | 0.90 ± 0.51* | 1.3±0.53* |
| Na (Meq/L) | 117 ± 1.3 | 127 ± 2.3* | 128 ± 4.5* | 142±5.4* |
| K (Meq/L) | 2.58 ± 0.12 | 3.65 ± 0.13 | 1.3 ± 0.8 | 5.00±0.80* |
| Cortisol (ng/dl) | 0.85 ± 0.23 | 0.88 ± 0.54 | 0.91 ± 0.39 | 1.5±0.45** |
| Glucose (mg/dl) | 52 ± 0.59 | 54.1 ± 0.50 | 68 ± 0.59 | 85±0.23** |
| Insulin (ng) | 7.6 ± 0.3 | 8.5 ± 0.4 | 11.7 ± 2.4 | 12.8±0.63** |
| Copper (mg %) | 181 ± 4.0 | 187 ± 2.3 | 168 ±1.3 | 148±0.45** |
| Iron (mg %) | 190 ± 1.26 | 176 ± 5.2 | 168 ± 3.3 | 151±4.3* |
| IgM Ng/MI | 0.85 ± 1.32 | 0.78 ± 1.20 | 0.63 ± 0.60 | 0.65±0.44* |

* $P < 0.01$

** $P < 0.05$

**Table 3.4: Effect of Low CHO Diet on Hematological Parameters in Fish Exposed to Malathion (4.5 mg/l) for 98 H**

| Time Groups | Parameters | | | | |
|---|---|---|---|---|---|
| | RBCs (106/mm³) | HB gm/dl | P.V.C.(%) | MCV Fl. | Reticulocyte % |
| Control | 3.2±0.34 | 7.7 ±033 | 8.7 ± 0.33 | 31± 0.51 | 1.21±0.2 |
| 24 hours | 3.3±0.34 | 8.6 ± 0.10 | 8.6 ± 0.11 | 37 ±0.41 | 1.92±0.3 |
| 38 hours | 3.9±0.63 | 8.7±0.17* | 7.87±0.11 | 38±0.73 | 2.3±0.4 |
| 98 hours | 3.7±0.62 | 8.3±0.28* | 6.3±0.37* | 39±0.83* | 2.4±0.4* |

* $P < 0.01$

**Table 3.5: Bacterial Isolates Recovered from Fish Exposed to Malathion (4.5 mg/l)**

| Bacterial Strain | External Surface | Kidneys | Liver | Gills |
|---|---|---|---|---|
| E. Coli | 2 X 10 | 3 X 10 | 2 X 10 | 1 X 10 |
| Aeromons Sp. | 3 X 10 | 6 X 10 | 3 X 10 | 2 X 10 |
| Vibrio/Sp. | 2 X 10 | 1 X 10 | 2 X 10 | 2 X 10 |

The present results agree with (Bruno & Stamps 1987) they observed that aquatic pollution with heavy metals cause immunosuppression and contribute to outbreaks of infections, and bacterial diseases in fish. We can say that Malathion can affect fish after 24h and there are some complications with this pesticide.

IgM level was determined to find out information about fish immune system, which was previously investigated in different species by many authors as (Matsubara *et al.*, 1985) and (Fuda *et al.*, 1991).

There is a significant decrease in IgM level in fish with Malathion, if compared with control groups. Anderson *et al.*, 1982 found a relation between corisol and IgM as when cortisol increased IgM decrease.

IgM is one of the most important factors in the immune factor to neutralize bacteria and render them more susceptible to phagocytosis (Mona S. Zaki *et al.*, 2003). It is well known that in mammals immunoglobulin production is closely related to endocrine status for example thyroid hormone enhances the production of immunoglobulin (Chen, 1980) cortisol intensity suppress immunoglobulins production (Pickering & Pottinger, 1983).

In conclusions Malathion will reduce humoral immune response as detected by decrease of IgM level and cortisol elevation.

## REFERENCES


1. Areechon and Plumb (2000). Sublethal Effects of Malathion on Channel Catfish, Ictalurus Punctatus. Bull. Environ. Contain. Toxicol. 44: 435-442.
2. Areechon, N. and Plumb, J.A. (1990) Sublethal Effects of Malathion on Channel Catfish, Ictalurus punctatus, Department of Fisheries and Allied Aquacultures and Alabama Agriculture Experiment station, Auburn University, Alabama 36849, USA.
3. Anderson, D.P. (1990). Immunological Indicators Effects of Environmental Stress on Immune Protection and Decrease Outbreaks. Am. Fish Soc. Symp.8, 38-43.
4. Anderson, D.P.; Roberson, B.S. and Dixon, O.W. (1982). Immunosuppression Induced by Corticosteroid or an Alkylating Agent in Rainbow Trout. Dev. Comp. Immol. Suppl. 2, 197-200.
5. Barham, W.T.; Smit, G.J. and Schoobee, H.J.J. (1972). Determination of Iron in Serum Fish Boil. 17, 275.

6. Bartels,H.; Bohmer, M.and Heierli, C.(1972). Clinical Chemistry Acta, 37, 139.
7. Barton, B.A. and Iwama, G.K. (1991). Physiological Changes in Fish from Stress in Aquaculture with Emphasis on the Response and Effects of Corticosteroids. Annual Review of Fish Disease, 1, 43-49.
8. Bennett, R.O. and Wolke, R.F. (1987a). The Effect of Sublethal Endrin Exposure on Rainbow Trout, Salmo Garidneri Richardson, I. Evaluation of Serum Cortisol Concentrations and Immune Responsiveness. J. Fish Biol. 31: 375-379.
9. Brenner, L.(1992) Journal of Pesticide Reform, Volume 12, Number 4, Winter 1992.

   Northwest Coalition for Alternatives to Pesticides, Eugene, OR
10. Bruno, D. and Stamps, D.J. (1987). Fry Journal of Fish Diseases, 10, 513. Bull. NRC, Egypt. Vol. 28, No. 2, pp. 245-257.
11. Cabello, G. et,al. (2001).A Rat Mammary Tumor Model Induced by the Organophosphorus Pesticides Parathion and Malathion Possibly Through Acetylcholinesterase Inhibition. Environ. Health Perespect, 101: 471-479.
12. Chen, Y. (1980). Effect of Thyroxine on the Immune Response of Mice in vivo and vitro. Immunol. Org. 9, 269.
13. Drabkin, D.J. (1946). Biol. Chem. 164, 703.
14. Fuda, H.; Sayano, K. Yamaji, F. and Haraj (1991). Serum Immunoglobulin N. (IgM) during Early Development of masu salmon on corhyrchus masu. Comp. Biochem. Physiol. 99A, 637.
15. Gad, S.C. and Weil, C.S. (1983). Statistics for Toxicologists. In Hayes, A.W. 2nd Ed. Principles and Methods of Toxicology. Raven Press, New York, pp. 273-320.
16. Giri, Set, al. (2002). Genotoxic Effects of Malathion: An Organophosphorus Insecticide, Using Three Mammalian Bioassays in vivo, 514: 223-231. Journal of Pesticide Reform, 23 (4).
17. Hara, A. (1976). Iron Binding Activity of Female Specific Serum Proteins Rainbow Trout Salmo and Chum Salman Ocorchynchus. J. of Biochem. And hysiology, 427, 549.
18. Hermre, Torrissen, O. and Waagba, R. (1999). Comparative Biochemistry and Physiology, (In press).
19. Hu, H., Kotha,S. and Brennan, T (1995) The Role of Nutrition in Mitigating Environmental Insults: Policy and Ethical Issues Environmental Health Perspectives Volume 103, Supplement 6, September 1995.
20. Joseph, A. and Roger, W.G. (1979). Clinical Chemistry Principles and Procedures 4th Boston, pp. 168-197.
21. Matsubara, A.; Mihara, S. and Kusuda, R. (1985). Quantitation of Yellow Tail Immunoglobulin by Enzyme-linked Immunosorbent Assay (Elisa). Bull. Japan Sac. Sci. Fish, 51, 921-927.
22. Mona, S. Zaki, Osfor, M.H. Bayomi, F.S. and Abouel-Gheit,.E.N. (2003). Impact of Low Dietary Carbohydrate Diets on some Nutritional and Clinicopathological Parameters of Tiliptia Nilotica Infected with Saprolegnia Parastitia and Exposed to Copper Sulphate Applied Bull. NRC, Egypt, 28.No(2); 245-257.

23. Nagae, M.; Fuda, H.; Hara, A.; Hamuchi, A. (1993). Changes in Serum Immunoglobulin M. (IgM) Concentrations during Early Development of Churm Salmon as Determined by Sensitive ELISA. Comp. Biochem. Physiology, 602-613.

24. Patton, C.J. and Crouch, S.R. (1988). Analytical chemistry, 49, 64. c.f. Bio-Merieus Laboratory Reagents and Products France Kit.

25. Pickering, A.D. and Duston, J. (1983). Analysis of Cortisol Hormone J. Fish Biol. 23, 163-172.

26. Ckering A.D. and Puttinger, P. (1983).Analysis of hormone Gen. Com. Endocrinal, 49, 232-239.

27. Reitman, S. and Frankel, S. (1957). Analysis of Liver Function Am. J. Clin. Pathol. 28, 56-64.

28. Roberts, R.J. (1989). Nutritional Pathology of Teleosts. In Fish Pathology. (Ed. By R.J. Roberts) pp. 337-362 Bailiere Tindail London.

29. Silversmit, A.B. (1965). For Determination of Serum Sodium and Potassium Med. 45, 175-177.

30. Trinder, P. (1969). For Determination of Serum Glucose Ann. Clin. Biochem. 6, 24-26.

31. Vergut, C. and Studnicka, M. (1994). Effects of Lindane Exposure on Rainbow Trout Immunity III. Effect on Non-specific Immunity and B Lymphocyte Functions Ecotoxicol. Environ. Safty 27: 324-328.

32. Yalow, R. and Bawman, W.A. (1983). Plalsma Insulin in Health and Disease. In "Diabetes Mellius. Theory and Practicle pp. 119-150 (Eds.) Ellelnberg M. and H. Riking Exerpta Medica, New York.

4

# Metals Estimation in Phytoplankton at Nainital Lake, India

**Rashmi Yadav**, ***India***

***ABSTRACT***

Phytoplankton is the primary producer of any aquatic ecosystem, which is an indicator of water quality and biological productivity. Plankton may vary at place to place and season to season depends the changing water quality parameters and others ecological factors.

The problems of the portable water treatment and its safety are directly related to the degree of eutrophication of the lake. Surface water with blue green algal bloom may be unfit for human consumption as they may contain toxins released form algae. These toxins are lethal to cattle and have been shown to produce human gastrointestinal problems.

The samples were analyzed for trace metals in the laboratory by Atomic Absorption Spectrophotometer (AAS) using air-acetylene flame. Quantification of metals was based upon calibration curves of standard solutions of respective metals. These calibration curves were determined several times during the period of analysis.

*Keywords:* Phytoplankton, aquatic ecosystem, Lake Nainital, heavy metals.

## INTRODUCTION

Nainital town is generously endowed with transcendental beauty, which is unveiled in its sylvan landscape with lofty snow-capped peaks, green valleys. The town is divided into two segments, Tallital and Mallital. This region has several lakes of large size and scenic beauty (Nevill, 1922). Lakes are naturally formed hollows and depressions on the surface of the earth which get filled with water. The water quality of lake Nainital influenced not only by the complex nature of the catchment geology but also by the anthrópogenic activities.

The resident population of the town is considerably low (approx. 50,000 residents). The lake is a summer resort in North India and attracts nearly 2, 00,000 tourist annually. Tourism is the major industry of this region there is no agricultural or industrial activity within the lake catchments area; however, a significant increase in population occurs during summer and autumn due to more influx of tourists. Apart from the tourism related activities the need for drinking water supply has put the lake to undue strees that is reflected in the deteriorationg water quality. In the town, the population is mainly concentrated around the lake on hills and their activities have direct bearing on it. As a result, large quantities of organic and inorganic nutrients are added directly into the Nainital lake. The lake being the only source of drinking water, has significant impact upon the economy of the region. After basic treatment, the lake water is supplied to the local inhabitants for drinking and domestic purposes.

The water quality of lake Nainital is mostly governed by the sub surface inflow and flow that takes place through major drains including sediments. However, the continous supply of various major or minor trace elements have created the deposits of these elements at the bottom which circulates every year during waiter mixing. The circulation of these elements make the concentration of few elements beyond the permissible limits. Apart from demographic pressure, the erosion has been one of the major stresses to the aquatic ecosystem in Indian hills. Today, the rate of erosion in the Himalayas is amongst the highest in the world. In the central Himalayas, high sediment production has caused siltation in lakes, reservoirs and canal systems and has led to aggregation, instability and flooding in the low-land river channels. The siltation rate in the Nainital lake has increased 5-7 times compared to that in the Quaternary and Prehistoric periods (Rawat, 1987). The main reason for accelerated erosion is loss of vegetation cover, construction activities, terraced cultivation, overgrazing, forest fires and population pressure. The area is receiving incredibly large amount of sediments every year by mass movements, devastating landslides, rock-fall, debris flow and severe erosion in the catchments of lake zone. As a result, the lakes are diminishing fast and natural springs are drying up. Highly crushed, sheared and shattered rocks, recurrently experiencing the mass movements and erosion resulting in environmental degradation and increased flooding, characterize the catchments. Extensive human settlements related to agriculture, monoculture plantation, deforestation and excavation of roads have intensified the erosion and have triggered slope failures on these highly unstable lake catchments.

Substances, because these are intrinsic component of environment. At high concentration, all the metals are toxic to animals and plant both (Rai and Chandra, 1992; Sinha *et al.*, 1997).

Phytoplankton is the primary producer of any aquatic ecosystem, which is an indicator of water quality and biological productivity. Dissolved oxygen is decreasas or incresease in an aquatic ecosystem due to the plankton. Plankton takes sunlight directly and makes food for the total ecosystem through the photosynthesis process. Plankton may vary at place to place and season to season depends the changing water quality parameters and others ecological factors.

Eutrophication is another important water quality problem in lentic as well as lotic aqutic ecosystem. It has resulted accumulation of nutrients in a natural processes, resulting serious impairment of water quality. The lake receives toxic metals, organic and inorganic pollutants from different sources viz., high soil erosion, illegal construction activities, tourism development, heavy litter inputs, automobile exhaust, domestic discharge and recreational uses of lake water etc. As a result of the accelerated rate of man's cultural activities in the catchment area of the lake, the lake has turned in to eutrophic state and polluted (Rai *et al.,* 2004). It is important to know that the term eutrophic does not mean bad, but it is only a descriptive of the state or condition of the lake. The problems of the portable water treatment and its safety are directly related to the degree of eutrophication of the lake. According to the Martin (1993) some organic molecules either loaded to or produced within the lake, produced mutagenic or carcinogenic compounds when chlorinated for drinking purpose. Surface water with blue green algal bloom may be unfit for human consumption as they may contain toxins released form algae. These toxins are lethal to cattle and have been shown to produce human gastrointestinal problems.

## METHODOLOGY

Nainital lake is the third largest lake (48.0 ha) situated in the heart of Nainital township on the elevation of this lake 1937 msl in the state of Uttarakhand, India. The maximum length and width of the lake are 1.4 and 0.45 km while maximum and mean depth of the lake is 27.3 and 16.5 m, respectively. Lake Nainital is a cup shaped water body surrounded by steep mountain slope. The Nainital fault and associated fractures have caused shearing of the rocks responsible for hill slope instability. Almost half of the areal extend of the lake basin is covered with debris generated by mass movements (Kumar *et al.,* 1999).

The following sampling locations have been selected for the study:

1. *Mallital zone:* The upper part of the lake is called mallital zone and government offices like high court of uttarakhand situated here.
2. *Central zone:* It is the middle part of the lake. It receives toxic substances through various open drains in the catchments of the lake.

3. *Tallital zone:* It is the lower part the lake, a dam has been constructed at tallital for prevent excessive water flow during rainy season.

Approximately 100 mg fresh weight of each aquatic plants from experimental and control aquariums were taken for metals estimation. The plants were washed and kept in an oven at 105°C for 48 h. The dried plants samples were digested in concentrated $HNO_3$ : $HClO_4$ (v/v 3:1) at 80°C temperature on hot plate and the final volume was maintained with double distilled water in volumetric flasks. Digested solutions were analyzed for trace metals by Atomic Absorption spectrophotometer (AAS) 4129 model (Singh *et al.*, 1987; APHA, 1998 and ECIL Methods Manual, 2004). ) using air-acetylene flame. Operational conditions were adjusted in accordance with the manufacturer's guidelines to yield optimal determination. Quantification of metals was based upon calibration curves of standard solutions of respective metals. These calibration curves were determined several times during the period of analysis. The detection limits for iron, manganese, copper, nickel, chromium, lead, cadmium and zinc are 0.003, 0.001, 0.001, 0.004, 0.002, 0.01, 0.0005 and 0.0008 mg/L respectively.

## RESULTS AND DISCUSSIONS

Metals estimation in algal blooms at Mallital zone and Tallital zone presented in Table 4.1 and 4.2 (*See Tables on page No. 43, 44*) respectively and concentration of heavy metals at Tallital zone presented in fig. 4.1.

The utilization of prriphyton community for the removal of heavy metals from enriched lake ecosystem has been examined. In the experiment some metals were removed continuously (Ni, Cr, Fe and Mn), other metals were removed more rapidly during the first hour or first two hours of the experiment and then only slightly removal continued (Cu,Pb,Cd,Co). The highest decrease of uptake was observed in Cu, Cr,Co and Cd described by Vymazal (2004). Algae are able to absorb pollutants from the aquatic environment and biotransform organic compounds and immobilize inorganic elements to make them less toxic (Pflugmacher et al., 1999; Sa´nchez-Rodri´guez et al., 2001). Besides, it is well known that they are at the basis of pollutant biomagniûcation and the transfer to upper levels of the food web have been considered (Sandermann, 1992; Nystro¨n et al., 2002).

The level of metals in algal blooms varied significantly throughout the year, The level of metals in algal blooms were recorded - Cr, 2.16-6.09; Cu, 18.07-35.46; Fe, 843.1-1836.80; Mn, 122.4-421.34; Ni, 9.18-21.49; Pb, 26.4-52.46; Zn, 25.9-42.08; Cd, 3.08-7.29 (ug/g) respectively. The level of some these metals like Fe, Mn, Pb and Zn were recorded higher quantity than other metals in algal communities from lake water. All the metals found in low concentration during winter season and maximum found in pre monsoon season at all the zones of the lake. All the metals concentration was high at Mallital zone and central zone I of the lake and minimum at Tallital Zone.

Table 4.1: Metals Estimation in Algal Blooms (μg/g) of Mallital Zone of Lake Nainital

| Months | Cr | | Cu | | Fe | | Mn | | Ni | | Pb | | Zn | | Cd | |
|---|---|---|---|---|---|---|---|---|---|---|---|---|---|---|---|---|
| | Mean | S.D | Mean | S.D | Mean | S.D | Mean | S.D | Mean | S.D | Mean | S.D | Mean | S.D | Mean | S.D |
| November | 2.95 | 0.07 | 20.67 | 0.10 | 1207.3 | 0.09 | 220.6 | 0.08 | 16.67 | 0.10 | 38.2 | 0.08 | 30.6 | 0.08 | 4.08 | 0.08 |
| December | 2.77 | 0.10 | 22.75 | 0.07 | 1308.7 | 0.07 | 269.2 | 0.07 | 18.75 | 0.07 | 41.6 | 0.08 | 33.9 | 0.09 | 3.77 | 0.08 |
| January | 2.16 | 0.08 | 18.07 | 0.10 | 843.1 | 0.08 | 122.4 | 0.08 | 9.18 | 0.09 | 26.4 | 0.08 | 23.6 | 0.06 | 3.08 | 0.07 |
| February | 3.58 | 0.11 | 25.26 | 0.08 | 987.4 | 0.10 | 174.4 | 0.07 | 14.96 | 0.08 | 32.0 | 0.06 | 32.3 | 0.08 | 4.60 | 0.09 |
| March | 6.88 | 0.11 | 36.66 | 0.08 | 1838.0 | 0.06 | 422.6 | 0.10 | 22.42 | 0.13 | 53.6 | 0.07 | 43.1 | 0.07 | 7.98 | 0.08 |
| April | 3.96 | 0.08 | 33.87 | 0.09 | 1652.2 | 0.10 | 328.9 | 0.09 | 18.55 | 0.07 | 49.9 | 0.08 | 36.0 | 0.07 | 5.76 | 0.10 |
| May | 3.17 | 0.10 | 24.65 | 0.10 | 1108.7 | 0.08 | 249.2 | 0.10 | 15.91 | 0.08 | 37.8 | 0.10 | 26.7 | 0.08 | 4.14 | 0.08 |
| June | 2.76 | 0.10 | 18.59 | 0.05 | 948.6 | 0.09 | 197.6 | 0.08 | 13.30 | 0.08 | 31.9 | 0.06 | 25.9 | 0.08 | 4.03 | 0.08 |
| July | 3.32 | 0.09 | 21.38 | 0.08 | 997.4 | 0.08 | 204.3 | 0.11 | 13.06 | 0.08 | 33.6 | 0.08 | 25.9 | 0.08 | 4.29 | 0.09 |
| August | 4.94 | 0.08 | 28.05 | 0.07 | 1187.6 | 0.09 | 297.3 | 0.08 | 19.41 | 0.06 | 46.4 | 0.07 | 34.8 | 0.09 | 5.89 | 0.08 |
| September | 4.51 | 0.08 | 25.17 | 0.10 | 958.5 | 0.08 | 234.9 | 0.09 | 15.45 | 0.07 | 38.3 | 0.11 | 30.1 | 0.07 | 5.94 | 0.07 |
| October | 2.66 | 0.08 | 22.10 | 0.08 | 952.1 | 0.02 | 209.0 | 0.08 | 13.26 | 0.08 | 35.1 | 0.07 | 26.3 | 0.09 | 3.82 | 0.08 |

**Table 4.2: Metals Estimation in Algal Blooms (µg/g) of Central Zone of Lake Nainital**

| Months | Cr | | Cu | | Fe | | Mn | | Ni | | Pb | | Zn | | Cd | |
|---|---|---|---|---|---|---|---|---|---|---|---|---|---|---|---|---|
| | Mean | S.D | Mean | S.D | Mean | S.D | Mean | S.D | Mean | S.D | Mean | S.D | Mean | S.D | Mean | S.D |
| November | 2.53 | 0.07 | 20.38 | 0.08 | 1207.08 | 0.07 | 220.28 | 0.08 | 16.38 | 0.08 | 37.81 | 0.09 | 30.09 | 0.08 | 3.79 | 0.07 |
| December | 2.39 | 0.08 | 22.50 | 0.11 | 1308.33 | 0.09 | 268.95 | 0.09 | 18.29 | 0.10 | 41.30 | 0.07 | 33.55 | 0.11 | 3.65 | 0.10 |
| January | 2.09 | 0.10 | 17.83 | 0.09 | 842.60 | 0.08 | 122.09 | 0.07 | 9.09 | 0.07 | 26.16 | 0.09 | 23.18 | 0.09 | 2.92 | 0.08 |
| February | 3.23 | 0.08 | 25.09 | 0.08 | 987.07 | 0.07 | 174.07 | 0.08 | 14.59 | 0.08 | 31.69 | 0.09 | 31.93 | 0.08 | 4.34 | 0.08 |
| March | 6.62 | 0.08 | 36.21 | 0.08 | 1837.62 | 0.08 | 422.33 | 0.10 | 22.19 | 0.07 | 53.22 | 0.11 | 42.75 | 0.09 | 7.76 | 0.10 |
| April | 3.69 | 0.08 | 33.54 | 0.09 | 1651.91 | 0.08 | 328.58 | 0.16 | 18.31 | 0.11 | 49.08 | 0.08 | 35.48 | 0.08 | 5.39 | 0.08 |
| May | 3.07 | 0.08 | 24.32 | 0.09 | 1108.32 | 0.08 | 248.64 | 0.08 | 15.39 | 0.08 | 37.31 | 0.10 | 26.23 | 0.07 | 3.89 | 0.08 |
| June | 2.29 | 0.09 | 18.39 | 0.08 | 948.28 | 0.07 | 197.28 | 0.07 | 12.94 | 0.07 | 31.39 | 0.08 | 25.36 | 0.09 | 3.73 | 0.10 |
| July | 3.07 | 0.06 | 21.20 | 0.09 | 997.07 | 0.06 | 203.96 | 0.09 | 12.73 | 0.09 | 33.25 | 0.08 | 25.29 | 0.09 | 4.09 | 0.08 |
| August | 4.65 | 0.08 | 27.63 | 0.10 | 1187.40 | 0.10 | 296.62 | 0.08 | 19.14 | 0.08 | 46.08 | 0.10 | 34.39 | 0.08 | 5.68 | 0.08 |
| September | 4.24 | 0.07 | 24.93 | 0.08 | 958.29 | 0.09 | 233.61 | 0.07 | 15.18 | 0.09 | 37.94 | 0.08 | 29.65 | 0.08 | 5.78 | 0.09 |
| October | 2.32 | 0.08 | 21.92 | 0.07 | 951.81 | 0.10 | 208.70 | 0.07 | 13.11 | 0.09 | 34.51 | 0.08 | 25.94 | 0.07 | 3.54 | 0.08 |

Metals found in algal blooms in these sequences Mallital zone > Central zone I > Central zone II > Tallital zone. Sharma *et al.*, (1982) observed the growth of phytoplankton often forming visual algal blooms except during the winter. The phytoplankton community was mainly consituted by green algae. Thus the phytoplankton community in nainital is truly characterized by blooms of blue green algae. Iron and manganese are essential elements to physiological processes of algae, plant and animals and it is to be expected that organic circulation of manganese can influence its occurances in natural water. In some instances depletion of dissolved trace elements in lakes also coincides with increased phytoplankton production reported by Wrench and Measures (1982), Wangersky (1986), Reynolds and Taylor (1992) and Rico et al. (1993). Experimental studies showed that phytoplankton blooms can remove metals from solution described by Slauenwhite and Wangersky (1991) and Apte et al. (1986).

Phytoplankton uptake may include adsorption of metals to the new surface area provided by algal bloom and (or) may involve active metal incorporation into cells. Large pro- portions of Cd and Zn, compared to many metals, are taken up into a labile intracellular fraction of phytoplankton (the cytosol), analogous to some nutrients also observed in water bodies by Collier and Edmonds (1984), Reinfelder and Fisher (1991).

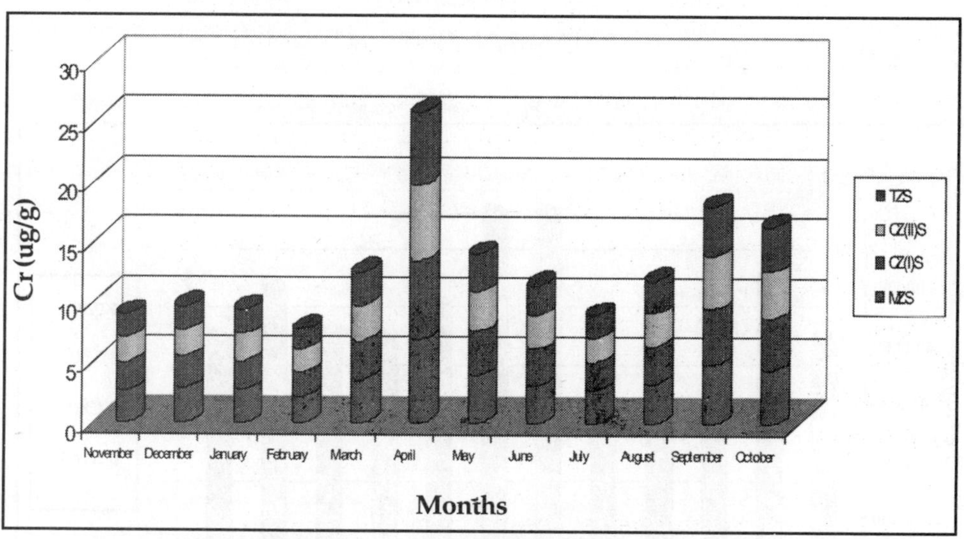


**Fig. 4.1: Monthly Variations of Chromium in Algal Blooms at Different Surface Water Zones in Lake**

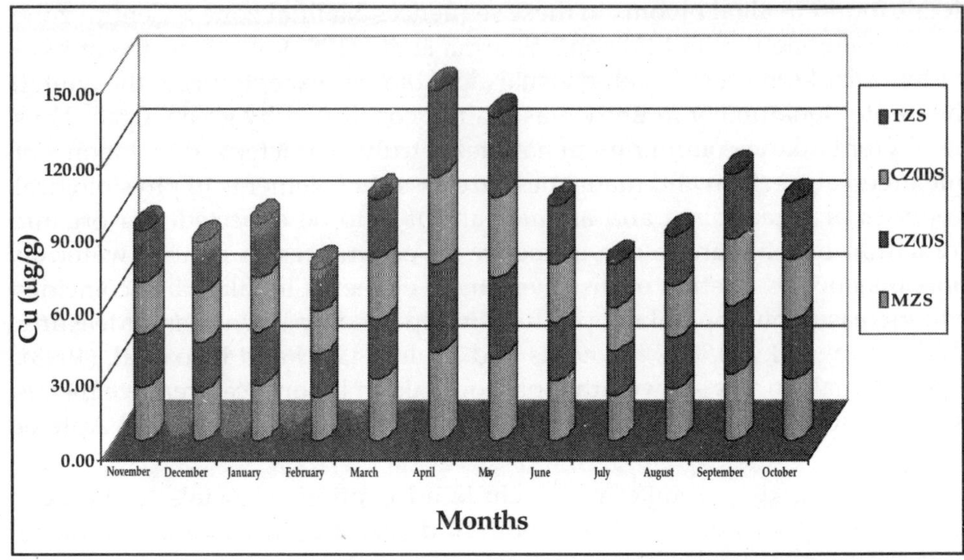


**Fig. 4.2: Monthly Variations of Copper in Algal Blooms at Different Surface Water Zones in Lake**

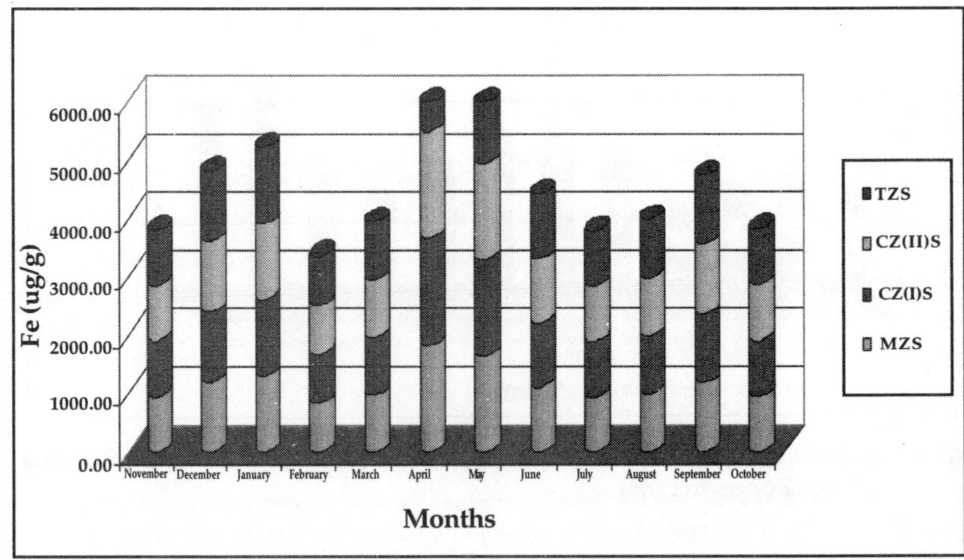


**Fig. 4.3: Monthly Variations of Iron in Algal Blooms at Different Surface Water Zones in Lake**

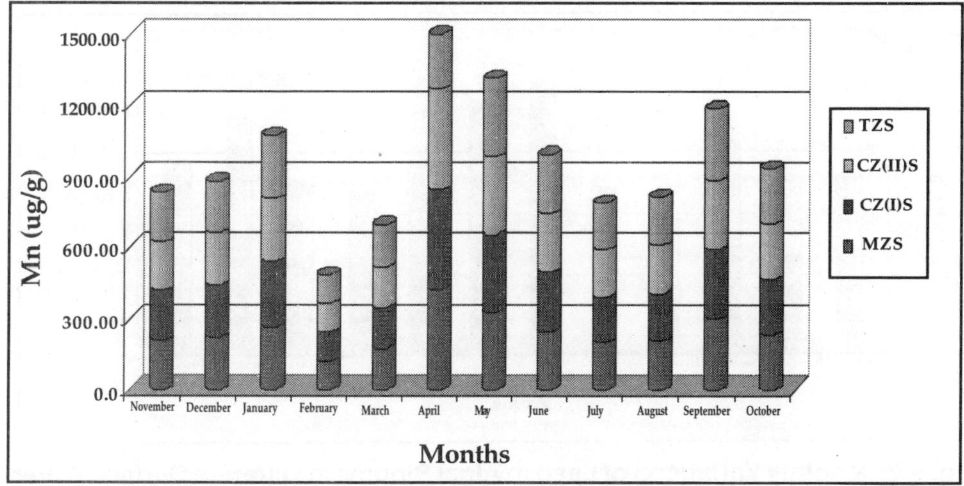


**Fig. 4.4: Monthly Variations of Manganese in Algal Blooms at Different Surface Water Zones in Lake**

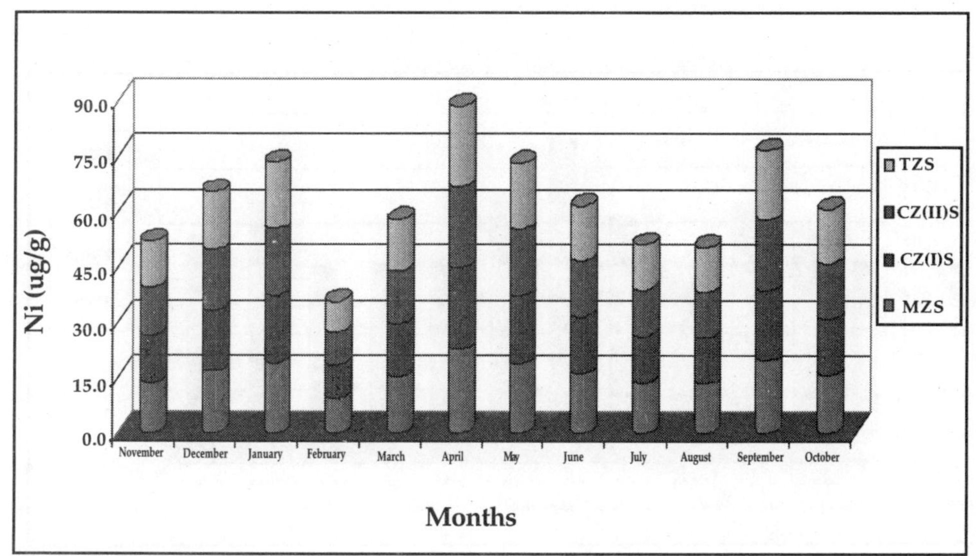


**Fig. 4.5: Monthly Variations of Nickel in Algal Blooms at Different Surface Water Zones in Lake**

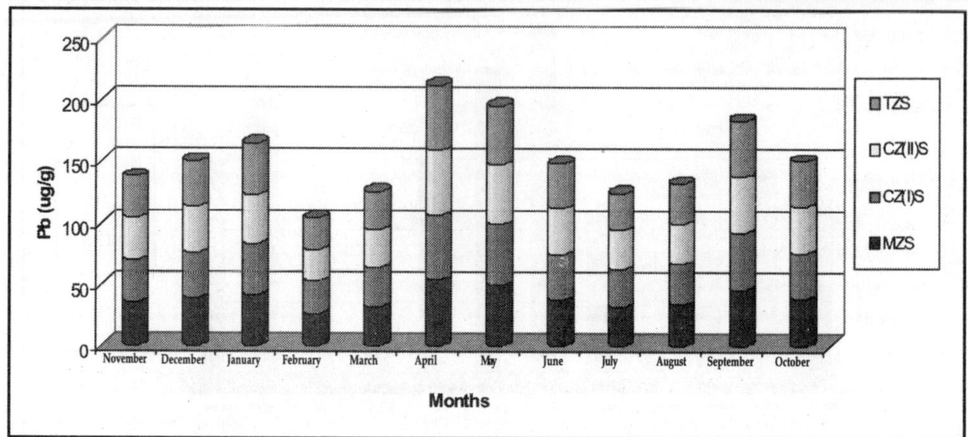


**Fig. 4.6: Monthly Variations of Lead in Algal Blooms at Different Surface Water Zones in Lake**

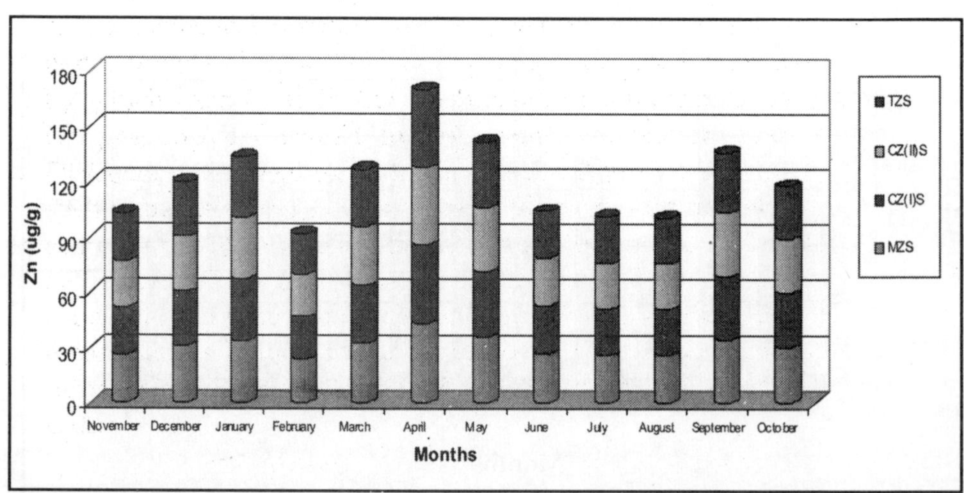


**Fig. 4.7: Monthly Variations of Zinc in Algal Blooms at Different Surface Water Zones in Lake**

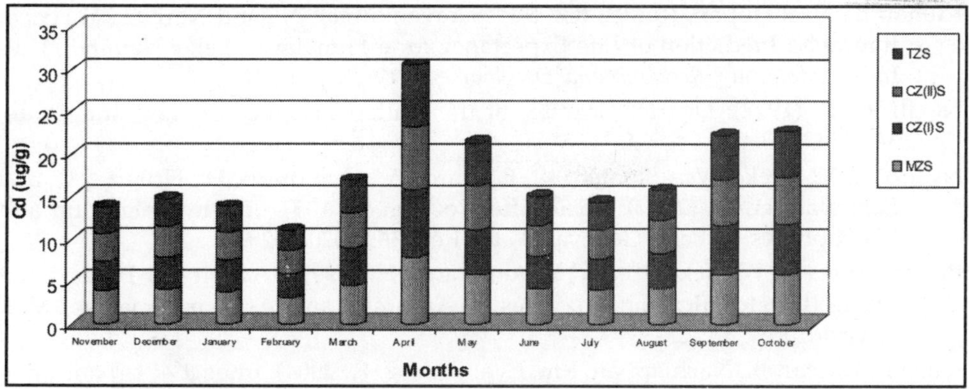


**Fig. 4.8: Monthly Variations of Cadmium in Algal Blooms at Different Surface Water Zones in Lake**

## CONCLUSION

The Nainital lake has a very significant importance for lake water utility, tourism, socio cultural and environmental ethics at National and International level. The present study will be provide basic scientific guidelines focused on toxic metal pollution, their accumulation pattern in surface & bottom water. The metal contents of various biotic components could be used for biomonitoring purpose and definitely contributing the remedial measures for restoration of lake water quality, enhancement of biological productivity, conservation and management of Nainital lake ecosystem.

## REFERENCES

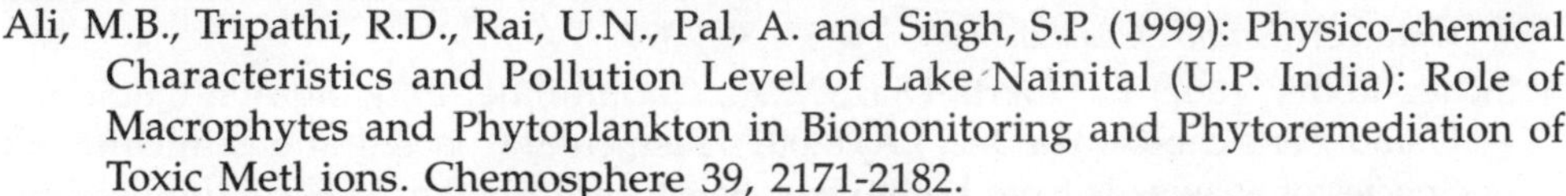

Ali, M.B., Tripathi, R.D., Rai, U.N., Pal, A. and Singh, S.P. (1999): Physico-chemical Characteristics and Pollution Level of Lake Nainital (U.P. India): Role of Macrophytes and Phytoplankton in Biomonitoring and Phytoremediation of Toxic Metl ions. Chemosphere 39, 2171-2182.

APHA (1998): Standard Methods for the Examination of Water and Waste Water, *American Public Health Association,* 19th Edition, 1015, Fifteenth Street, NW, pp: (1-1) – 10-150.

Apte, S.C., Howard, A.G., Morris, R.J. and McCartney. (1986): Arsenic, Antimony and Selenium Speciation during a Spring Phytoplankton Bloom in a Closed Experimental Ecosystem. *Mar. Chern*. 20: 119-130.

Collier, R., and Edmonds, J. (1984): The Trace Element Geochemistry of Marine Biogenic Particles. *Prog. Oceanogr*. 13: 113-199.

ECIL Methods Manual (2004) Methods Manual, Atomic Absorption Spectrophotometer, AAS 4129, *Electronic Corporation of India Limited*, Hyderabad-500 062, pp: 85.

Jan Vymazal, (2004): Short Term Uptake of Heavy Metals by Periphyton Algae, *Hydrobiologia*, 119: 171-179.

Kumar, B., Nachiappan, Rm. P., Rai, S.P., Saravankumar, N., and Narda, S.V. (1999): Improved Prediction of Life Expectancy for a Himalayan Lake: Nainital , U.P., India. *Mountain Research and Development*. 19(2): 113-121.

Nevill, H. R. (1922): District Gazetter of the United Province of Agra and Oudh, 34: 255.

Nystro¨ n, B., Becker-Van Slooten, K., Be´ rard, A., Grandjean, D., Druart, J-C. and Leboulanger, C. (2002): Toxic Effect of Irgarol 1051 on Phytoplankton and Macrophytes in Lake Geneva. Water Res. 36, 2020-2028.

Pflugmacher, S., Wiencke, C. and Sandermann, H. (1999): Activity of Phase I and Phase II Detoxification Enzymes in Antarctic and Artic macroalgae. Mar. Environ. Res. 48, 23-36.

Rai, S.P., Kumar, B., Nachiappan, Rm. P., and Garg, P. (2004): Impact of Urbanisation on Chemical Characteristics of Lake Nainital in Kumaun Lesser Himalaya. In C.K. Jain, R. C. Trivedi & K. D. Sharma (Eds *(.), Water Quality Monitoring, Modelling and Prediction*: 241-251.

Rai, U.N. and Chandra, P. (1992): Accumulation of Copper, Lead, Magnese and Iron by Field Population of Hydrodictyon Reticulatum (linn.). Lagerheim. Sci. *Total Environ*. 116: 203-211.

Rawat, J.S., (1987): Morphology and Morphometery of Naini Lake, Kumaon, Lesser Himalaya. *Jour.Geol.Soc. India*. 30: 493-498.

Reinfelder, J. R., and Fisher, N. S, (1991): The Assimilation of Elements Ingested by *Marine Copepods. Science* 251: 794-796.

Reynolds, G.L. and Hamilton-Taylor, J. (1992): The Role of Planktonic Algae in the Cycling of Zn and Cu in a Productive Soft-water Lake. *Limnol. Oceanogr*. 37: 1759-1769.

Rico, R.D., Le Corre, P., Madec, C., Birrin, J.L. and Quental, E. (1993): Seasonal Variation of Copper, Nickel and Lead in Western Brittany Coastal Waters (France). *Estuar. Coastal Shelf Sci*. 37: 313-327.

Sa´nchez-Rodrý´guez, I., Huerta-Diaz, M.A., Choumiline, E., Holguý´n-Quinones, O and Zertuche-Gonza´ lez, J.A. (2001): Elemental Concentrations in Different Species of Seaweeds from Loreto Bay, Baja California Sur, Mexico: Implications for the Geochemichal Control of Metals in Algal Tissue. Eviron. Pollut. 114, 145-160.

Sandermann Jr., H. (1992): Plant Metabolism of Xenobiotics. Trends Biochem. Sci. 17, 82-84.

Sharma, A.P., Jaiswal, S., Negi, N. and Pant, M.C. (1982): Phytoplankton Community Analysis in Lakes of Kumaun Himalayas, Arch. Hydrobiol. 93, pp. 173-193.

Singh, K.P. Takroo, R. and P.K. Roy (1987): Pesticides and Heavy Metal Residue Analysis in Water, ITRC Manual. *ITRC,* Lucknow, pp: 1-160.

Sinha, S., Gupta, M. and Chandra, P. (1997): Oxidative Strees Induced by Iron in Hydrilla Verticillata (D.F) Royle: Response of Antioxidants Ecotoxicol. *Env. Safety* 38: 286-291.

Slauenwhite, D.E. and Wangersky, P.J. (1991): Behaviour of Copper and Cadmium during a Phytoplankton Bloom: A me- socosm Experiment. *Mar. Chem*. 32: 37-50.

Volterra, L. and Conti, M.E. (2000): Algae as Biomarkers, Bioaccumulators and Toxin Producers. Int. J. Environ. Pollut. 13, 92-125.

Wangersky, I.J. (1986): Biological Control of Trace Metal Residence Time and Speciation: A Review and Synthesis. *Mar. Chem*. 18: 269-297.

Whitton, B.A. and Kelly, M.G., (1995): Use of Algae and Other Plants for Monitoring Rivers. Aust. J. Ecol. 20, 45-56.

Wrench, J.J. and Measures, C.I. (1982): Temporal Variations in Dissolved Selenium in a Coastal Ecosystem. *Nature,* 299: 4431-4433.

# Clinico-pathological and Biochemical Studies on *Tilipia zilli* Exposed to Cadmium Chloride

**Mona Saad Zaki,** ***Egypt*****; Ahmed Hassan Osman,** ***Egypt***
**Olfat Mohamed Fawzi,** ***Egypt*****; Suzan Omar Mostafa,** ***Egypt***
**Nagwa Said Ata,** ***Egypt*****; Medhat Khafagy,** ***Egypt***

**_ABSTRACT_**

Heavy metals are recognized as cumulative toxic substances causing serious health hazards to man depending on their concentration. Fourty fish (Tilipia Zilli) were collected from Abbassa Sharkia government and fed commercial fish diet. Thirty fish were exposed to cadmium chloride) 0.25 p.p.m.) And 30° temp. For 21 days. Ten fish were kept without treatment (control). Haematological analysis of the exposed group demonstrated a marked elevation in serum glutamic oxaloacetic transaminase, serum glutamic pyruvic transaminase, serum glucose, urea, creatinine, sodium, potassium and phosphorus, while serum calcium, haemoglobin and PCV were reduced. Histopathological examination of the fish exposed to cadmium chloride revealed necrobiotic changes of hepatocytes and epithelial lining of renal tubules spleen showed depletion of melanomacrophage centre. Necrosis of the gill filaments was also noticed. It could be concluded that cadmium chloride at 0.25 p.p.m induced deleterious effects in fish such as damage of liver, Kidney, spleen and gills, which were reflected on the biochemical and hematological parameters. Heavy metals induced cumulative effect; therefore equivalent lesions of fish may occurr in humans. Moreover, immune suppression could play an important role in predisposing for further infections conditions.

*Key words:* Pollution – cadmium, fish, immunity.

## INTRODUCTION

Heavy metals are persistent contaminants in the environment that come to the forefront of dangerous substances such as cadmium, lead, mercury, copper and zinc causing serious health hazard in humans and animals [1-10]. The agricultural and industrial wastes partially treated or without treatment are being discharged into surface water [11-16]. Such metals are absorbed from polluted water through gills, skin and digestive tract of fish by bio-concentration and bio-magnification. Chronic cadmium toxicity or "itai-itai" disease was recorded [17-20].

Cadmium toxicity was interfered with calcium/phosphorus ratio [21, 22] Suppression of cell mediated and humoral response of mammals exposed to sublethal dose of cadmium has been reported [23-26].

Histophathological examination of fish exposed to cadmium showed edema of secondary gill lamellae, degeneration of hepatocytes and epitheliallining of renal tubules. Degeneration and necrosis in the gill lamellae of fish xposed to cadmium were noticed [13-19].

Heavy metals are recognized as cumulative toxic substances causing serious health hazards to man depending on their concentration.

## MATERIALS AND METHODS

### Experimental Design

Total of fourty fish 100-200 gm body weight of each was acclimatized a tized to laboratory conditions for two weeks before use. They were divided into control group (10 fish) and experimental group (30 fish) that was exposed to cadmium chloride at a concentration of 0.25 p.p.m. and 30° temp. for 21 days.

Blood samples were collected from the caudal vein after 7 and 21 days of exposure. Serum for biochemical analysis and heparinized blood for hematological investigations were obtained from each sample.

### Biochemical Analysis

Test kits of Bio Merieux (France) were used for evaluation of serum glutamic pyruvic transminase and glutamic oxaloacetic transaminase [20]. Serum glucose was assessed according to Trinder [23]. Serum urea and creatinine were determined using kits of Bio Merieux (France). The concentration of cadmium, sodium, potassium and calcium were detected by using atomic spectrophotometry according to Forstner [13].

### Hematological Examination

Blood hemoglobin (Rb) was assessed by Drabkin [12]. Hematocrit value was carried out by using microhaematocrit capillary tubes, centrifuged at 1200 r.p.m. for 5 min.

## Bacteriological Examination

Bacterial isolation was done from skin, liver and kidney of fish on blood tryptose agar, MacConcky agar and tryptic soy agar plates. The plates were incubated aerobically and anaerobically. The bacterial isolates were identified morphologically and biochemically, according to Nomiyama [18].

The serum IgM was measured according to Fuda et. al. [15]. Antisera for fish were prepared by immunizing rabbits as previously described by Fuda et.al [15]. The procedure for labeling antibody fragment with enzyme was performed.

Elisa assay procedure: Assay was carried out in 96-well polystyrene ELISA microtiter plates (Titertex, Horsham, P A). The microtiter plates were coated with rabbit antigrey mullet IgM and were fractionated by DE-52 at a concentration of 40 $\mu$g/ml in 0.01 MPBS. A volume of 150$\mu$l was dispensed into each well and incubated for 4 hrs at 4°C.

Blocking was achieved after one washing with 200 $\mu$ l of 0.01 MPBS + 0.1 per cent 20 $\mu$ l per well and two washings with 200 $\mu$ l of PBS +1 per cent PBS. 0.01 per cent thiomerosol was added to each well and incubated for 2 hrs. at room temperature.

Incubation of samples and standards after washing was carried out as described above. 100 $\mu$ l of sample and standard were placed into the appropriate wells in the microtiter plates and incubated at room temperature.

Incubation with peroxidase labeled antibody after washing was done as described above, each well received 150 $\mu$ l of peroxidase labeled antibody 1:1600 in PBSBSA, followed by incubation for 12 hrs at room temperature.

## Histopathological Examination

Specimens from gills, liver, Kidney and spleen were collected from both control and exposed groups at the end of experiment. The samples were fixed in 10 per cent neutral buffered formalin. Five-micron thick paraffin sections were prepared and stained with H&E for microscopic examination [27]

Statistical analysis: The obtained data were subjected to the student T test.

# RESULTS

## Serum Biochemical Analysis

Fish exposed to cadmium chloride (0.25 p.p.m) showed a significant icrease of SGPT and SGOT activity with pronounced elevation of urea and creatinine by 1st, 2nd, 3rd week of exposure. High level of sodium and potassium in serum of exposure fish was noticed (Table 5.1). Hyperglycaemia and hypocalcemia were noticed along the experimental period with-marked elevation of serum cadmium (Table 5.2).

**Table 5.1: Effect of Cadmium Chloride .25 p.p.m. on Kidney and Liver Function of Tilipia Zilli**

| Exposure Time | SGOT U/L | SGPT U/L | Urea mg/dl | Creatinine mg/dl | Sodium Meg | Potassium Meg |
|---|---|---|---|---|---|---|
| 1st week (control) | 90.0 ± 0.17 | 20.7 ± 1.7-5 | 3.29 ± 0.27 | 0.76 ± 0.72 | 124 ± 0.57 | 4.19 ± 0.07 |
| 1st week of exposure | 91.00 ± 2.40 | 25.5 ± 0.73 | 3.90 ± 0.34 | 0.81 ± 0.01 | 131 ± 0.76 | 4.60 ± 0.02 |
| 2ndst week (control) | 90.00 ± 0.10 | 22.1 ± 1.48 | 3.30 ± 0.28 | 0.75 ± 30 | 120.3 ± 4.8* | 4.33 ± 0.58 |
| 2ndst week of exposure | 125 ± 0.45* | 29 ± 2.1* | 3.91 ± 0.13** | 0.90 ± 0.19** | 138 ± 0.70** | 5.9 ± 0.08 |
| 3rd week (control) | 90 ± 2.2 | 20.00 ± 0.05 | 3.20 ± 0.27 | 0.72 ± 0.27 | 126 ± 4.2 | 4.1 ± 0.09 |
| 3rd week of exposure | 136 ± 2.46* | 35 ± 1.56* | 4.6 ± 24* | 0.99 ± 0.18** | 148 ± 7.6 | 6.25 ± 0.13 |

* Segnificant P< 0.05

** Highly significant P < 0.01

**Table 5.2: Some Hematological and Biochemical Changes in Tilipia Zilli Exposed to Cadmium Chloride**

| Exposure Time | P.C.V % | Hemoglobin gm/dl | Glucose mg % | Cadmium p.p.m | Calcium mg/dl | Phosphonis mg/dl |
|---|---|---|---|---|---|---|
| 1st week (control) | 21.00 ± 0.06 | 8.7 ± 0.3 | 62 ± 1.20 | 0.05 ± 0.01 | 5.6 ± 0.32 | 4.2 ± 0.07 |
| 1st week of exposure | 17.9 ± 0.05 | 8.1 ± 0.01 | 68 ± 0.46 | 0.08 ± 0.016 | 4.00 ± 0.87 | 6.1 ± 0.21 |
| 2ndst week (control) | 22 ± 0.29 | 8.1 ± 0.36 | 60 ± 0.05 | 0.054 ± 0.068 | 5.4 ± 0.91 | 4.1 ± 0.66 |
| 2nd week of exposure | 17 ± 1.97 | 7.00 ± 0.98** | 70 ± 1.93** | 0.12 ± 1.03* | 4.2 ± 0.73* | 6.4 ± 0.12* |
| 3rd week (control) | 20.0 ± 1.32 | 8.1 ± 0.07 | 62.2 ± 0.70 | 0.04 ± 0.01* | 4.4 ± 0.73 | 3.9 ± 0.1 |
| 3rd week of exposure | 16.9 ± 0.8 | 6.91 ± 0.23* | 84 ± 0.02* | 0.16 ± 082* | 3.5 ± 0.88* | 6.1 ± 0.6* |

* Segnificant P< 0.01

** highly significant P < 0.05

## Haematological Profile

Reduction of Hb concentration and P.C.V value were observed (Table 5.2).

## Bacteriological Examination

Pure culture of *Streptococcus spp., Staphylococcus spp. Agrobacterium spp., Flavobacterium spp. and Lactobacillus spp.* were isolated from the internal and external organs of exposed fish (Table 5.3).

**Table 5.3: Bacteriological Recovered in Tilipia Zilli Exposed to Cadmium Chioride (0.25 p.p. m)**

| Bacterial Strain | External Surface | Internal Organs | Internal Organs Liver | Gills |
|---|---|---|---|---|
| *Agrobacterium spp.* | $4.1 \times 10^7$ | $3.8 \times 10^6$ | $3 \times 10^4$ | $5 \times 10^7$ |
| *Flavobacterlum spp.* | $7 \times 10^7$ | $6.2 \times 10^6$ | $6 \times 10^3$ | $7.3 \times 10^8$ |
| *Staphylococcus spp.* | $6 \times 10^5$ | $5 \times 10^4$ | $6.2 \times 10^3$ | $4.2 \times 10^6$ |
| *Streeptococcus spp.* | $5 \times 10^7$ | $9 \times 10^5$ | $7 \times 10^6$ | $3 \times 10^7$ |
| *Lactobacillus spp.* | $3.3 \times 10^3$ | $4.4 \times 10^6$ | $2 \times 10^3$ | $2 \times 10^6$ |

## Determination of Fish IgM

There was a significant decrease in total protein and IgM level from the first week of exposure until the end of last week (Table 5.4).

**Table 5.4: Influence of Cadmium Chloride 0.25 p.p.m on 1gM and Protein Level**

| Exposure Period | 1gM/Old | Total Protein/neg/dl |
|---|---|---|
| Control | $0.98 \pm 0.13$ | $7.84 \pm 0.23$ |
| 1st week of exposure | $0.80 \pm 0.23^{**}$ | $7.00 \pm 0.69^{*}$ |
| 2st week of exposure | $0.74 \pm 0.84^{*}$ | $6.42 \pm 0.29^{*}$ |
| 3st week of exposure | $0.68 \pm 0.44^{*}$ | $6.2 \pm 0.48^{*}$ |

* Segnificant P< 0.01

** highly significant P < 0.05

± Standard errors

## Pathological Findings

Macroscopical lesions of exposed fish revealed congestion in all internal organs after 21 days. Liver appeared friable and dark red. Peticheal haemorrhages around the operculum, and abdominal cavity were observed. Congestion and edema of gill lamellae were seen (Fig. 5.1).

Histopathological examination revealed necrobiotic changes in hepatocytes and disorganisation of hepatic cord (Fig. 5.2). Kidney showed shrinkage of glomerular tufts and degeneration of proximal tubular epithelium (Fig. 5.3). The anterior Kidney showed depletion of melanomacrophage center (Fig. 5.4). Sloughing of epithelial lining of secondary gill lamellae with lymphocytes, oesinophils, polymoph infiltration were observed (Fig. 5.5).

Necrosis of both primary and secondary gill lamellae was sometimes seen (Fig. 5.6). Hyperplasia of primary and secondary lamellar epithelium associated with shortening and fusion of gill lamellae with obliteration of interlamellar space were noticed (Fig. 5.7). Rupture of pillar cells and capillaries associated with lamellar telangiectasis were also observed (Fig. 5.8).

**Fig. 5.1: Congestion of All Internal Organs of Exposed Fish**

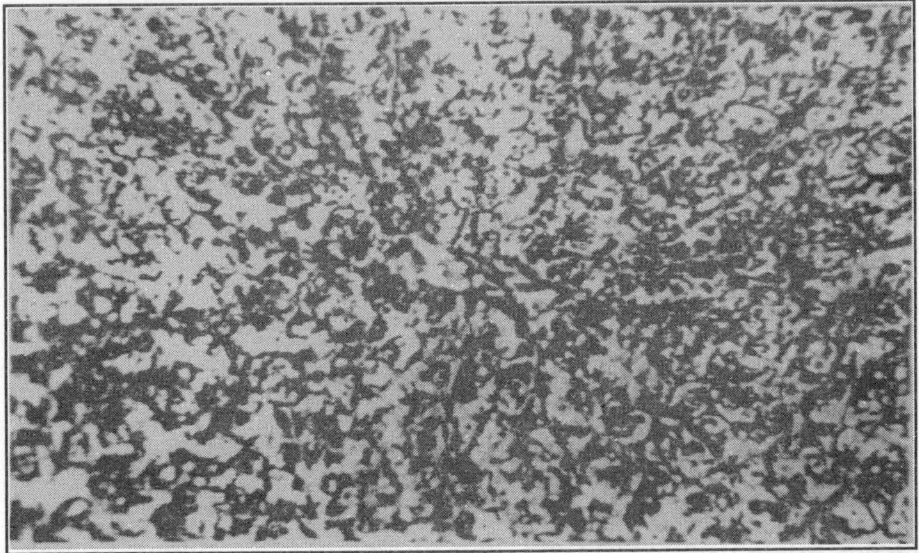

**Fig. 5.2: Liver Showing Neerobiotic Changes of Hepatocytes (H & E x 400)**

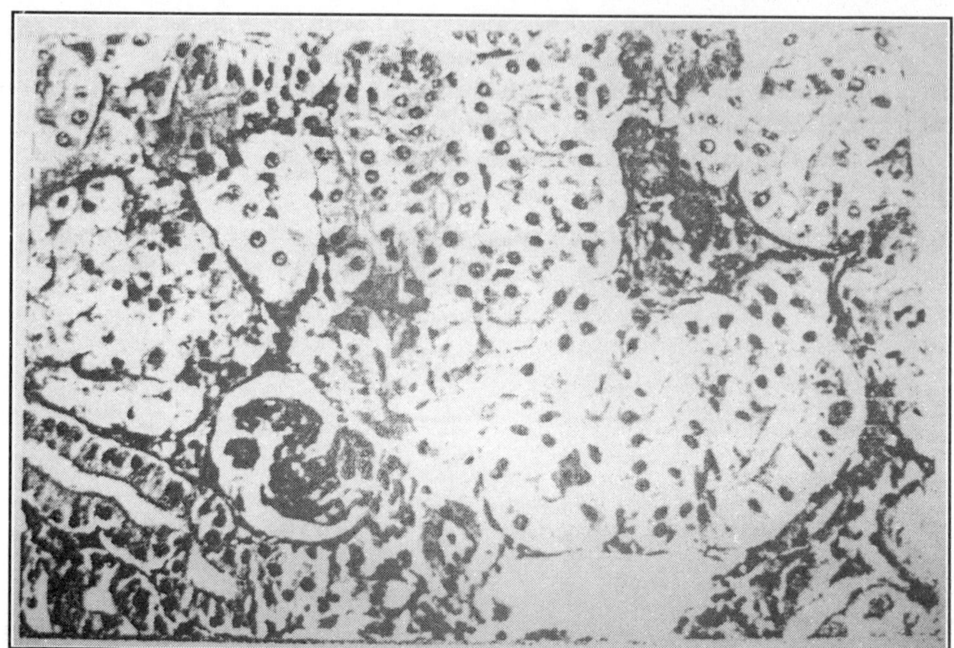

**Fig. 5.3: Kidney Showing Shrinkage of Glomerular Tufts and Degeneration of Tubular Epithelium (H & E x 400)**

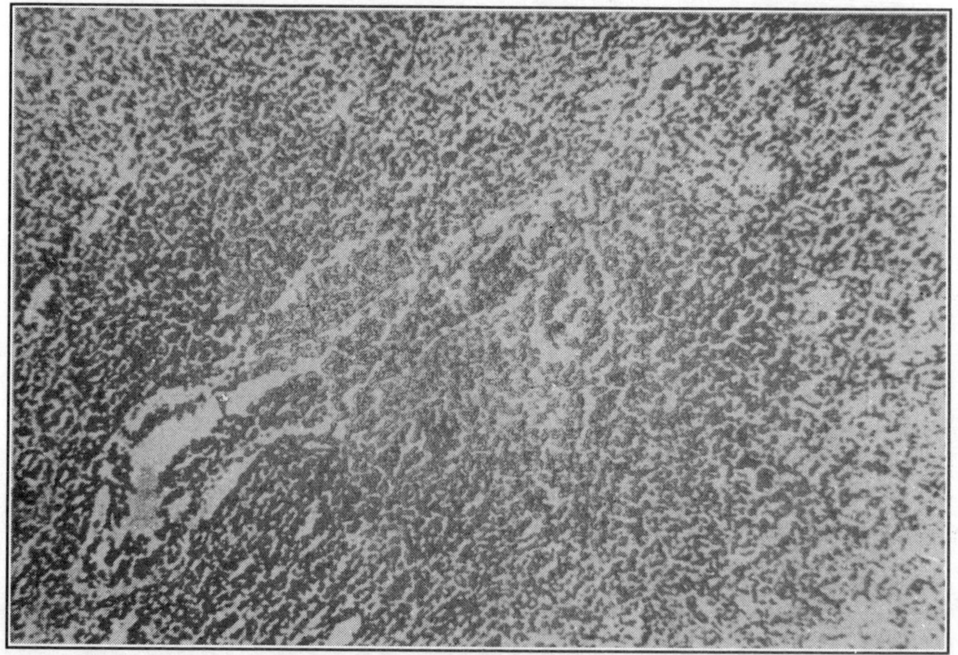

**Fig. 5.4: Spleen Showing Depletion of Melanomacrophage Center and Haemopoietic Elements (H & E x 100)**

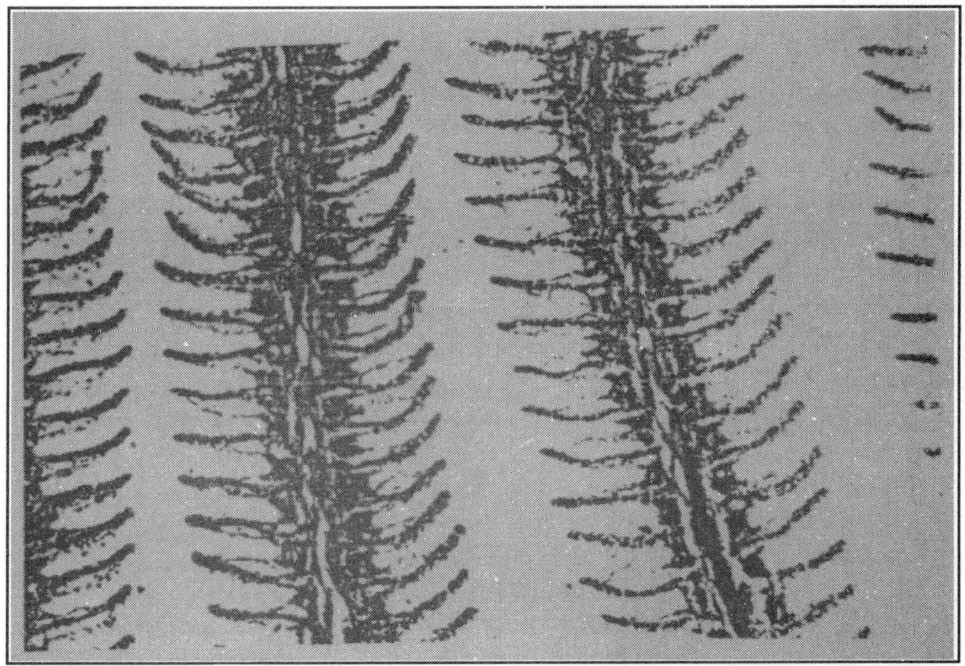

Fig. 5.5: Sloughing of Epithelial Lining of Secondary Gill Lamellae (H & E x 100)

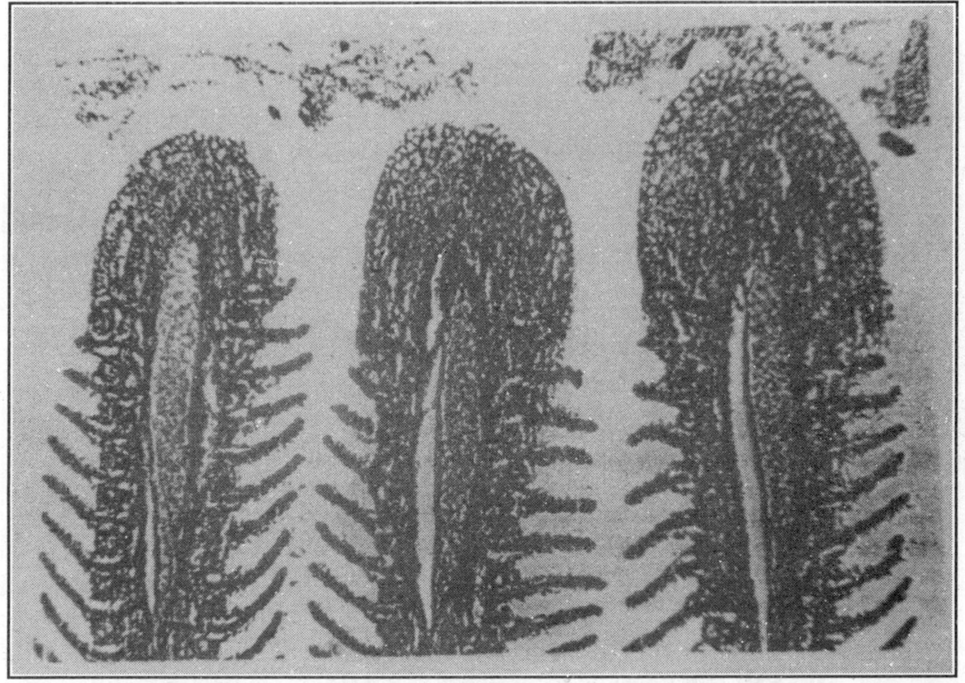

Fig. 5.6: Hyperplasia and Fusion of Secondary Gill Lamellae (H & E x 200)

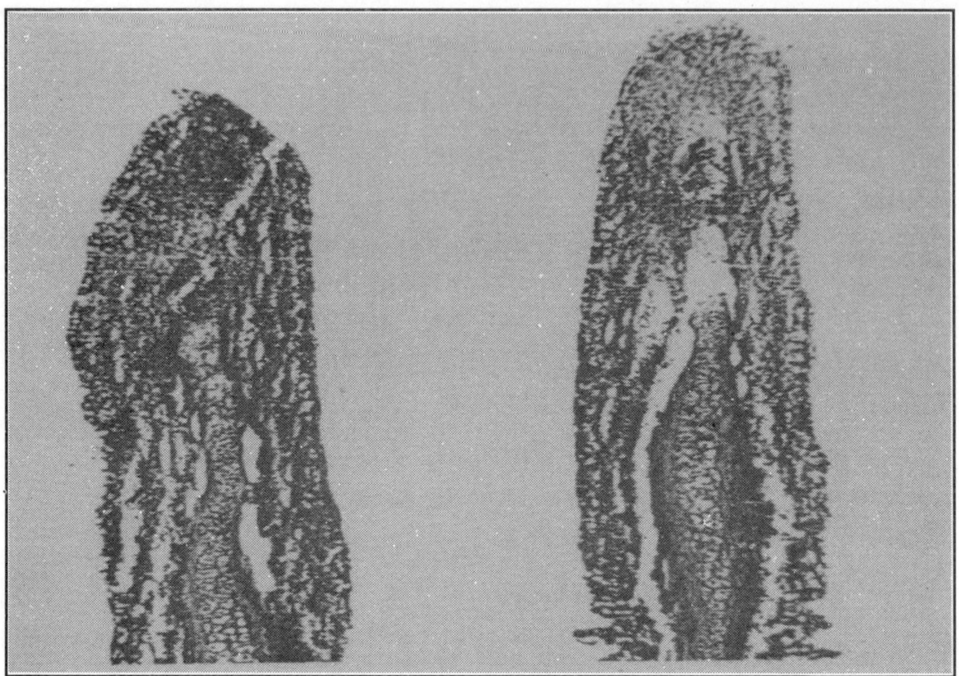

Fig. 5.7: Necrosis of Both Primary and Secondary Gill Lamellae ( H & E x 200)

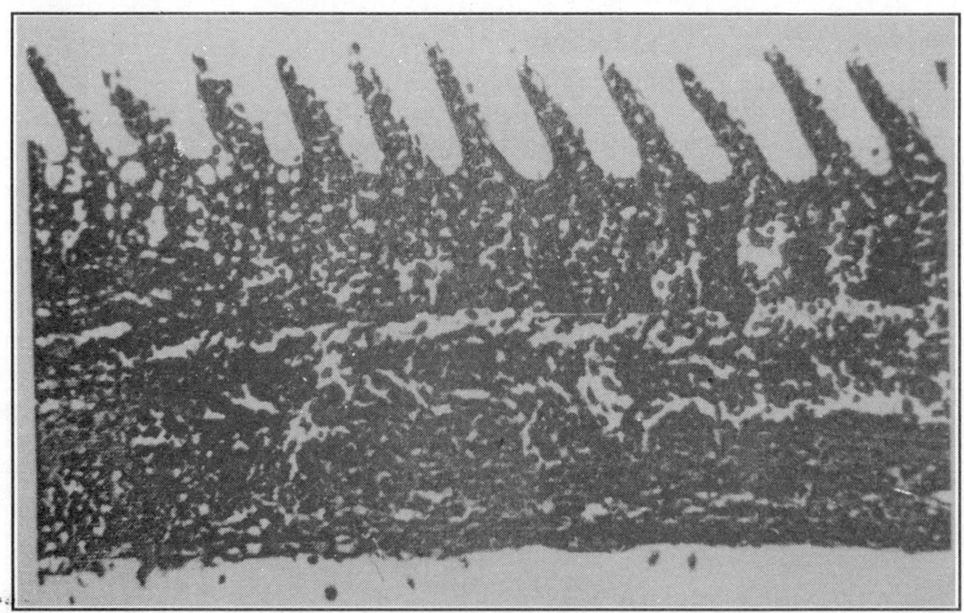

Fig. 5.8: Gill Lamellae Showing Telangiectasis (H & E x 400)

## DISCUSSION

Aforementioned data of exposed fish to cadmium chloride (0.25 p.p.m) for 3 weeks revealed an elevation of serum GPT, GOT, urea and creatinine.

These findings are in agreement with previous results. Elevation of urea and creatinine beside liver enzymes in cadmium-exposed fish may be attributed to liver and kidney injury. Reduction of calcium level in serum may have resulted from its increased excertion in urine through inhibition of calcium ATPase enzyme. On the other hand, increase of the phosphorus level in serum of exposed fish was noticed. Cadmium chloride toxicity leads to disturbance in blood electrolytes followed by skeletal changes [23, 25]. Hyperglycemia was observed in the present work which coincides with that obtained in Rainbow traut and salmogaidneri [25]. The blood glucose level was affected by the rate of carbohydrate metabolism under hypoxia and stress conditions. Hyperglycemia is attribute to stress stimuli followed by rapid secretion of both glucocorticoids and α-techolarnines from the adrenal tissue [2]. Regarding to hematological profile exposed fish, hemoglobin and P.C.V. values were decreased. These results are in agreement with previous findings [17, 18]. The erythropenia resulted from reduction of Hb concentration and P.C.V. value in Kwait Mullet due to disturbance of osmoregulatory mechanism accompanied with destruction of gill membrane and failure of gas exchange [19]. Cadmium interfered with sulpha-hydride groups of essentials enzymes [4, 25]. Heavy metals are recognized as cumulative substances leading to serious health hazards to man and animals [6-9].

In the present study, a significant decrease of IgM and total protein during the experimental period were observed. Reduction of IgM level indicated that the cadmium chloride toxicity leads to suppression of immune system of exposed fish which become susceptible to any infective agents [15, 20]. There is a significant decrease in IgM level in fish exposed to cadmium chloride if compared with control which may have resulted from high cortisol secretion that was indicated by hyperglycemia in exposed fish.

Macroscopical examination of fish exposed to cadmium chloride for 21 days revealed a congestion of all internal organs and friable bloody liver. These findings are in agreement with those mentioned by other authors [1-9].

Degeneration and necrosis of hepatocytes may be attributed to the cumulative effect of cadmium and to the increase of its concentration in the hepatic tissue during experimental period. These results agreed with Frolin et al. [14], who stated that liver has an important detoxical role of exogenous waste products as well as externally derived toxins such as heavy metals.

Necrobiotic changes of epithelial lining of renal tubules were observed especially the proximal convoluted tubules that were reflected on electrolytes reabsorption such as calcium, phosphorus, potassium and sodium. These findings come parallel to those previously reported.

It could be concluded that cadmium chloride at 0.25 p.p.m induced deleterious effect in fish such as damage of liver, kidney, spleen and gills, which were reflected on the biochemical and hematological parameters. Heavy metals induced cumulative effect; therefore equivalent lesions of fish may occur in humans. Moreover, immune suppression could play an important role in predisposing for further infections conditions.

Gills showed sloughing of epithelial lining and necrosis of some lamellae. Hyperplasia, shortening and fusion of the secondary gill lamellae that may lead to a great disturbance of gas exchange and ionic regulation were noticed [28]. Lamellar telangictasis resulted from rupture of pillar cells and capillaries under effect of chronic irritation of cadmium chloride and leads to an accumulation of erythrocytes in the distal portion of the secondary lamellae [29]. The subepithelial space of the secondary gill lamellae was infiltrated with inflammatory cells. This finding is in agreement with that previously mentioned [29, 30]. Mucinous metaplasia of lamellar epithelial lining is considered as adaptive mechanism against heavy metal toxicity. These alterations are in agreement with those previously mentioned [31].

It could be concluded that cadmium chloride at 0.25 p.p.m induced deleterious effects in fish such as damage of liver, Kidney, spleen and gills, which were reflected on the biochemical and hematological parameters. Heavy metals induced cumulative effect; therefore equivalent lesions of fish may occurr in humans. Moreover, immune suppression could play an important role in predisposing for further infections conditions.

## REFERENCES

[1] Abbas, H.H., K.H. Zaghloul, and M.A. Mousa, 2002. Effect of Some Heavy Metal Pollutants on Some Biochemical and Histopathological Changes in Blue Tilapia, *Oreochromis aureus*. Egypt. J. Agric. Res., 80(3): 1395-1411.

[2] Abbas, W.T. 2006. Fish as an Indicator for Pollutants in Aquatic Environment. Ph.D. Thesis, Zoology Department, Faculty of Science, Cairo University, Egypt, 144 pp.

[3] Abdel-Baky, T.E. 2001. Heavy Metals Concentrations in the Catfish, *Clarias gariepinus* (Burchell, 1822) from River Nile, El-Salam Canal and Lake Manzala and Their Impacts on Cortisol and Thyroid Hormones. Egypt. J. Aquat. Biol. & Fish., 5(1): 79-98.

[4] Abernthy A.R. and P.M., Cutnbie 1999. Bull Environ. Contoam. Toxicol. 17: 595 (1999).

[5] Abou El-Gheit, E.N., M.S., Zaki, A.A., Abo El-Ezz, H.A. El-Cherei, 2001. Vertebral Column Curvature Syndrome in Common Carp *Cyprinus Carpio* L. Fish. J. Egypt. Vet. Med. Ass., 61(5): 57-69.

[6] Abou El-Naga, E.H.; K.M. El-Moselhy, and M.A. Hamed, 2005. Toxicity of Cadmium and Copper and Their Effect on Some Biochemical Parameters of Marine Fish *Mugil seheli*. Egypt. J. Aquat, Res., 31(2): 60-71.

[7] Ahmed, Y.F.; M.M., Mohamed, I.Z., El-Nemer, K.I. El-Desoky, and S.S. Ibrahim, 1998. Some Pathological Studies on the Effect of Cadmium and Mercuric Chlorides on the Gonads of Catfish (*Clarias lazera*). Egypt. J. Comp. Pathol. Clin. Pathol., 11: 72-81.

[8] Authman, M.M.N. 2008. *Oreochromis Niloticus* as a Biomonitor of Heavy Metal Pollution with Emphasis on Potential Risk and Relation to some Biological Aspects. Global Veterenaria, 2(3): 104 -109.

[9] Authman, M.M.N., E.M. Bayoumy, and A.M. Kenawy, 2008. Heavy Metal Concentrations and Liver Histopathology of *Oreochromis niloticus* in Relation to Aquatic Pollution. Global Veterenaria, 2(3): 110-116.

[10] Bahnasawy, M.H. 2001. Levels of Heavy Metals in Catfish, *Clarias gariepinus* from Different Habitats and Their Effects on Some Biochemical Parameters. Egypt. J. Aquat. Biol. & Fish., 5(1): 99-125.

[11] Burger, J., M. Gochfeld, C., Jeitner, S.Burke, and T. Stamm, 2007. Metal Levels in Flathead Sole (*Hippoglossoides elassodon*) and Great Sculpin (*Myoxocephalus polyacanthocephalus*) from Adak Island, Alaska: Potential Risk to Predators and Fishermen. Environmental Research, 103: 62-69.

[12] Drabkin, D., l964. Bio Chem., 164,̇ 703.

[13] Forstner N. and G.T.W., Wittmann 2007. Metal Pollution in the Aquatic Environment. Springer-Verlag, Belin.

[14] Frolin, L, C. Haux, L., Karkson-Norgren, P. Runn, and A. Larsson 1986. Aquatic Toxicol. 8:51.

[15] Fuda, H., K., Sayano, F. Yamaji, and Haraj, 1991. Comp Brioche, Physiol, 99 A 637-643.

[16] Gad, S.C. and C.S., Weil, 1986. Statistics for Toxicologists. In Hayes. A. W. 2nd.

[17] Matsubara, A., S. Mihara, and R., Kusuda, 1985. Bull Japan Sac, Sic. Fish. 51m 921.

[18] Nomiyama, K., 1988. "Bacteriological Test Book". Vol. 2 pp. 15-23 Pergamon.

[19] O'Neill, J.G., 1981. Bull. Env. Contam. Toxico!., 27: 42-48.

[20] Reitman, S.,and S. A., Frankel, 1957. Am. J. Clin. Pathol. 28, 56.

[21] Stephen, W.I. 2004. Zinc, Cadmium, Mercury and Lead. Stephen, W.I. Ed.; Blackwell Scientific Publications.

[22] Stostiof, M.K. 1993. "Fish Medicine" W.B. Saunders Company, Philadelphia, Lonion, Toronto, Montreal, Sydney, Tokyo (1993).

[23] Trinder, P., 1960. Ann. CUn Brioche. 6, 24.

[24] Vinodhini, R., and M. Narayanan, 2008. Bioaccumulation of Heavy Metals in Organs of Fresh Water Fish *Cyprinus carpio* (Common Carp). Int. J. Environ. Sci. Tech., 5 (2): 179-182.

[25] Vosyliene, M.Z. and A. Jankaite, 2006. Effect of Heavy Metal Model Mixture on Rainbow Trout Biological Parameters. Ekologija., 4: 12-17.

[26] Zaki, M.S., and A.H. Osman, 2003. Clinicopathological and Pathological Studies on Tilapia Nilotica Exposed to Cadmium Chloride (0.25 ppm) Bull. NRC, Egypt., 28 (1): 87-100.

[27] Carleton H., "Carleton's; Histopathological Technique" 4th Ed. London, Oxford University, Press, New York, Toronto. (1979).

[28] Balah, A.M., El-Bouhy, Z.M. and Easa, M.E.I.S., Histopathlogical Studies in the Gills of Tilipia Nilotica "Oreochromis Niloticus" Under the Effect of Some Heavy Metals. Zagazig Vet. J., Vol. 21, No. 3 pp. 351-364. (1993).

[29] Randi, A.S., Monserrat J.M., Rodrigue E.M and Romano L.A. , J. of Fish Diseases 19, 311 (1996).

[30] Pascoe, D., Evans, S.A. and Woodworth, J., Arch. Env. Contam. Toxicol., 15: 481. (1986).

[31] Stostiof, M.K. "Fish Medicine". W.B Saunders Company, Philadelphia, London, Toronto, Montreal, Sydney, Tokyo (1993).

6

# Technologies in Aquatic Bioremediation

**Vikas Phulia, *India*; Ankur Jamwal, *India*; Neha Saxena, *India***
**N.K. Chadha, *India*; A.P. Muralidhar, *India*; A.K. Prusty, *India***

## INTRODUCTION

Rivers were the cradle of civilizations and even today the river banks and coastal regions continue to be the most densely populated on this earth. Of all, it is perhaps the aquatic habitat that has borne the brunt of expanding human civilization the most. While agricultural revolution derived water from these water sources to feed the ever growing human population, industrial revolution made water bodies a dumping ground for the waste that could not have been disposed in any other manner. In addition to these conscious attempts to use water as a sink for the waste generated, accidents like oil spills and nuclear plant disasters as in Chernobyl and the recently in Fukushima have left our water bodies with a heavy load of contaminants. Human civilization perhaps would have never bothered to clean these water bodies had the health of the aquatic environment not affected the survival of humans. Due to implications of contamination of water bodies it has become a huge responsibility to revive the aquatic environment to its original condition.

Treatment of water and cleaning the after effects of accidents like oil spills and nuclear disasters, leeching of agricultural chemicals and fertilizers leading to eutrophication is not only costly but the compliance to the regulations is also very difficult. Water treatment, at certain regions where excavation may be required to set up treatment plants or setting up of treatment unit over a large water body, would certainly be very costly thereby deterring the efforts to clean up. Under such conditions organic methods to treat the aquatic habitats is perhaps the most appropriate one and is widely known as bioremediation.

Bioremediation can be defined as restoration of the conditions in natural environment, contaminated or fouled, to its pristine state by use of biological agents such as microorganisms, algae and green plants or their enzymes. Bioremediation can be a natural process of degradation so as to ensure the reduction in the contaminant concentration with time (bioattenuation), it might be an intentional stimulation of xenobiotic-degrading bacterial that may have such effects attributed to oxidation or reduction of the contaminant, hydrolysis or nutrient addition (bioaugmentation) or there can be man-made efforts to reduce the contaminants in environment by addition of laboratory grown bacteria that have appropriate degradative abilities (bioaugmentation) (Madsen 1991, Madsen *et al.* 1991).

The idea of bioremediation is with the nature itself. Due to contamination in a particular region, some organisms may die, growth of few others might get retarded but there would be certain organisms that would thrive well on the contaminants by metabolizing it. Bioremediation would involve identification of such organisms and fostering their growth, naturally or by inoculation, so as to breakdown the contaminants into less harmful metabolites. This technology being cheaper and nature friendly is certainly a technology for future. But, like other technologies this too is not a panacea to all the maladies of environmental contaminants; toxic metals like cadmium obliterate complete flora and fauna of the contaminated area and hence it is not possible to use biological agents to treat them. Microbes require oxygen as an electron acceptor hence in aqueous phase; oxygen concentration below 1mg/l restricts the process of bioremediation. Similarly many other limitations would be discussed later.

With the progress of biological sciences many bioengineered strains of microbes are being designed that are more capable of utilizing the contaminants. Bioengineered strains can use the contaminants better and hence there is a chance of obliteration of local flora and fauna thereby causing a concern for biodiversity among biologists and environmentalists alike.

At present, this technology is being used to treat aquatic habitat contaminated with heavy metals, oil spills, radioactive materials, fertilizers and agricultural discharge, aquaculture waste water, sewage, industrial effluents and discharge loaded with toxic hydrocarbon residues and tackling the issue of eutrophication which is responsible for development of algal load in water bodies causing hypoxic conditions and making them unfit for fish and shell fish survival along with aerobic microbes. Uses of bioremediation for various purposes and little recent advancement in this field would be discussed under various headings in this chapter.

## METAL BIOREMEDIATION

As far as health effects of metals on aquatic flora and fauna is concerned, there are two categories of metals; one, which are nutritionally important but exceeding concentrations tend to be toxic and other category of metals have no role in the physiology of body and are toxic even at low levels. Cu, Zn, Fe, Ni, Co, Se, Mo and Cr are the metals belonging to the first category of metals having biological roles (Bury, Walker and Glover, 2003) while Ag, Al, Cd, Pb, Hg, As, Sr, and U belong to the second category. There are other toxic metals too but these are the major elements which have aroused lot of public sentiments and have been extensively studied by the researchers. Maintaining the optimal levels of the elements mentioned by pumping and treating is not only expensive but also less effective (NRC, 1994).

Therefore, bioremediation is a viable option but the toxicity of contaminants to microorganisms and plants to be used for such purpose have to be considered. Another factor to be considered while using biological agents for cleanup is the bioavailability of the metals. Water pH affects the speciation and bioavailability to a considerable level, for example, at pH 7, 68µM of cobalt is predicted to exist in the free ionic form while only 4.1 µM of nickel remains in this form (Sandarin and Hoffman, 2007). Hence, using a buffering system to maintain pH or using lime to increase pH or alum to reduce pH is advisable.

## MICROBIAL BIOREMEDIATION OF METALS

Organic compounds are detoxified or removed by the microbes by converting them into harmless water, carbon dioxide and other volatile gases but metals are just transformed by the microbes to less soluble or bioavailable form (Lovley & Coates, 1997). This generally is made possible by converting inorganic forms into organic forms by redox conversions and coupling in respiratory pathways (Lovley & Coates, 1997; Tebo *et al.* 1997). Microbes have capabilities to immobilize metals by bioaccumulation and biosorption. The process of active uptake of metals by bacteria is termed as bioaccumulation while passive uptake is called biosorption (Unz & Shuttleworth, 1996).

**Bioaccumulation** is an interaction between the microorganism and the metal ion in relation to metabolic pathways. Metal ions required for biological functions are actively taken up by the microbes and converted into organic forms. Accumulation of radio nucleotides through the pathways of their stable isotopes or of chemical homologous elements can be considered as bioaccumulation. One such example is of accumulation of cesium by potassium channels (Avery, 1995).

**Biosorption** is simply a physiochemical process of accumulating metal species by sorption, surface complexion, ion exchange and entrapment (Gadd, 2004; Le Cloirec & AndrÃ, 2005). The biosorption qualities of *Saccharomyces cerevisiae* have a special mention. This is a by-product of fermentation and brewery industry and is hence quite cost effective to treat water bodies dissolving certain metals (Lovley & Coates, 1997; Unz & Shuttleworth, 1996). In fact, the dehydrated yeast *Candida utilis* demonstrated improved chromium sorption (Simmons, Tobin & Singleton, 1995). *Micrococcus luteus, Pseudomonas aeruginosa* and *Escherichia coli* have also been attributed with biosorption properties of metals like chromium, copper, nickel and cobalt (Churchill & Churchill, 1995).

Peptidoglycan carboxylic groups of the gram-positive bacteria phosphate groups in gram-negative bacteria (Beveridge & Doyle, 1989; McLean, Lee, & Beveridge, 2002; Schultze-Lam, Fortin, Davis, & Beveridge, 1996), chitin in fungal cell walls, chitosan and other chitin derivatives (Simmons *et al.*, 1995) have been attributed with metal adsorptive properties. Fungal phenolic polymers and melanins possess many potential metal binding sites with oxygen-containing groups such as carboxyl, phenolic and alcoholic hydroxyl, carbonyl and methoxyl groups (G. M. Gadd & White, 1993). Due to its cost effectiveness and easy availability of raw material, this technology is being widely appreciated and accepted. This method not only remediates effluents and water in the water bodies but recovery of soluble metals is also possible (Gavrilescu, 2004). This technology is being used as immobilized living biomass mainly in the form of bacterial biofilms on inert supports in a variety of bioreactor configurations such as rotating biological contactors, fixed bed reactors, trickle filters, fluidized beds and air-lift bioreactors (G. M. Gadd, 2001; G. M. Gadd & White, 1993; Macaskie & Dean, 1989; Schiewer & Volesky, 2000).

Not only microorganisms but also other biosorbent substrates like tamaring shell, rice husk, cottonseed hull, corncobs, almond and peanut hulls have been shown to remove heavy metal ions (Johnson *et al.* 2002; Kumar & Bandyoadhyay, 2006; Rao Popuri *et al.* 2007; Shen & Duvnjak, 2005).

Bioremediation of certain metals by microbes can be affected by mobilization (G. M. Gadd, 2004). Microorganisms can affect dissolution of metals by leaching, chelation while they are metabolized by action of siderophores. Once leached or chelated, the metals become unavailable for biological functions in water. Processes such as methylation of certain metals can also volatilize them facilitating the removal from water. In general, mobilization is affected by various methods like chemoorganotrophic leaching, autotrophic leaching, siderophores, biomethylation and redox transformations.

## CHEMOORGANOTROPHIC LEACHING (HETEROTROPHIC)

Microorganisms maintain their charge balance through H+ efflux through H+-ATPase pumps so as to neutralize metabolic carbon dioxide. This proton efflux causes the microenvironment surrounding the biofilm to get acidic and lead to metal release from the soil (G. M. Gadd, 2004). There is a dynamic equilibrium between the metals adsorbed in the soil and metal ions dissolved in water. Acidification of water shifts the equilibrium and causes the release of ions into water from soil. Microbes also release some organic acids that are formed during metabolic processes which supply water with protons and metal-complexing anions (Burgstaller & Schinner, 1993; G. M. Gadd, 1999). Citrate and oxalate ions have the ability to form complexes with a wide variety of elements (G. M. Gadd, 2001).

Metallocitrate ions are very stable and hard to break thereby removing many metals from water (Francis, Dodge & Gillow, 1992). Oxalate forms stable complexes with Al, Li, Mn and Fe (Strasser, Burgstaller, & Schinner, 1994). Acid producing fungi is a better approach for bioremediation as they can tolerate a wider fluctuation in pH than bacteria (Burgstaller & Schinner, 1993). Some of the acid producing fungi are *Yarrowia lipolytica* (citric), *Mucor spp.*(fumaric and gluconic), *Rhizopus spp.* (lactic, fumaric and gluconic), *Aspergillus niger* (citric, oxalic, gluconic), *Aspergillus spp.* (citric, tartaric, malic, α-ketoglutaric, itaconic, aconitic), *Penicillium spp.* (citric, tartaric, malic, α-ketoglutaric, gluconic) and *Schizophyllum commune* (malic) (Burgstaller & Schinner, 1993).

## AUTOTROPHIC LEACHING

Some bacteria oxidize ferrous ions or reduce sulphur so as to obtain energy. Such a chemical change results in solublization of metals as the end product is usually Fe(III) or $H_2SO_4$ which are soluble (Rawlings, 1997; Schippers & Sand, 1999). Such bacterial are called chemoautotrohic, chemolithotrophic and acidophilic bacteria which fix carbon by obtaining energy from such chemical reactions (G. M. Gadd, 2001). Organic acids act as carbon substrates which are oxidized completely to $CO_2$ or to some other organic intermediates. The ATPs are produced through electron transport chain with sulphur as terminal electron acceptor which is reduced to sulphide (Hansen, 1993; Peck Jr, 1993). The sulphide so generated form metal sulphide and gets precipitated. Sulphur reducing bacteria are essentially anaerobic (White, Shaman, & Gadd, 1998). Some of the bacterial species used in bioremediation are: sulphur oxidizing *Thiobacillus thioxidans*, Iron and sulphur oxidizing *T. ferroxidans*, Iron oxidizing *Leptospirillum ferroxidans* (Bosecker, 2006; Ewart & Hughes, 1991). Autotrophic reduction of sulphuric acid causes metals to soublize from sewage and sludge (Sreekrishnan & Tyagi 1994; White *et al.*, 1998). Both sulphate and iron reducing bacteria have been used to treat the mine waste water in artificial wet lands (Hammack & Edenborn, 1992).

## SIDEROPHORES

Siderophores (from the Greek: "iron carriers") are defined as relatively low molecular weight, ferric ion specific chelating agents released by bacteria and fungi growing under low iron stress (Neilands, 1995). Bacteria producing siderophores have been used to treat metal contaminated sandy soils.

*Alcaligenes eutrophus* is used to solublize metal from contaminated soils which can be removed by biosorption techniques as mention earlier. This method has been used effectively for reduction of Cd, Zn and Pb from contaminated soils (Diels, De Smet, Hooyberghs, & Corbisier, 1999).

## BIOMETHYLATION

Microbes can methylate metals so as to yield volatile derivatives such as dimethylselenide and trimethylarsine (Brady, Tobin, & Gadd, 1996; Dungan & Frankenberger, 1999; G. Gadd, 1993). Selenium methylation has been widely discussed and the probable mechanism is by transfer of methyl group to selenium by S-adenosyl methionine system (G. Gadd, 1993). Mediation of Hg, As, Se, Sn, Te and Pb by bacteria has been discussed by Gadd, (2004).

## BIOREMEDIATION OF PETROLEUM CONTAMINANTS

Petroleum and its components drive the present civilization and are the major energy sources. But, where there is use there is a chance for abuse too. Hence, being the prime source of energy, petroleum is also a major environment pollutant. Since 1992, there have been 21 major oil spills causing huge economic and immeasurable non-economic losses (Cedre, 2012. http://www.endgame.org/oilspills.htm). Petroleum contamination is quite harmful for the higher organisms (Cheong *et al.*, 2011; Janjua, Kasi, Nawaz, Farooqui, & Khuwaja, 2006; Lyons, Temple, Evans, Fone, & Palmer, 1999) but it is fortunate that microorganisms can thrive on it and assimilate (Atlas, 1995; de Oliveira *et al.*, 2012). Soon after major oil spill incident is reported, the efforts are concentrated at physical removal of oil but they rarely achieve complete clean up. As per Office of Technology Assessment (OTA; USA), such mechanical methods are efficient at removing no more than 10-15 per cent of oil after a major spill. In such cases, bioremediation has a major role to play in neutralizing the harmful effects of oil in the open environment. The basic principle is to use organisms that can use petroleum as carbon source and hence, break them down to harmless end products.

Like any other technology that uses biological agents, success of bioremediation of petroleum contamination also depends on establishing and maintaining conditions that favour proliferation of petroleum scavenging microorganisms. Bioaugmentation and Biostimulation are the two main approaches followed in this regard. Bioaugmentation refers to inoculating the affected area with degrading microorganisms while biostimulation would require favouring growth of such microorganism through addition of nutrients or by providing other growth-limiting substrates (e.g. oxygen, surf washing etc.). As petroleum is hydrophobic in nature, its bioavailability becomes a major constraint in the process of bioremediation. Use of biosurfactants is a common approach to increase the bioavailability. Requirements of a successful bioremediation process of petroleum contamination are as follows:

The very first requirement is the availability of microorganisms that can utilize oil as a metabolic substrate. Finding and transplanting such an organism to the site of contamination would be the first approach. Jones *et al.*, in 1983 reported for the first time biodegraded petroleum byproducts in marine sediments (Das & Chandran, 2010). Enzymatic degradation of petroleum can be achieved by bacteria, algae or fungi. Different organisms have varied degradation capabilities and act on different substrates. As petroleum is an assortment of different components, it is advisable to use a cocktail of organisms to effect remediation. Bacteria are the most efficient of all organisms that can degrade hydrocarbons (Rahman *et al.*, 2003; Brooijmans 2009. Floodgate, (1984) mentioned 25 genera of hydrocarbon degrading bacteria and 25 genera of hydrocarbon degrading fungi which were isolated from marine environment.

Some of the bacteria recognized as hydrocarbon degrading are *Arthrobacter, Burkholderia, Mycobacterium, Pseudomonas, Sphingomonas, Rhodococcus, Pseudomonas fluorescens, P. aeruginosa, Bacillus subtilis, Bacillus sp., Alcaligenes sp., Acinetobacter lwoffi, Flavobacterium sp., Micrococcus roseus,* and *Corynebacterium sp.* (Jones *et al.*, 1983; Adebusoye *et al.*, 2007). Some fungal genera utilized for this purpose are *Amorphoteca, Neosartorya, Tal aromyces, Graphium, Candida lipolytica, Yarrowia, Pichia, Aspergillus, Cephalosporium, Rhodotorula mucilaginosa, Geotrichum sp, Trichosporon mucoides and Pencillium* (Boguslawska-Was & Dabrowski, 2001; Chaillan *et al.*, 2004; Singh, 2006). After the potential scavengers have been identified, the conditions for their survival and proliferation have to be ascertained.

Among the physical factors temperature is most important one determining the survival of microorganisms and composition of the hydrocarbons (Das & Chandran, 2010). At higher temperature some fraction may get evaporated and the oil would tend to spread while in low temperature the slick would be more viscous and retention of otherwise volatile fractions thereby delaying the bioremediation process. For freshwater bioremediation process 20-30 °C is the ideal temperature while for marine 15-20 °C is recommended. For high molecular weight polycyclic hydrocarbons, which are otherwise difficult to degrade, higher temperatures may be required (Bartha and Bossert, 1984; Cooney, 1984). As temperature has effect on enzymatic turnover rate "$Q^{10}$" hence, higher temperature would favour bioremediation. It was reported that the rate of hydrocarbon remediation was maximum in the range of 30-40 °C in general and above this, the membrane toxicity effect of hydrocarbons was found to inhibit the survival of microorganisms (Bartha and Bossert., 1984). As there is a close relationship between temperature and oil bioremediation, it is easy to understand why an oil leak disaster would be dangerous in polar regions.

The first step in degrading hydrocarbons is action of oxygenase which requires molecular oxygen (Das & Chandran, 2010). By the action of monooxygenases (on aliphatic and certain aromatic hydrocarbons) or dioxygenases (on aromatic hydrocarbons), one or two oxygen atoms, respectively, are directly incorporated from $O_2$ leading to hydroxylated products (Widdel & Rabus, 2001). As hydrocarbons are less denser than water, they would form a layer over water and oxygen limitation would rarely be encountered. But, under the condition of large spill and extensive bacterial colonies thriving on it, oxygen may get depleted soon leading to anaerobic conditions (Thapa, KC, & Ghimire, 2012). Oxygen though usually not a rate determining step may become limiting when aquatic sediments are deeper or water movement through small pores of sediment is restricted so that oxygen is not replenished (Salleh *et al.*, 2003). Though contrbution of anaerobic bacteria to bioremediation is still considered negligible, Widdel and Rabus, (2001) report that some anaerobic bacteria may still have some role to play while it is a matter of time till they are discovered. Some anaerobic bacteria that may have role to play in hydrocarbon degradation are *Syntrophus spp., Methanosaeta spp., Metanospirillum spp., Desulfotomaculum spp., Geobacter spp.* (Watanabe, 2001).

It is well known that nitrogen and phosphorus are the major nutrients for productivity in an aquatic habitat. At the time of oil spills, there is a sudden increase in the carbon and hence, nitrogen and phosphorus would become major rate limiting factors (Cooney *et al.*, 1985). A sudden increase in the carbon:nitrogen ratio or carbon:phosphorus ratio at the time of oil spill or contamination would restrict the growth of microbes (Leahy & Colwell, 1990) hence, it would be vital to restore the balance by adding oleophilic fertilizers. The optimum nutrient balance required for hydrocarbon remediation is Carbon: Nitrogen: Phosphorus equals 100:10:4 (Thapa *et al.*, 2012). However, in the regions where there is high nitrogen background, nutrition addition has no or rather negative effect on bioremediation rates and hence, fertilization is recommended only for those regions that are deficient in nutrients (Oudot *et al.*, 1998).

Microbial communities have salinity tolerance and this aspect is important for aquatic ecosystems as salinity is very much relevant when bioremediation of water comes into discussion. While freshwater and estuarine communities can survive in sea water, the inverse is not successful (Salleh *et al.*, 2003). As sea water is buffered and salinity is constant in deeper regions maintenance is required only in expanses where freshwater dilutions may vary with time. Salinity maintenance is required for the inland regions where salinities may change with surface runoff. In sea water, the autochthonous communities degrade hydrocarbons efficiently and the degradation can be significant till the salinities are in the range of 0.1 to 2.0 M NaCl, 0.4 M NaCl being the salinity level of natural sea water (Salleh *et al.*, 2003). Ward and Brock, (1978) established a negative relation between salinity and biodegradation of petroleum containants owing to less survival of microbial communities in very high salinities. However, some bacteria like *Streptomyces albaxialis* (Kuznetsov *et al.*, 1992) for crude oil degradation and *Halobacterium spp.* (Kulichevskaya, Milekhina, Borzenkov, Zvyagintseva, & Belyaev, 1992) for degradation of n-alkanes (C10-C30) have been identified. Kapley *et al.*, 1999 cloned *E. coli* pro U operon, which is responsible for osmoregulation, into some bacterial consortium which can attack various fractions of crude oil making them salinity tolerant upto 6 per cent NaCl.

pH also had an implication on biodegradation rates. The rates were found to be highest at neutral pH (Leahy & Colwell, 1990). Lower pH at around 5.0 (Patrick Jr & DeLaune, 1977) as seen in salt marshes reduces oil mineralization but the rates were satisfactory at pH above 6.5 (Hambrick, DeLaune, & Patrick, 1980). Octadecane mineralization improved further at pH 8.0 (Leahy & Colwell, 1990).

Bioavailability of petroleum is a major problem that limits the rate of biodegradation. In order to enhance bioavailability, it is must that solubilization be increased. Such a task is accomplished by certain microorganisms that secrete surfactants which is a group of surface active chemicals that increase the bioavailability of petroleum floating on the water column by increasing their solubilisation (Das & Chandran, 2010). Biosurfactants increase the oil surface area and hence, the amount of oil that is actually available for degradation to the bacteria. Due to this property of enhancing biodegradation of oil such surfactant producing bacteria have potential to be used in bioremediation (Cameotra & Singh, 2008). A consortium of bacteria was used for evaluation of surfactants and their composition by Camoetra & Singh, 2008. The surfactant was found to be a conglomerate of 11 rhamnolipid family members and found that crude biosurfactant addition to the oil contamination was very effective in degradation process. Genus *Pseudomonas* is widely known for efficient surfactant production properties (Rahman *et al.*, 2007; Cameotra & Singh, 2008; Beal & Betts, 2000; Pornsunthorntawee *et al.*,2008). Some of the bioactive species that have been identified and their source are mentioned in Table 6.1.

**Table 6.1: Surfactant Species and Their Source Organism**

| Surfactant Species | Source Organism | Reference |
|---|---|---|
| Sophorolipids | *Candida bombicola* | Davery & Pakshirajan, 2009 |
| Rhamnolipids | *Pseudomonas aeruginosa,*<br>*P. fluorescens* | Kumar *et al.*, 2008<br>Muthusamy *et al.*, 2008 |
| Lipomann | *C. tropicalis* | Mahmound *et al.*, 2008 |
| Sufactin | *Bacillus subtilis* | Youssef *et al.*, 2007 |
| Glycolipid | *Aeromonas sp.*<br>*Bacillus sp* | Iluri *et al.*, 2005<br>Tabatabaee *et al.*, 2005 |

(Modified from Das & Chandran, 2010)

Obbard *et al.*, (2004) demonstrated that addition of crude palm oil and myristic, oleic, linoleic and palmitic acids (0.5% dry weight equivalent) enhanced the degradation rate of Arabian light crude oil contamination by 170 times through metabolic enhancement of microbial communities.

## BIOREMEDIATION OF PESTICIDES

Today, intensification of agriculture has increased the risk of losses due to improper crop health making agriculture sector heavily dependent upon the use of pesticides to prevent losses from pests. Pesticides are usually applied as a spray over the crop in aqueous or some non-polar solvent medium of which only 5 per cent is estimated to be utilized for the intended purpose and the rest remains in the environment as residues. These residues may get washed off and either seep into the ground water or reach water bodies along with the runoff. Once reaching the water bodies, the process of bio-magnification begins. Vaccari *et al.* (2006) estimated that pesticide Dichlorodiphenyldichloroethane (DDD) may get accumulated 85,000 times more in a predatory fish than at concentration it enters in water.

Some pesticides may get decomposed sooner after they are dissolved in a solvent but the most commonly used organochlorides have a very long half-life making them threatening to the ecosystem and human beings. Pesticides may get accumulated in the human adipose tissue which enter the system orally, through inhalation and some are even absorbed dermally. In humans, pesticides may cause irritation, affect mental health, affect digestion and even cause carcinosis (Green and Hoffnagle, 2004). Concern of this chapter would only be limited to persistent organic pesticides which have a very long half-life and are recalcitrant. UNEP's (United Nations Environment Programme) list of persistent organic pollutants, including aldrin, chlordane, DDT, dieldrin, endrin, heptachlor, hexachlorobenzenes, mirex and toxaphene.

Sometimes the pesticide used may be less toxic than the degraded product that is produced from it. Hence, an effective bioremediation technique would be one that acts fast so as to prevent the degradation process and the end product that results from bioremediation is either non-toxic or less toxic. Bioremediation of metal contaminants or hydrocarbon contaminants is easier as the organisms that can survive in excess of metals and hydrocarbons can be naturally found but this is not the case with pesticide as these are artificial chemicals intended to kill. Hence, identification of organisms that may help in bioremediation process is crucial. Usually four remediation technologies are followed at the pesticide contaminated regions - Low temperature desorption, Incineration, Bioremediation and Phytoremediation. All these techniques have their own advantages and disadvantages. While incineration and low temperature desorption are faster technologies they are usually very expensive. Bioremediation and phytoremediation on the other hand are very efficient and cheaper technologies but the time taken for remediation is very long and hence a major drawback. Since our concern is aquatic habitat, bioremediation and phytoremediation are by far the best technologies that can remove pesticide load from water and the water-soil interface.

White-rot fungi, particularly those of the family Phanerochaete, are becoming recognized for their ability to efficiently biodegrade toxic contaminants. Most studies focus on the ability of *Phanerochaete chrysosporium* to degrade persistent compounds, but *Phanerochaete sordida, Pleuotus ostreatus, Phellinus weirii,* and *Polyporus versicolor* have also been successful in laboratory studies (Safferman et al,. 1995). Watanabe *et al.*, (2008) reported anaerobic microbial strains that have the ability to degrade various types of POPs, such as HCB, dieldrin, endrin, aldrin, and heptachlor. Amongst the aerobic organic pesticide degrading bacteria, *Pseudomonas sp., Bacillus sp., Trichoderma viride* (Matsumura and Boush, 1967), *Aerobacter aerogenes* (Wedemeyer 1968), *Mucor alternans* (Anderson *et al.*1970), and *Trichoderma koningi* (Bixby *et al.* 1971) were isolated as dieldrin-degrading and *Pseudomonas sp., Micrococcus sp.*, and several other unidentified bacteria and yeast (Matsumura *et al.* 1971) were found to be endrin degrading microorganisms.

Principal compound among the organic solvent-soluble metabolites was 6,7-trans-dihydroxydihydroaldrin produced by *Pseudomonas sp., Bacillus sp.* (Matsumura and Boush, 1967), *A. aerogenes* (Wedemeyer, 1968), and *T. viride* (Matsumura and Boush, 1968). Microbial genes (*atz, trz, psb, tri, tfd, puh, and ndo*) encoding different groups of enzymes like dehalogenase, dehydrogenase, dehydro-chlorinase, hydrolase, haloperoxidase, urease, cytochrome P450, deaminase, dioxygenase, isomerases, reductases, and glutathione S transferases were found to have been involved in herbicide degradation and are also involved in pesticide degradation (Hussain *et al.*, 2009). Sutherland *et al.*, (2002) reported gene Esd in *Mycobacterium spp.* capable of mineralising â-endosulfan. *Ese* gene from *Arthrobacter spp.* isolated by Weir *et al.* (2006) is capable of mineralizing both á and â form of endosulfan and endosulfate. A group of lin genes (*lin, lin*A, *lin*B, *lin*C, *lin*D, *lin*E, *lin*X), which encode several enzymes like dehalogenase, dehydrogenase, dehydrochlorinase, and hydrolase, have been reported in numerous gram-negative Hexacholorohexane degrading soil bacteria (Boltner *et al.*, 2005; Cérémonie *et al.*, 2006).

*Nocardia spp.* was identified to have *trz*N gene responsible for initial dechlorination of atrazine into hydroxyatrazine which is further dealkylated in two step reaction (Smith, 2005). Gene *atz*C is required for ring cleavage and was found in *Agrobacterium tumefaciens, Caulobacter crescentus, Pseudomonas putida, Sphingomonas yaniokuyae, Nocardia sp., Rhizobium sp., Flavobacterium oryzihabitans,and Variovorax paradoxus*. Similarly many, other genes have been discovered that characterize the utility of microbes for bioremediation of organic pesticides. Such genes have been summarized by Hussain *et al.*, 2009.

As mentioned earlier, there are different methods to carry out remediation of pesticide contamination and which method to adopt is crucial. Bioremediation techniques are effective and can act even on very small amount of contamination but when the contamination is severe and affects the immediate survival of organisms in the affected area then other methods like incineration and desorption may have to be used so as to provide immediate relief and the residues from such treatments may be left for bioremediation. Therefore, different techniques may be used so as to effectively remove the pesticide contaminants.

## BIOREMEDIATION OF ORGANIC XENOBIOTICS

Organic xenobiotics in aquatic habitats have a varied origin - industrial effluents, incomplete combustion of fuels, forest and grass fires, biosynthesis of hydrocarbons by aquatic or terrestrial organisms, post-depositional transformation of biogenic precursors, diffusing from the mantle, petroleum source rocks or reservoirs (Perelo, 2010). Persistent organic pollutants (POP) are a major source of concern amongst these organic xenobiotics due to very long half-life that makes them almost indestructible for years and years under natural conditions. Perelo, (2010) classified organic xenobiotics in aquatic sediments under four headings: *(a)* Polycyclic aromatic hydrocarbons (PAH), *(b)* Polychlorinated biphenyls (PCBs), *(c)* Polychlorinated dibenzo-p-dioxins and dibenzofurans (PCDD/Fs), and *(d)* others.

### (a) Polycyclic aromatic hydrocarbons (PAH)

Over hundred PAH have been identified which have their origin from incomplete combustion of organic substances and rarely are of industrial use, except for a few PAHs used in medicines and the production of dyes, plastics and pesticides (US-EPA, 2008). They are highly hydrophobic making them insoluble in water, hence, they tend to get adsorbed on the aquatic sediments where they usually do not get decomposed and get accumulated later on in aquatic flora and fauna. PAH are carcinogenic and highly mutagenic (Perelo, 2010). Chronic toxic effects from high PAH concentrations in sediments on benthic and aquatic organisms have been reported (Jerónimo *et al.*, 2008).

### (b) Polychlorinated biphenyls (PCBs)

These are used widely in industry and get into the aquatic system through industrial discharge and spillage. Perhaps, they are most toxic and highly persistent nature and are classified as the most dangerous of all the POPs. They are toxic and carcinogenic, have wide distribution and degrade at very slow rate. As per a very old NRC report there are hundred thousand tonnes of commercial PCB persistent in aquatic sediments and the quantity might have magnified since then (NRC, 1979).

**(c) Polychlorinated dibenzo-p-dioxins and dibenzofurans (PCDD/Fs)**

Though they were deposited decades ago under the sediments but are still found buried due to their high recalcitrant nature and non-bioavailability. Chlorine substitutions at 2, 3, 7 and 8 position makes them highly toxic and carcinogenic to humans (Kaiser, 2000).

**(d) Others**

Under this classification are included chlorinated compounds such as trichloroethane, carbontetrachloride and pentachlorophenols which are of industrial use and get into atmosphere through leakage or disposal of old machinery. Such chlorinated compounds are also used as industrial solvents.

Physical remediation of xenobiotics require processes such as dredging and excavating which may reduce the environmental load of pollutants but tamper with the ecosystem and may cause harm. Bioremediation is by and large non-invasive technique and results in complete mineralization of pollutants in an economical way. Naphthalene being the simplest PAH is most widely studied. The biochemical sequence and enzymatic reactions leading to the degradation of naphthalene were first presented by Davies and Evans, (1964). The principal mechanism for the aerobic bacterial metabolism of PAHs is the initial oxidation of the benzene ring by the action of dioxygenase enzymes to form *cis*-dihydrodiols. These dihydrodiols are dehydrogenated to form dihydroxylated intermediates, which can then be further metabolised via catechols to carbon dioxide and water (Bamforth & Singleton, 2005).

Usually gram-negative bacteria belonging to genus *Pseudomonas* have been attributed with PAH degradative properties though other genera like *Mycobacterium, Corynebacterium, Aeromonas, Rhodococcus* and *Bacillus* have also been found to have to such properties (Allard & Neilson, 1997; Annweiler *et al.*, 2000; Cerniglia, 1984). A naphthalene oxygenase has also been isolated from cells of *Corynebacterium renale*, which was able to use naphthalene as a main source of carbon and energy (Cerniglia, 1984). Like any other polar hydrocarbon, PAH are not biologically available for degradation which makes the application of bioremediation difficult. To overcome such difficulties, usage of surfactants is suggested. SDS, TritonX-102, Brij 35, Marlipal 013/90 and Genapol X150 are some of the surfactants that increases the concentration of hydrophobic compounds in the water phase by solubilization or emulsification.

Solubilization occurs above a specific threshold of surficant, the critical micellar concentration (CMC) where surfactant molecules aggregate to micelles. Usage of organic solvents have also been tried to increase the bioavailability of organic xenobiotics. Lee *et al.*, (2001) using acetone and ethanol found that total PAH biodegradation rates for soils pretreated with these solvents were estimated to be about twice faster than soils without solvent pretreatment. Using such solvents in water may not be good idea if it is found that such solvents themselves are of polluting nature, however, low molecular weight solvents are usually volatile and can be removed once their job is done.

Swampy habitats can be remediated by the use of bacteria or by inoculating them with ligninolytic or non-ligninolytic fungus. Ligninolytic fungi, such as *Phanerochaete chrysosporium*, are commonly associated with woody materials; however these fungi can be enriched in a soil by the addition of straw, wood chips and other lignin rich substrates (Bamforth & Singleton, 2005). Ligninolytic and non-lignolytic fungus have different mode of action. The first step in the metabolism of PAHs by nonligninolytic fungi is to oxidise the aromatic ring in a cytochrome P450 monoxygenase enzyme catalyzed reaction to produce an arene oxide (Sutherland *et al.*, 1995). Arene oxide is subsequently hydrated via an epoxide-hydrolase catalysed reaction to form a trans-dihydrodiol (Jerina,1983). In addition, phenol derivatives may be produced from arene oxides by the non-enzymatic rearrangement of the compound, which can act as substrates for subsequent sulfation or methylation, or conjugation with glucose, xylose, or glucuronic acid (Mueller *et al.*, 1996). Such conjugates are usually the end products of the fungal action and are less toxic than the parent compound. Complete mineralization by non ligninolytic fungi is usually not seen. *Chrysosporium pannorum, Cunninghamella elegans and Aspergillus niger* are examples of non-ligninolytic fungi that use a P450 monoxygenase enzyme-mediated oxidative pathway for PAH degradation (Bamforth & Singleton, 2005).

Ligninolytic fungi or white rot fungi are found on wood and have lignolytic enzymes capable of oxidizing lignin and other organic material present in wood. Peroxidases and laccases are two types of ligninolytic enzymes secreted extracellularly and oxidise organic matter via a non-specific radical based reaction (Kirk & Farrell, 1987; Mester & Tien, 2000). Lignin peroxidase (LP) and manganese peroxidase (MnP) are two types of peroxidase enzymes both of which are capable of oxidising PAHs (Mester & Tien, 2000). Lacasses are basically phenol oxidase enzymes and are also capable of oxidizing PAHs. There is significant interest surrounding the use of ligninolytic fungi to degrade PAHs, owing to their low substrate specificity and hence the capability to degrade even the most recalcitrant of compounds. Also, the enzymes involved are extracellular, and are theoretically able to diffuse into the soil or sediment matrix and potentially oxidise PAHs with low bioavailability (Bamforth & Singleton, 2005).

## FACTORS AFFECTING BIOREMEDIATION OF ORGANIC XENOBIOTICS

### (a) Temperature

Like petroleum bioremediation, organic xenobiotic bioavailability also increases thereby increasing their bioremediation rates. PAH degradation has been reported over a wide range of temperatures from 0° C in seawater to temperature as high as above 75 °C in spent-mushroom compost (Lau *et al.*, 2003; Siron *et al.*,1995).

**(b) pH**

Indigenous bacteria and other microorganisms usually do not act in acidic or alkaline conditions on organic xenobiotics. Phenanthrene degradation in liquid culture with *Burkholderia cocovenenas*, an organism isolated from a petroleum-contaminated soil was found to be better near neutral pH (Wong *et al.*, 2002). A similar result was obtained with *Sphingomonas paucimobilis* (strain BA 2) for the degradation of the PAHs phenanthrene and anthracene (Kastner *et al.*, 1998). Bioremediation at higher and low pH does occur but the rates are lower than the near neutral atmosphere hence liming so as to normalize pH is suggested.

**(c) Oxygen**

Though it has been confirmed that PAH degradation may occur even under anaerobic conditions, bioaugmentation of microbial communities by aeration usually has been found to speed up the remediation rates. Under high temperatures oxygen solubility reduces hence artificial aeration of affected sites may be required along with a rise in temperature so as to speed up the bioremediation reactions.

**(d) Nutrient availability**

Nutrient availability for organic xenobiotics is considered to be similar to the requirement for petroleum bioremediation. Carbon being in rich quantities other nutrients like nitrogen and phosphates might be a limiting factor thus fertilization is required.

**(e) Bioavailability**

Bioavailability can be defined as the effect of physicochemical and microbiological factors on the rate and extent of biodegradation and is believed to be one of the most important factors in bioremediation (Bamforth & Singleton, 2005). These compounds are hydrophobic and therefore, poor bioavailablity. Moreover, organic xenobiotics can undergo rapid sorption to mineral surfaces (i.e. clays) and organic matter (i.e. humic and fulvic acids) in the soil matrix. Longer the PAH is in contact with soil, the more irreversible the sorption, and the lower is the chemical and biological extractability of the contaminant. This phenomenon is known as 'ageing' of the contaminant. Application of surfactants or use of organic solvents as discussed previously is usually done to increase the bioavailability.

## PHYTOREMEDIATION

Plants have long been exposed to different climatic and environmental conditions and therefore have been overcoming various stressors. Plants have evolved various ways to survive by utilizing different substrates and cleaning up their vicinity so as to perpetuate. Phytoremediation makes use of this characteristic of plants to survive on different substrates. Phytoremediation consists of a set of innovative technologies for environmental cleanup that takes advantage of the unique extractive and metabolic capabilities of plants. There are four characteristics preferred in a plant for phytoremediation techniques. The first is that the plant should be able to accumulate the pollutants to be extracted. Secondly, the plants should have enough tolerance to be able to not only survive in polluted soils, but to carry pollutants within their shoots. Thirdly, the species should be fast growing with an amplified ability to accumulate toxins. Lastly, the plant should be easily harvestable for simple disposal (Kärenlampi *et al.*, 2000).

Phytoremediation consists of a collection of four different plant-based technologies based on different mechanism of action.

1. Phytostabilization- plants used to stabilize rather than cleaning contaminated soil.
2. Phytovolatilization- use of plants to extract certain metals from soil and then release them into the atmosphere through volatilization.
3. Phytoextraction/Rhizofiltration- plants absorb metals from soil and translocate them to the harvestable shoots where they accumulate.

### 1. Phytostabilisation

This is not a cleaning up technology as such but is used where inactivation of contaminants is required. It reduces the risks presented by a contaminated soil by decreasing contaminants' bioavailability using plants, eventually in combination with soil amendments (Vangronsveld *et al.* 1995; Vangronsveld and Cunningham 1998). Plants help to stabilize contaminants by accumulating and precipitating toxic trace elements in the roots (or root zone) or by adsorption on root surfaces. Plants may also alter the chemical form of the contaminants by changing the soil environment (e.g., pH, redox potential) around plant roots which is usually achieved by the action of microorganisms (bacteria and mycorrhiza) living in the rhizosphere of these plants. These bacteria not only change the physio-chemical properties of the soil around the roots but they also prevent phytotoxicity (Van der Lelie *et al.* 1999; Mastretta *et al.* 2006).

### 2. Phytovolatilisation

Some metals like arsenic (As), mercury (Hg) and selenium (Se) may exist in gaseous form in the atmosphere. Plants take up such metals, convert them into gaseous form and excrete them through transpiration. This technique of remediating water or sludge is controversial as elements like arsenic and mercury are harmful even in gaseous form. This technique, hence, is used away from human habitation. Some plants of family Brassicaseae is capable of releasing Se into atmosphere through aerial parts. Aquatic plant, cattail (*Typha latifolia*) is also known to have Se excretion capacities in gaseous form *Arabidopsis thaliana* L. and tobacco (*Nicotiana tabacum* L.) have been genetically modified with bacterial organ mecurial lyase (*mer*B) and mercuric reductase (*mer*A) genes. Hybrid poplar and Eastern cottonwood is also known to have phytovolatalisaiton capacities.

### 3. Phytoextraction

This technique involves use of plant that is known to accumulate contaminants in its vascular tissue and later this plant is properly disposed, usually by incineration. Rhizofiltration is the term used in the context of aquatic ecosystem. This technique is usually used for accumulation of heavy metals and radioactive nuclides. Marine algae, water hyacinth (*Eichhornia crassipes*) are known to have phytoextraction properties. Cyanide CN, is commonly used in extraction of silver and gold in the industries. After the extraction, solvent is usually discharges in to water bodies which keep accumulating CN. Such water bodies can use water hyacinth which take up and store cyanide. Phytoextraction can also be used for economic purposes where suitable plants can be grown for phytomining. Algae along the coasts are known to accumulate radionuclides and other trace metals too.

## GENETICALLY MODIFIED ORGANISMS IN BIOREMEDIATION

With acceptance of genetically modified organisms for food like *Bt*-cotton and *Bt*-brinjal there is an attempt to look into other aspects where biotechnology can be used so as to utilize more and more aquatic habitats for food production. Water bodies have traditionally been the dumping grounds for anthropogenic waste but with rising population there is a demand to increase the area under crop cultivation. It is necessary that we efficiently utilize our water bodies to produce fish/shellfish/aquatic plant for human consumption. Remediation of contaminated sites and water bodies can help in reclaiming the lost regions again for food production. It is possible that a contaminated site may not be congenial for inoculating with a microorganism or a plant that is capable of effective bioremediation hence transforming a locally available species would be an excellent idea. Many genes have been identified in bacteria and in plants that help in survival of these organisms in contaminated.

A major problem in utilizing microorganisms for bioremediation is the acceptance. Release of more competent microorganisms into atmosphere may change the biodiversity of the region and hence we may lose our objective of site restoration to quite an extent. In such cases it is wise to develop GM-plant which is easier to control than bacteria or fungi. Another approach would be to develop bioremediation competency in symbiotic bacteria which remain in relationship with roots of plants and hence do not spread. Another approach can be to develop bioremediation capable endophytes. Trichloroethylene (TCE)-degrading bacteria have been proven to protect host plants against the phytotoxicity of TCE and to contribute to a significant decrease in TCE evapotranspiration. Mass accumulators like *Thlaspi caerulescenscan* take up sufficient amounts of metals through its roots but such plants usually have low biomass.

Development of larger mass bioaccumulators is another approach. Incorporation of bacterial genes in plants so as to produce enzymes capable of degrading pollutants has been followed (Meagher, 2000; Rugh et al,. 1996). Most common approach in plant biotechnology has been to target enzymes involved in metal metabolism like metallothioneins, phytochelatins, glutathione (Clemens *et al.* 2002; Kotřba, *et al.* 1999). Manipulation of plant enzymes involved in phytochelation of metals has also been tried. Over expression of ATP sulfurylasein mustard plant facilitates increased selenium reduction and its storage as sulphated form which is less toxic in addition to this the storage metabolite methylselenocysteine is anticarcinogenic hence increasing the commercial value of the plant (Banuelos, 2005; Pilon-Smits, 1998). Nicotianamine synthase gene involved in the formation of phytosiderophore has been identified to be incorporated into plants so as to increases the bioavailability of metals to plants (Higuchi *et al.*1999; Rudolph *et al.* 1985).

Metabolism of organic POP requires cytochrome $P_{450}$ hence the gene responsible for this factor has been worked upon to increase the efficiency. Transgenic plants containing cytochrome $P_{450}$ 2E1 was shown to have increased hydrocarbon metabolizing efficiency (Doty et al 2000).Over expression of peroxidase in tomato has also shown increased phenol phytoremediation (Stiborova and Anzenbacher, 1991).

It was perhaps by Strong *et al.*, 2000 that the first genetically modified bacteria were used for bioremediation on field. Killed and whole cell suspension of *Escherichia coli* encapsulating over expressed atrazine chlorohydrolase, *Atz*A was used and it was found that atrazine levels reduced by 52-77 per cent after a period of eight weeks as compared to control. Diaz et al, 2003 utilized *opd* gene encoding organophosphatehydrolase (OPH) in *Escherichia coli* for biodegradation of methyle parathion. Organophosphorus hydrolase (OPH) degrades organophosphorus pesticides (OP) such as chlorpyrifos, paraoxon, parathion, disulfoton, dimeton, and carbophenothion.

After elucidation of biochemical pathways of metabolism of contaminants many more genes have been identified and tied for bioremediation. Commercial products for treatment of oil slick have received special attention due to lot of money involved in clearing up the oil spread. This field is open but the response from legislators, environmentalists and people keeps the excitement low. Perhaps, to allay the fear of people development of GM plants or symbiotic microbes is a safer option as they can be controlled after the cleaning is achieved.

## CONCLUSION

Industrial revolution and increased handling of heavy metals, POPs and similar hazardous chemicals has raised the chances of accidents. Nuclear disasters at Fukushima and other previous similar incidents have raised lot of questions about the usage of such hazardous chemicals. One thing is clear that with rising population and rising demand for food and energy will certainly rule out utilization of hazardous metals and other chemical but we can certainly develop technologies that can help in mopping them up so that impact on biodiversity and on human population can be minimized. Bioremediation is one such method which is ecofriendly, cost effective and cleans up the contaminants to quite an extent efficiently. But, slow pace and threat from genetically modified organisms to biodiversity may be deterrents to this technology. Bioremediation by itself may not be a complete solution to the problem of contamination but mixing physical and chemical remediation techniques with bioremediation may be an answer to complete remediation of natural resources.

## REFERENCES


Adebusoye, S.A., Ilori, M.O., Amund, O.O., Teniola, O.D., and Olatope, S. (2007). Microbial Degradation of Petroleum Hydrocarbons in a Polluted Tropical Stream. *World Journal of Microbiology and Biotechnology*, 23(8): 1149-1159.

Allard, A.S., and Neilson, A.H. (1997). Bioremediation of Organic Waste Sites: A Critical Review of Microbiological Aspects. *International Biodeterioration and Biodegradation*, 39(4): 253-285.

Annweiler, E., Richnow, H., Antranikian, G., Hebenbrock, S., Garms, C., Franke, S., Michaelis, W. (2000). Naphthalene Degradation and Incorporation of Naphthalene-Derived Carbon into Biomass by the Thermophile *Bacillus Thermoleovorans*. *Applied and Environmental Microbiology*, 66(2): 518-523.

Atlas, R.M. (1995). Bioremediation of Petroleum Pollutants. *International Biodeterioration and Biodegradation*, 35(1): 317-327.

Avery, S.V. (1995). Microbial Interactions with Caesium—Implications for Biotechnology. *Journal of Chemical Technology and Biotechnology*, 62(1): 3-16.

Bamforth, S.M., Singleton, I. (2005) Bioremediation of Polycyclic Aromatic Hydrocarbons: Current Knowledge and Future Directions. *Journal of Chemical Technology and Biotechnology* 80: 723-736.

Banner Jr, W., and Tong, T.G. (1986). Iron Poisoning. *Pediatric Clinics of North America*, 33(2): 393.

Banuelos, G. (2005) Field Trial of Transgenic Indian Mustard Plants Shows Enhanced Phytoremediation of Selenium-contaminated Sediments. *Environment Science and Technology* 39: 1771-1777.

Bartha R. and Bossert I. (1984). The Treatment and Disposal of Petroleum Wastes. *Petroleum Microbiology*, R.M.Atlas, Ed., pp. 553-578, Macmillan, New York, NY, USA.

Beal R. and Betts W. B. (2000). Role of Rhamnolipid Biosurfactants in the Uptake and Mineralization of Hexadecane in *Pseudomonas Aeruginosa. Journal of Applied Microbiology* 89(1): 158-168.

Beveridge, T.J., and Doyle, R.J. (1989). Metal Ions and Bacteria: Wiley-Interscience.

Boguslawska-Was, E., and Dabrowski, W. (2001). The Seasonal Variability of Yeasts and Yeast-like Organisms in Water and Bottom Sediment of the Szczecin Lagoon. *International journal of hygiene and environmental health,* 203(5): 451-458.

Boltner, D., Moreno-Morillas, S., and Ramos, J.L. (2005). 16S rDNA Phylogeny and Distribution of lin Genes in Novel Hexachlorocyclohexane-degrading *Sphingomonas* strains. *Environ. Microbiol.*, 7: 1329-1338.

Bosecker, K. (2006). Bioleaching: Metal Solubilization by Microorganisms. *FEMS Microbiology Reviews,* 20(3 4): 591-604.

Brady, J.M., Tobin, J.M., and Gadd, G.M. (1996). Volatilization of Selenite in Aqueous Medium by a *Penicillium* Species. *Mycological Research,* 100(8): 955-961.

Brooijmans, R., Pastink, M., and Siezen, R. (2009). Hydrocarbon-degrading Bacteria: The Oil-spill Clean-up crew. *Microbial Biotechnology,* 2(6): 587.

Bumpus, J.A., and Aust S.D. (1987). Biodegradation of DDT [1,1 1-Trichloro-2,2-Bis(4-Chlorophenyl)Ethane] by the White Rot Fungus *Phanerochaete chrysosporium. Applied and Environmental Microbiology* 53: 2000-2008.

Burgstaller, W., and Schinner, F. (1993). Leaching of Metals with Fungi. *Journal of Biotechnology,* 27(2): 91-116.

Bury, N.R., Walker, P.A., and Glover, C.N. (2003). Nutritive Metal Uptake in Teleost Fish. *Journal of Experimental Biology,* 206(1): 11-23.

Cameotra S.S. and. Singh P (2008). Bioremediation of Oil Sludge Using Crude Biosurfactants. *International Biodeteriorationand Biodegradation,* 62(3): 274-280.

Cérémonie, H., Boubakri, H., Mavingui, P., Simonet, P., and Vogel, T.M. (2006). Plasmid-encoded γ -hexachlorocyclohexane Degradation Genes and Insertion Sequences in *Sphingobium Francense* (ex-*Sphingomonas paucimobilis* Sp+). *FEMS Microbiology Letters,* 257: 243-252.

Cerniglia, C.E. (1984). Microbial Metabolism of Polycyclic Aromatic Hydrocarbons. *Advances in Applied Microbiology,* 30: 31-71.

Chaillan, F., Le Flèche, A., Bury, E., Phantavong, Y.H., Grimont, P., Saliot, A., and Oudot, J. (2004). Identification and Biodegradation Potential of Tropical Aerobic Hydrocarbon-degrading Microorganisms. *Research in Microbiology,* 155(7): 587.

Cheong, H.K., Ha, M., Lee, J.S., Kwon, H., Ha, E.H., Hong, Y.C., Lee, S.M. (2011). Hebei Spirit Oil Spill Exposure and Subjective Symptoms in Residents Participating in Clean-up Activities. *Environmental Health and Toxicology,* 26.

Churchill, S., and Churchill, P. (1995). Sorption of Heavy Metals by Prepared Bacterial Cell Surfaces. *Journal of Environmental Engineering,* 121: 706.

Clemens, S. et al. (2002). A Long Way Ahead: Understanding and Engineering Plant Metal Accumulation. *Trends in Plant Science* 7: 309-315

Cooney J. J.(1984).The Fate of Petroleum Pollutants in Fresh Water Ecosystems. *Petroleum Microbiology, R.M.* Atlas, Ed., pp. 399-434, Macmillan, New York, NY, USA, 1984.

Cooney, J., Silver, S., and Beck, E. (1985). Factors Influencing Hydrocarbon Degradation in Three Freshwater Lakes. *Microbial Ecology*, 11(2): 127-137.

Dalzell, D., and Macfarlane, N. (1999). The Toxicity of Iron to Brown Trout and Effects on the Gills: A Comparison of Two Grades of Iron Sulphate. *Journal of Fish Biology*, 55(2): 301-315.

Das, N., and Chandran, P. (2010). Microbial Degradation of Petroleum Hydrocarbon Contaminants: An Overview. *Biotechnology Research International*, 2011.

Daverey A. and Pakshirajan K.(2009) "Production of Sophorolipids by the Yeast *Candida bombicola* Using Simple and Low Cost Fermentative Media," *Food Research International*,. 42(4): 499–504.

Daverey, A. and Pakshirajan, K. (2009). Production, Characterization, and Properties of Sophorolipids from the Yeast *Candida bombicola* Using a Low-cost Fermentative Medium. *Applied Biochemistry and Biotechnology*, 158, (3), 663-674.

Davies, J.I., Evans, W.C. (1964). Oxidative Metabolism of Naphthalene by Soil *Pseudomonas*. The Ring Fission Mechanism. *Journal of Biochemistry*. 91: 252.

De Oliveira, N. C., Rodrigues, A. A., Alves, M. I. R., Antoniosi Filho, N. R., Sadoyama, G., and Vieira, J. D. G. (2012). Endophytic Bacteria with Potential for Bioremediation of Petroleum Hydrocarbons and Derivatives. *African Journal of Biotechnology*, 11(12): 2977-2984.

Diaz, A.Z., Ha, J., Engler, C.R., and Wild, J.R. (2003). Biodegradation of Theorganophosphate Methyl Parathion by Recombinant *Escherichia coli*. *Am.Soc. Agric. Biol. Eng.*

Diels, L., De Smet, M., Hooyberghs, L., and Corbisier, P. (1999). Heavy Metals Bioremediation of soil. *Molecular Biotechnology*, 12(2): 149-158.

Doty, S.L. (2000) Enhanced Metabolism of Halogenated Hydrocarbons in Transgenic Plants Containing Mammalian Cytochrome $P_{450}$ 2E1. *Proc. Natl. Acad. Sci.* U.S. A. 97: 6287-6291.

Dungan, R., and Frankenberger, W. (1999). Microbial Transformations of Selenium and the Bioremediation of Seleniferous Environments. *Bioremediation Journal*, 3(3): 171-188.

Ewart, D.K., and Hughes, M. N. (1991). The Extraction of Metals from Ores Using Bacteria. *Adv. Inorg. Chem*, 36: 103-135.

Floodgate G. (1984). The Fate of Petroleum in Marine Ecosystems in Petroleum Microbiology, R. M. Atlas, Ed., pp. 355-398, Macmillion, New York, NY, USA, 1984.

Francis, A., Dodge, C., and Gillow, J. (1992). Biodegradation of Metal Citrate Complexes and Implications for Toxic-metal mobility. *Nature*, 356: 140-142.

Gadd, G. (1993). Microbial Formation and Transformation of Organometallic and Organometalloid Compounds. *FEMS Microbiology Reviews*, 11(4): 297-316.

Gadd, G. M. (1999). Fungal Production of Citric and Oxalic Acid: Importance in Metal Speciation, Physiology and Biogeochemical Processes. *Advances in Microbial Physiology*, 41: 47-92.

Gadd, G.M. (2001). Accumulation and Transformation of Metals by Microorganisms. *Biotechnology Set*, 225-264.

Gadd, G.M. (2004). Microbial Influence on Metal Mobility and Application for Bioremediation. *Geoderma*, 122: 109-119.

Gadd, G.M., and White, C. (1993). Microbial Treatment of Metal Pollution—A Working Biotechnology? *Trends in Biotechnology*, 11(8): 353-359.

Gavrilescu, M. (2004). Removal of Heavy Metals from the Environment by Biosorption. *Engineering in Life Sciences*, 4(3): 219-232.

Green, Cynthia, and Hoffnagle, Ana. (2004). Phytoremediation Field Studies Database for Chlorinated Solvents, Pesticides, Explosives, and Metals. Washington, DC: U.S. Environmental Protection Agency.

Hambrick, G.A., DeLaune, R.D., and Patrick, W. (1980). Effect of Estuarine Sediment pH and Oxidation-reduction Potential on Microbial Hydrocarbon Degradation. *Applied and Environmental Microbiology*, 40(2): 365-369.

Hammack, R.W., and Edenborn, H.M. (1992). The Removal of Nickel from Mine Waters Using Bacterial Sulfate Reduction. *Applied Microbiology and Biotechnology*, 37(5): 674-678.

Hansen, T. (1993). Carbon Metabolism of Sulfate-reducing Bacteria. The Sulfate-reducing Bacteria: Contemporary Perspectives. Springer, New York Inc.: S, 21-40.

Higuchi, K. (1999) Cloning of Nicotianamine Synthase Genes, Novelgenes Involved in the Synthesis of Phytosiderophores. *Plant Physiol*.119: 471-479.

http://clu-in.org./download/studentpapers/hoffnagle-phytoremediation.pdf

Hussain, S., Siddique, T., Arshad, M., Saleem.(2009). M.Bioremediation and Phytoremediation of Pesticides: Recent Advances. *Critical Reviews in Environmental Science and Technology*, 39: 843-907.

Ilori M.O., Amobi C.J., and Odocha A. C. (2005). Factors Affecting Biosurfactant Production by Oil Degrading *Aeromonas spp*. Isolated from a Tropical Environment, *Chemosphere*, 61(7): 985-992.

Janjua, N., Kasi, P., Nawaz, H., Farooqui, S., and Khuwaja, U. (2006). Acute Health Effects of the Tasman Spirit Oil Spill on Residents of Karachi, Pakistan. *BMC Public Health*, 6(1): 84.

Jerina DM. (1983). Metabolism of Aromatic Hydrocarbons by the Cytochrome $P_{450}$ System and Epoxide Hydrolase. *Drug Metab Dispos* 11: 1-4.

Johnson, P., Watson, M., Brown, J., and Jefcoat, I. (2002). Peanut Hull Pellets as a Single Use Sorbent for the Capture of Cu (II) from Wastewater. *Waste Management*, 22(5): 471-480.

Jones D.M., Douglas A.G., Parkes R.J., Taylor J., Giger W., and Schaffner C. (1983). "The Recognition of Biodegraded Petroleum-derived Aromatic Hydrocarbons in Recent Marine Sediments," *Marine Pollution Bulletin*, 14(3): 103-108.

Kaiser J.(2008). Just How Bad is Dioxin? *Science* 288 (2000) 1941-1944.

Kapley, A., Purohit, H. J., Chhatre, S., Shanker, R., Chakrabarti, T., Khanna, P., (1999). "Osmotolerance and Hydrocarbon Degradation by a Genetically Engineered Microbial Consortium." *Bioresource Technology* 67(3): 241-245.

Kärenlampi S.; Schat, H.; Vangronsveld, J.; Verkleij, J.A.C.; van der Lelie, D.; Mergeay, M.; and Tervahauta, A.I. (2000). Genetic Engineering in the Improvement of Plants for Phytoremediation of Metalpolluted Soils. *Environmental Pollution*. 107: 225-231.

Kastner M, Breuer-Jammali M and Mahro B. (1998). Impact Ofinoculation Protocols, Salinity, and pH on the Degradationof Polycyclic Aromatic Hydrocarbons (PAHs) and Survival of PAH-degrading Bacteria Introduced into Soil. *App Environ Microbiol* 64: 359-362.

Kirk TK and Farrell RL. (1987). Enzymatic 'Combustion': The Microbial Degradation of Lignin. *Annu Rev Microbiol* 41: 465-505.

Kotrba, P. et al. (1999) Heavy-metal Binding Peptides and Proteins Inplants. Collect. *Czech. Chem. Commun.* 64: 1057-1086.

Kulichevskaya, I., Milekhina, E., Borzenkov, I., Zvyagintseva, I., and Belyaev, S. (1992). Oxidation of Petroleum Hydrocarbons by Extremely Halophilic Archaebacteria. *Microbiology*, 60(3): 596-601.

Kumar M., Le´on V, De Sisto Materano A., Ilzins O.A., and Luis L. (2008). Biosurfactant Production and Hydrocarbon Degradation by Halotolerant and Thermotolerant *Pseudomonas* sp. *World Journal of Microbiology and Biotechnology*, 24(7): 1047-1057.

Kumar, U., and Bandyopadhyay, M. (2006). Sorption of Cadmium from Aqueous Solution Using Pretreated Rice Husk. *Bioresource Technology*, 97(1): 104-109.

Kuznetsov, V.D., Zaitseva, T.A., Vakulenko, L.V., Filippova, S.N. (1992) *Streptomyces albiaxalis sp* nov.; A New Petroleum Hydrocarbon Degrading Species of Thermo- and Halotolerant *Streptomyces. Microbiology* 61: 62-67.

Lau KL, Tsang YY and Chiu SW. (2003). Use of Spent Mushroom Compostto Bioremediate PAH-contaminated Samples. *Chemosphere* 52: 1539-1546.

Le Cloirec P, Andrès Y. (2005). Bioremediation of Heavy Metals Using Microorganisms, In: Bioremediation of Aquatic and Terrestrial Ecosystems. Science Publishers, India, pp: 97-140.

Leahy, J.G., and Colwell, R.R. (1990). Microbial Degradation of Hydrocarbons in the Environment. *Microbiological Reviews*, 54(3): 305-315.

Lee, P.H., Ong, S.K., Golchen, J., Nelson, G.L. (2001). Use of Solvents to Enhance PAH Bioremediation of Coal Tar – Contaminated Soils. *Wat. Res.* 35: 39-41.

Lovley, D.R., and Coates, J. D. (1997). Bioremediation of Metal Contamination. *Current Opinion in Biotechnology*, 8(3): 285-289.

Lyons, R.A., Temple, J., Evans, D., Fone, D.L., and Palmer, S. R. (1999). Acute Health Effects of the Sea Empress Oil Spill. *Journal of Epidemiology and Community Health*, 53(5): 306-310.

Macaskie, L., and Dean, A. (1989). Microbial Metabolism, Desolubilization, and Deposition of Heavy Metals: Metal Uptake by Immobilized Cells and Application to the Detoxification of Liquid Wastes. *Advances in Biotechnological Processes*, 12: 159.

Madsen, E.L. (1991) Determining *in situ* Biodegradation: Facts and Challenges. *Environ Sci Technol* 25: 1663-1673.

Madsen, E.L., Sinclair, J.L., Ghiorse, W.C. (1991) *In situ* Biodegradation: Microbiological Patterns in a Contaminated Aquifer. *Science* 252: 830-833.

Mahmound A., Aziza Y., Abdeltif A., and Rachida M. (2008). Biosurfactant Production by Bacillus Strain Injected in the Petroleum Reservoirs. *Journal of Industrial Microbiology and Biotechnology*, 35: 1303-1306.

Martínez-Jerónimo F., Cruz-Cisneros J.L. and García-Hernández L.(2008). A Comparison of the Response of *Simocephalus mixtus* (Cladocera) and *Daphnia magna* to Contaminated Freshwater Sediments, *Ecotoxicol. Environ.* Saf. 71: 26-31.

Mastretta C, Barac T, Vangronsveld J, Newman L, Taghavi S, van derLelie D (2006) Endophytic Bacteria and Their Potential Application to Improve the Phytoremediation of Contaminated Environments. In: Harding SE, Tombs MP (eds) Biotechnology and Genetic Engineering Reviews, Vol. 23. Lavoisier, Paris, pp. 175-207. ISBN 1-84585003-3.

Matsumura, F., Boush, G.M. (1967) Dieldrin: Degradation by Soil Microorganisms. Science, 156: 959-961.

Matsumura, F., Gotoh, Y., and Boush, G. M., 1971. Phenylmercuric Acetate. Metabolic Conversion by Microorganisms. Science, 173(3991): 49-51.

Matsumura, Fumio; Boush, Mallory G. Degradation of Insecticides by a Soil Fungus, Trichoderma Viride *Journal of Economic Entomology*, Volume 61, Number 3, June 1968, pp. 610-612(3).

McLean, J., Lee, J., and Beveridge, T. (2002). In: Interactions of Bacteria and Environmental Metals, Fine-grained Mineral Development and Bioremediation Strategies. IUPAC Series on Analytical and Physical Chemistry of Environmental Systems, 8: 227-262.

Meagher, R.B. (2000) Phytoremediation of Toxic Elemental and Organic Pollutants. *Curr. Opin. Plant Biol.* 3: 153-162.

Mester T and Tien M. (2000). Oxidation Mechanism of Ligninolytic Enzymes Involved in the Degradation of Environmental Pollutants. *Int Biodeterior Biodegrad* 46: 51-59.

Mueller JG, Cerniglia CE and Pritchard P H. (1996). In: Bioremediation of Environments Contaminated by Polycyclic Aromatic Hydrocarbons, in Bioremediation: Principles and Applications, edby Crawford RL and Crawford DL. Cambridge University Press, Idaho, pp. 125-194.

Muthusamy J., Gopalakrishnan S., Ravi T.K., and Sivachidambaram P. (2008). Biosurfactants: Properties, Commercial Production and Application. *Current Science*, 94(6): 736-747.

Neilands, J. (1995). Siderophores: Structure and Function of Microbial Iron Transport Compounds. *Journal of Biological Chemistry*, 270(45): 26723-26726.

Nikolopoulou M. and Kalogerakis N. (2009). Biostimulation Strategies for Fresh and Chronically Polluted Marine Environments with Petroleum Hydrocarbons. *Journal of Chemical Technology and Biotechnology*, 84(6): 802-807.

NRC National Research Council, Polychlorinated Biphenyls, 1979.

Obbard, J.P., Ng, K.L., Xu, R. (2004). Bioremediation of Petroleum Contaminated Beach Sediments: Use of Crude Palm Oil and Fatty Acids to Enhance Indigenous Biodegradation. *Water, Air* and *Soil Pollution* 157: 149-161.

Oudot, J., Merlin, F., and Pinvidic, P. (1998). Weathering Rates of Oil Components in a Bioremediation Experiment in Estuarine Sediments. *Marine Environmental Research*, 45(2): 113-125.

Patrick Jr, W., and DeLaune, R. (1977). Chemical and Biological Redox Systems Affecting Nutrient Availability in the Coastal Wetlands. *Geoscience and Man*, 18(13): 137.

Peck Jr, H. (1993). Bioenergetic Strategies of the Sulfate-reducing Bacteria. In: The Sulfate-reducing Bacteria: Contemporary Perspectives. Springer, New York Inc.: S, 41-76.

Perelo, L.W. (2010). Review: *In situ* and Bioremediation of Organic Pollutants in Aquatic Sediments. *Journal of Hazardous Materials* 177: 81-89.

Pilon-Smits, E.A. (1998). Overexpression of ATP Sulfurylase in Indian Mustard Leads to Increased Selenium Uptake, Reduction and Tolerance. *Plant Physiol.* 119: 123-132.

Pornsunthorntawee O., Wongpanit P., Chavadej S., Abe M., and Rujiravanit R. (2008). Structural and Physicochemical Characterization of Crude Biosurfactant Produced by Pseudomonas Aeruginosa SP4 Isolated from Petroleum— Contaminated Soil. *Bioresource Technology*, 99(6): 1589-1595.

Rahman, K.S.M., Rahman, T.J., Banat, I.M., Lord, R. and Street, G. (2007). Bioremediation of Petroleum Sludge Using Bacterial Consortium with Biosurfactant, In: Environmental Bioremediation Technologies. Springer Berlin Heidelberg New York, pp: 391-408.

Rao Popuri, S., Jammala, A., Naga Suresh Reddy, K. V., and Abburi, K. (2007). Biosorption of Hexavalent Chromium Using Tamarind (*Tamarindus indica*) Fruit Shell-a Comparative Study. *Electronic Journal of Biotechnology*, 10(3): 358-367.

Rawlings, D. (1997). Mesophilic, Autotrophic Bioleaching Bacteria: Description, Physiology and Role, DE Rawlings. In: Theory, Microbes and Industrial Processes Ed. Biomining: 229-245.

Rudolph, A. et al. (1985) The Occurence of the Amino Acid Nicotianamine in Plants and Microorganisms. A Reinvestigation. Biochem. *Physiol. Pflanzen* 180: 557-563.

Rugh, C.L. et al. (1996) Mercuric Ion Reduction and Resistance in Transgenic Arabidopsis Thaliana Plants Expressing a Modified Bacterial *Mer*A Gene. *Proc. Natl. Acad. Sci.* U.S.A. 93: 3182-3187.

Safferman, S.I., Lamar, R.T., Vonderhaar, S., Neogy, R., Haught, R.C., and E.R. Krishnan. (1995). Treatability Study Using *Phanerochaete Sordida* for the Bioremediation of DDT Contaminated Soil. *Toxicological and Environmental Chemistry*. 50: 237-251.

Salleh, A.B., Ghazali, F.M., Rahman, R., and Basri, M. (2003). Bioremediation of Petroleum Hydrocarbon Pollution. *Indian Journal of Biotechnology*, 2(3): 411-425.

Sandarin T.R. and Hoffman D.R. (2007). Bioremediation of Organic and Metal Contaminants, In: Environmental Bioremediation Technologies. Springer Berlin Heidelberg New York, pp: 2-18.

Schiewer, S., and Volesky, B. (2000). Biosorption Processes for Heavy Metal Removal. Environmental Microbe-Metal Interactions. ASM Press, Washington, DC, USA, 329-362.

Schippers, A., and Sand, W. (1999). Bacterial Leaching of Metal Sulfides Proceeds by Two Indirect Mechanisms via Thiosulfate or via Polysulfides and Sulfur. *Applied and Environmental Microbiology*, 65(1): 319-321.

Schultze-Lam, S., Fortin, D., Davis, B., and Beveridge, T. (1996). Mineralization of Bacterial Surfaces. *Chemical Geology*, 132(1): 171-181.

Shen, J., and Duvnjak, Z. (2005). Adsorption Kinetics of Cupric and Cadmium Ions on Corncob Particles. *Process Biochemistry*, 40(11): 3446-3454.

Simmons, P., Tobin, J. M., and Singleton, I. (1995). Considerations on the Use of Commercially Available Yeast Biomass for the Treatment of Metal-containing Effluents. *Journal of Industrial Microbiology and Biotechnology*, 14(3): 240-246.

Singh, H. (2006). Mycoremediation: Fungal Bioremediation: John Wiley and Sons.

Siron R, Pelletier E and Brochu H. (1995). Environmental Factors Influencing the Biodegradation of Petroleum Hydrocarbons in Cold Seawater. *Arch Environ Contam Toxicol* 28: 406-416.

Smith, D., Alvey, S., and Crowley, D.E. (2005). Cooperative Catabolic Pathways within an Atrazine Degrading Enrichment Culture Isolated from Soil. *FEMS Microbiol. Ecol.*, 53: 265-273.

Sreekrishnan, T., and Tyagi, R. (1994). Heavy Metal Leaching from Sewage Sludges: A Techno Economic Evaluation of the Process Options. *Environmental Technology*, 15(6): 531-543.

Stiborova, M. and Anzenbacher, P. (1991). What are the Principal Enzymes Oxidizing the Xenobiotics in Plants – Cytochromes $P_{450}$ or Peroxidases (A hypothesis)? *Gen. Physiol. Biophys.* 10: 209-216.

Strasser, H., Burgstaller, W., and Schinner, F. (1994). High-yield Production of Oxalic Acid for Metal Leaching Processes by *Aspergillus Niger. FEMS Microbiology Letters*, 119(3): 365-370.

Strong, L.C., McTavish, H., Sadowsky, M.J., and Wackett, L.P. (2000). Field-scaleremediation of Atrazine-contaminated Soil Using Recombinant *Escherichia coli* Expressing Atrazine Chlorohydrolase. *Environ. Microbiol.*, 2: 91-98.

Stumm, W., and Morgan, J. J. (1996). Aquatic Chemistry, Chemical Equilibria and Rates in Natural Water: New York, NY: Wiley-Interscience.

Sutherland J.B., Rafii F., Khan A.A. and Cerniglia C.E .(1995). Mechanisms of Polycyclic Aromatic Hydrocarbon Degradation, in Microbial Transformation and Degradation of Toxic Organic Chemicals, ed by Young LY and Cerniglia CE. Wiley-Liss,New York, pp. 269-306.

Sutherland, T.D., Horne, I., Harcourt, R.L., Russell, R.J., and Oakeshott, J.G. (2002). Isolation and Characterization of a Mycobacterium Strain that Metabolizes the Insecticide Endosulfan. *J. Appl. Microbiol.*, 93: 380-389.

Tabatabaee A, Assadi M.M., Noohi A. A., and Sajadian V.A. (2005). Isolation of Biosurfactant Producing Bacteria from Oil Reservoirs. *Iranian Journal of Environmental Health Science and Engineering*, 2(1): 6-12.

Tebo, B.M., Ghiorse, W.C., van Waasbergen, L.G., Siering, P.L., and Caspi, R. (1997). Bacterially Mediated Mineral Formation; Insights into Manganese (II) Oxidation from Molecular Genetics and Biochemical Studies. *Reviews in Mineralogy and Geochemistry*, 35(1): 225-266.

Thapa, B., KC, A.K., and Ghimire, A. (2012). A Review on Bioremediation of Petroleum Hydrocarbon Contaminants In Soil. *Kathmandu University Journal of Science, Engineering and Technology*, 8(1): 164-170.

Unz, R.F., and Shuttleworth, K.L. (1996). Microbial Mobilization and Immobilization of Heavy Metals. *Current Opinion in Biotechnology*, 7(3): 307-310.

US-EPA Great Lakes National Programme Office, Realizing Remediation: A Summary of contaminated Sediment Remediation Activities in the Great Lakes Basin, 1998.

Vaccari, Strom, and Alleman. (2006). Environmental Biology for Engineers and Scientists.

Van der Lelie D, Corbisier P, Diels L, Gilis A, Lodewyckx C, MergeayM, Taghavi S, Spelmans N, Vangronsveld J. (1999). The Role of Bacteria in the Phytoremediation of Heavy Metals. In: Terry N, Banuelos G (eds) Phytoremediation of Contaminated Soils and wate. CRC, Boca Raton, pp. 265-281. ISBN 1-56670450-2.

Vangronsveld J, Cunningham SD (1998) Introduction to the Concepts. In: Vangronsveld J, Cunningham SD (eds) Metal-contaminatedsoils: *In-situ* Inactivation and Phytorestoration. Springer, Berlin, pp. 1-15. ISBN 1-57059-531-3.

Vangronsveld J, Van Assche F, Clijsters H (1995) Reclamation of Abare Industrial Area Contaminated by Nonferrous Metals—*in situ* Metal Immobilization and Revegetation. *Environ Pollut* 87: 51-59.

Ward, D.M., and Brock, T.D. (1978) Hydrocarbon Biodegradation in Hypersaline Environments. Appl. Environ. *Microbiol.,* 35, 353-359.

Watanabe K, Yoshikawa H, Goto M, Furukara K (2007) Enrichment and Isolation of Novel Anaerobic Microorganisms Capable of Degrading Various Kinds of POPs. *Organohalogen Compounds.* 69: 2500-2503.

Watanabe, K. (2001). Microorganisms Relevant to Bioremediation. *Current Opinion in Biotechnology,* 12(3): 237-241.

Wedemeyer. G. Partial Hydrolysis of Dieldrin by *Aerobacter aerogenes. Appl Microbiol.* 16(4); Apr 1968.

Weir, K.M., Sutherland, T.D., Horne, I., Russell, R.J., and Oakeshott, J.G. (2006). A Single Monooxygenase, *Ese,* is Involved in the Metabolism of the Organochlorides Endosulfan and Endosulfate in an *Arthrobacter sp. Appl. Environ.Microbiol.,* 72: 3524-3530.

White, C., Shaman, A.K., and Gadd, G.M. (1998). An Integrated Microbial Process for the Bioremediation of Soil Contaminated with Toxic Metals. *Nature Biotechnology,* 16(6): 572-575.

Widdel, F., and Rabus, R. (2001). Anaerobic Biodegradation of Saturated and Aromatic Hydrocarbons. *Current Opinion in Biotechnology,* 12(3): 259-276.

Wong J.W.C., Lai K.M., Wan C.K., Ma K.K. and Fang M .(2002). Isolation and Optimisation of PAH-degradative Bacteria from Contaminated soil for PAH Bioremediation. *Water Air Soil Pollution,* 139: 1-13.

Youssef N., Simpson D. R., Duncan K. E. (2007). *In situ* Biosurfactant Production by *Bacillus* Strains Injected into a Limestone Petroleum Reservoir. *Applied and Environmental Microbiology,* 73(4): 1239-1247.

7

# Ameliorate the Drastic Effect of Ochratoxin A by Using Yeast and Whey in Cultured *Oreochromus niloticus* in Egypt

**Mansour, T.A,** ***Egypt*****; Safinaz, G.Mohamed,** ***Egypt***
**Soliman, M.K.,** ***Egypt*****; Eglal, A. Omar,** ***Egypt*****; Srour, T.M.,** ***Egypt***
**Mona S. Zaki,** ***Egypt*****; Shahinaz, M.H. Hassan,** ***Egypt***

***ABSTRACT***

Ochratoxin A is one of the most important mycotoxins in fish feed. In the present study the effects of OTA on cultured *Oreochromus niloticus* were evaluated. Trials for ameliorate the drastic effect of OTA were done by using active life yeast and whey. The results indicted that significant ($p<0.05$) decrease in RBCS, WBCS, phagocytic activity and phagocytic index were occurred in both levels of OTA. Hypoalbuminemia, hypoproteinemia, decrease of globulin, and antibody titer as well as increase of liver enzymes, creatinine and uric acid were noticed. The histopathological examination showed that OTA caused diffuse hydropic degeneration and advanced fatty changes in liver. Tubular necrosis and hydropic degeneration of the kidneys were observed. The activation of melano macrophage centers (MMCs) were recorded. The results proved that OTA produce serious physiological, immunological and pathological effects on, *O.niloticus*. Morovere active life yeast and whey were succeed to neutralize the drastic toxic effects of OTA.

*Keywords:* Ameliorate; Drastic Effect; Ochratoxin; Oreochromus niloticus; Egypt.

## INTRODUCTION

Ochratoxin is a group of secondary metabolites produced by fungi of two genera: *Penicillium* and *Aspergillus*, this group include Ochratoxin A; Ochratoxin B; Ochratoxin C; Ochratoxin α, and the most toxic member is Ochratoxin A (OTA) )Ringot *et al.*, 2006).

Manning *et al.*, (2005) indicated that juvenile channel catfish fed OTA had greater mortality when challenged with *Edwardsiella ictaluri* compared with control group. Saad (2002) reported that OTA has immunosuppressive effect on *O. niloticus* and Common carp in acute (50 µg/kg fish) and chronic toxicity (10 µg/kg fish).

The role of microorganisms on detoxification of OTA has a lot of concern because they promote the hydrolysis of OTA to its nontoxic form [Ochratoxin á (OTα)] in case of ruminant (Sreemannarayana *et al.*, 1988) and non ruminant (Madhyastha *et al.*, 1992).

In many studies on OTA detoxification by yeast showed antagonistic effect on the production of OTA by fungi. Petersson *et al.*, (1998) showed that *Saccharomyces cerevisiae* inhibit production of toxin from *Penicillium verrucosum*. Péteri *et al.* (2007) found that yeast strain, *Phaffia rhodozyma*, degraded more than 90 per cent of OTA in 15 days at 20°C where hydrolysis it to OTα.

Moreover, yeast enhanced immune response of treated fish (Elkafoury, 2006; Reyes-Becerril *et. al.*, 2008). Useful microflora in the intestine such as Lactobacillus and Bifidobacterial can utilize the lactose for proliferation (Naghton *et al.*, 2001).

The proliferation of this species causes increase in the acidity of intestine by producing lactic acid and short-chain fatty acids formed unsuitable environment to pathogen bacteria like *Salmonida* and *Escherichia coli* (Juven *et al.*, 1991). This competition leads to excluding harmful bacteria out of the gut (Nurmi and Rantal, 1973). Consequently digestion and absorption increased and feed utilization improved (Tellez *et al.*, 1993). No available studies conducted to investigate the effect of whey on fish.

Moreover, whey protein concentrates enhanced ex-vivo lymphoid cell proliferative responses and increased in vivo antibody production (Knowles and Gill, 2002).

The aim of the present study is to investigate the effects of OTA on cultured *O. niloticus* and attempt to ameliorate the drastic effect of OTA by using yeast and whey as diet supplementations.

## MATERIALS AND METHODS

Apparently healthy 210 *O. niloticus* with an average body weight of 40 ±5 g/fish were used. Fish was obtained from private fish farm in Alexandria governorate and kept for 21 days in circular fiberglass tanks (800L) for acclimatization and fed on a diet contained 30 per cent crude protein.

Water temperature was ranged 25-27C. Continuous aeration was maintained in each tank using an electric air pumping compressor.

The 210 *O. niloticus* fish were randomly allotted in fourteen fiberglass tanks (two tanks/treatment) with fifteen fish per tank. The fish treated by Ochratoxin A (OTA) in two doses according to Saad (2002), 80 µg/kg fish as low dose (LOTA) and 160 µg/kg fish as high dose (HOTA). The OTA doses performed by stomach intubations once in day zero of the experiment in all fish groups by dissolving OTA in chloroform according to Trucksess and Pohland (2001) then dissolved in corn oil (Abdel-Wahhab *et al.*, 2005) and left to evaporate the chloroform before using. The individual stomach) intubations performed by using syringe attached with butterfly cannula to get the doses through the stomach of the fish (Abdel-Wahhab *et al.*, 2005). Fish in control group which fed basal diet received 0.5 ml corn oil.

Yeast (Tonilisat®): Active live yeast (China Way Corporation, Taiwan kindly supplied by EL Zahra Vetrinary), *Saccharomyces cerevisiae*, ($8 \times 10^9$ cells/gram) was used. The yeast added in the ration by incorporating 0.5 kg/ton ration after coating it with oil according to (Elkafoury, 2006). Fish were kept under daily observation for 8 weeks.

Whey: Whey powder (Dairy Farmers Company of America New Wilmington, PA 16142 U.S.A) free fats were used in the experiment. The whey incorporated into the diet at 14 per cent. The whey contained 11, 62, 0.5 and 11 per cent of Protein, Lactose, Fiber and Ash, respectively.

Seven experimental treatments were designed as follows: the basal diet (BD), BD with LOTA dose (80 µg OTA/kg fish), BD with HOTA dose (160 µg OTA/ kg fish), AY diet (0.5 g/kg diet) and LOTA dose,AY diet (0.5 g/kg diet) and HOTA dose, W diet (14% of diets) and LOTA dose and W diet (14% of diets) and HOTA dose.

Every two weeks, blood samples were taken from the caudal vasculature of - fish after anesthetized with MS222 (ten fish/treatment) for hematological assay and serum separation. Total red blood cell (RBCs), white blood cell (WBCs) were performed according to the methods of Anderson and Siwicki (1995) and Hesser (1960) respectively.

**Determination of Phagocytic Activity and Phagocytic Index**

Phagocytic activity was determined according to Kawahara *et al.* (1991) and Safinaz, (2001). Phagocytosis was estimated by determining the proportion of macrophages which contained intracellular yeast cells in a random count of 300 phagocytes and expressed as percentage of phagocytic activity (PA). The number of phagocytized organisms was counted in the phagocytic cells and called phagocytic index.

Clinico-biochemical determination was used to examine total protein, albumin, globulin and albumin/globulin ratio, alkaline phosphatase, glutamic-oxaloacetic transaminase, uric acid and creatinine were done according to Saad (2002) and Safinaz (2001) by using commercial kits (Biodiagnostic, Cairo, Egypt).

### Evaluation of Immune Response of *O. niloticus* Against *Aeromona. hydrophila* Bacterin

*Aeromonus hydrophila* isolate was used in the bacterin preparation according to the method described by (Sakai *et al.*, 1984)

The preparation of bacterin for injection was carried out according to the method of Badran (1990). The formalin inactivated bacterin cells were mixed with an equal volume of 0.85 per cent sterile saline. Bacterial number was adjusted to Fit MacFarlan's No. 2

At the 4$^{th}$ week one hundred and five *O. niloticus* fish exposed to both dose of OTA and control were inoculated intraperitoneally (IP) with 0.2 ml/fish of formalin inactivated bacterin. One hundred and five *O. niloticus* fish were similarly injected IP with 0.2 ml/fish sterile saline. After 2 weeks, the injected fish received booster dose from bacterin. After 1, 2, 3 and 4 weeks post-injection with inactivated bacterin blood collection was carried out from the caudal vasculature of inoculated fish after anesthetized with MS222 for antibody determination by microagglutination test according to the method described by Badran (1990).

### Histopathological Studies

At the end of experiment specimen from kidneys, spleens and livers were removed from fish of the experimental groups and rapidly placed in adequate amount of 10 per cent neutral buffered formalin for at least 24 hrs and used for histopathological studies according to Culling (1983).

### Statistical Analysis

Statistical analysis of the experimental results was conducted according to SPSS (version 16.00). Duncan's (1955) multiple range test was carried out to test the significance levels among means of treatments.

## RESULTS

The effects of OTA, yeast and whey on red blood cells (RBCs), white blood cells (WBCs) count PA and PI are demonstrated in (*See Table 7.1 on next page*). The red blood cells count differ significantly (***P***> 0.05) all over experimental period, where OTA presented severe decrease of RBCs especially with HOTA dose and showed anemia. Meanwhile, addition of yeast and whey with both OTA doses increased RBCs count and improved the body health condition.

Significant (***P*** >0.05) differences were observed after two weeks of treatment and showed decrease of WBCs count with LOTA and HOTA doses significantly than control group and reduced insignificantly than yeast and whey treatments all over the experimental period.

**Table 7.1: Effect of Ochratoxin A (OTA), Yeast and Whey on Red Blood Cells (RBCs), White Blood Cells (WBCs) Phagocytic Activity (PA) and Phagocytic Index (PI) of Blood of *O. niloticus* Through Out Experimental Period ($\overline{X} \pm SE$)**

| Items | Treatments | Week 2 | Week 4 | Week 6 | Week 8 | Total Mean |
|---|---|---|---|---|---|---|
| Total protein (g/dl) | Control | 4.39±0.21 | 4.37±0.10 | 4.39±0.12$^{a}$ | 4.46±0.06$^{a}$ | 4.40±0.06$^{A}$ |
| | LOTA dose | 4.14±0.31 | 4.05±0.22 | 3.73±0.08$^{cd}$ | 3.55±0.09$^{bc}$ | 3.87±0.11$^{BC}$ |
| | HOTA dose | 3.91±0.10 | 3.69±0.17 | 3.42±0.04$^{d}$ | 3.06±0.06$^{d}$ | 3.52±0.09$^{D}$ |
| | LOTA dose + yeast | 4.34±0.17 | 4.29±0.12 | 4.12±0.13$^{ab}$ | 3.84±0.14$^{b}$ | 4.15±0.08$^{AB}$ |
| | HOTA dose + yeast | 4.31±0.32 | 4.14±0.06 | 3.88±0.14$^{bc}$ | 3.44±0.08$^{bcd}$ | 3.94±0.12$^{BC}$ |
| | LOTA dose + whey | 4.22±0.18 | 4.20±0.18 | 4.02±0.20$^{bc}$ | 3.65±0.25$^{bc}$ | 4.02±0.11$^{BC}$ |
| | HOTA dose + whey | 4.18±0.12 | 3.98±0.25 | 3.70±0.03$^{cd}$ | 3.42±0.10$^{cd}$ | 3.82±0.10$^{C}$ |
| | Total Mean | 4.21±0.08$^{A}$ | 4.10±0.07$^{AB}$ | 3.90±0.07$^{B}$ | 3.63±0.09$^{C}$ | 3.96 |
| Albumin (g/dl) | Control | 3.10±0.11 | 3.16±0.21 | 3.06±0.10$^{a}$ | 3.13±0.08$^{a}$ | 3.11±0.06$^{A}$ |
| | LOTA dose | 3.03±0.23 | 2.87±0.03 | 2.73±0.06$^{b}$ | 2.52±0.04$^{c}$ | 2.79±0.07$^{B}$ |
| | HOTA dose | 2.95±0.04 | 2.76±0.14 | 2.65±0.08$^{b}$ | 2.47±0.05$^{c}$ | 2.71±0.06$^{B}$ |
| | LOTA dose + yeast | 3.09±0.25 | 2.97±0.13 | 2.81±0.14$^{b}$ | 2.73±0.05$^{b}$ | 2.90±0.08$^{B}$ |
| | HOTA dose + yeast | 3.04±0.33 | 2.87±0.09 | 2.75±0.06$^{b}$ | 2.76±0.07$^{b}$ | 2.84±0.09$^{B}$ |
| | LOTA dose + whey | 3.06±0.12 | 2.92±0.09 | 2.79±0.07$^{b}$ | 2.73±0.06$^{b}$ | 2.87±0.05$^{B}$ |
| | HOTA dose + whey | 3.00±0.04 | 2.81±0.06 | 2.67±0.04$^{b}$ | 2.52±0.06$^{c}$ | 2.75±0.05$^{B}$ |
| | Total Mean | 3.04±0.06$^{A}$ | 2.91±0.05$^{AB}$ | 2.78±0.04$^{BC}$ | 2.69±0.04$^{B}$ | 2.85 |
| Globulin (g/dl) | Control | 1.29±0.17 | 1.21±0.22 | 1.34±0.11 | 1.33±0.11$^{a}$ | 1.29±0.07$^{A}$ |
| | LOTA dose | 1.11±0.38 | 1.18±0.22 | 0.99±0.12 | 1.03±0.12$^{ab}$ | 1.08±0.11$^{A}$ |
| | HOTA dose | 0.96±0.10 | 0.92±0.26 | 0.77±0.11 | 0.59±0.07$^{b}$ | 0.81±0.08$^{B}$ |
| | LOTA dose + yeast | 1.25±0.22 | 1.33±0.23 | 1.31±0.07 | 1.11±0.17$^{ab}$ | 1.25±0.09$^{A}$ |
| | HOTA dose + yeast | 1.27±0.07 | 1.27±0.12 | 1.12±0.12 | 0.73±0.13$^{b}$ | 1.10±0.08$^{A}$ |
| | LOTA dose + whey | 1.16±0.24 | 1.29±0.27 | 1.24±0.26 | 0.92±0.31$^{ab}$ | 1.15±0.13$^{A}$ |
| | HOTA dose + whey | 1.18±0.15 | 1.17±0.21 | 1.03±0.03 | 0.89±0.10$^{ab}$ | 1.07±0.07$^{A}$ |
| | Total Mean | 1.17±0.07$^{A}$ | 1.19±0.08$^{A}$ | 1.12±0.06$^{AB}$ | 0.94±0.07$^{B}$ | 1.11 |
| A/G Ratio | Control | 2.55±0.36 | 3.01±0.74 | 2.33±0.20 | 2.42±0.26 | 2.58±0.21 |
| | LOTA dose | 4.00±1.54 | 2.68±0.46 | 2.87±0.34 | 2.60±0.44 | 3.04±0.41 |
| | HOTA dose | 3.17±0.34 | 4.18±1.47 | 3.84±0.87 | 4.48±0.71 | 3.92±0.44 |
| | LOTA dose + yeast | 2.75±0.55 | 2.53±0.57 | 2.16±0.17 | 2.66±0.48 | 2.53±0.22 |
| | HOTA dose + yeast | 2.43±0.33 | 2.36±0.35 | 2.55±0.31 | 4.46±1.34 | 2.95±0.40 |
| | LOTA dose + whey | 3.00±0.58 | 2.63±0.62 | 2.67±0.68 | 4.50±1.54 | 3.20±0.47 |
| | HOTA dose + whey | 2.69±0.36 | 2.74±0.62 | 2.59±0.11 | 2.95±0.39 | 2.74±0.19 |

Values in the same item with different letters are significantly different.
LOTA dose (80 µg OTA/ kg fish). HOTA dose (160 µg OTA/ kg fish).

The significant (*P*>0.05) differences of PA were observed at week four until the end of the experiment. The PA of HOTA dose reduced significantly than other treatments. Meanwhile, insignificant (*P*<0.05) differences were observed among LOTA dose and detoxification treatments.

The phagocytic index differ significantly from the second week of treatment, where HOTA dose recorded the lowest significant (*P*>0.05) PI and showed insignificant (*P* <0.05) differences with LOTA dose and HOTA dose plus whey all over the experiment. The addition of yeast ameliorate the drastic effect of OTA significant (*P*>0.05) on PI especially with LOTA dose. Meanwhile, slightly improve of PI observed with HOTA dose plus yeast and LOTA dose plus whey.

The significant effects of OTA, yeast and whey on total protein (*See Table 7.2 on page 98*) observed at week six to eight and showed significant (*P*<0.05) decrease of total protein with both LOTA and HOTA doses treatments. Meanwhile, the addition of yeast increased total protein values with both LOTA (significant *P*<0.05) and HOTA doses. Whey addition increased total protein but not significantly (*P* <0.05) with both LOTA and HOTA doses.

Regarding to albumin level, significant effects was observed at week six where each OTA treatments and detoxification treatments showed significant (*P* <0.05) decrease of albumin value (hypoalbuminemia) than control group although yeast and whey improved albumin levels insignificantly (*P*<0.05) than LOTA and HOTA doses.

Insignificant (*P* <0.05) decrease of globulin with LOTA and HOTA doses and increased in case of yeast and whey until sixth week were found. Meanwhile, at eighth week globulin decrease significant (*P*<0.05) with LOTA dose and HOTA dose.

The results of antibody titer of *O. niloticus* after vaccination with *A. hydrphila* and exposed to OTA and detoxification agents (yeast and whey) were 4, 2.67±0.33, 2±0.00, 3.33±0.33, 3±0.00, 3.67±0.33 and 3.00±0.00 in case of control, LOTA, HOTA, LOTA plus yeast, HOTA plus yeast, LOTA plus whey and HOTA plus whey respectively. The results indicated that significant (*P* <0.05) differences were observed among other treatments and control group. However, the addition of yeast and whey to the diet increased significantly antibody titare.

Data presented in (*See Table 7.3 on page 99*) showed the effect of OTA, yeast and whey on the liver and kidneys function. Significant differences of GOT were observed at the sixth week of treatment where GOT values with LOTA and HOTA doses increased significantly than control and yeast supplementation treatments.

In the same time the levels of liver enzymes in case of OTA plus yeast were less than OTA only.

**Table 7.2: Effect of Ochratoxin A (OTA), Yeast and Whey on the Total Protein, Albumin, Globulin and Albumin/Globulin Ratio (A/G Ratio) in serum of *O. niloticus* Through Out Experiment**

| Items | Treatments | Week 2 | Week 4 | Week 6 | Week 8 | Total Mean |
|---|---|---|---|---|---|---|
| Total protein (g/dl) | Control | 4.39±0.21 | 4.37±0.10 | $4.39 \pm 0.12^{a}$ | $4.46 \pm 0.06^{a}$ | **$4.40 \pm 0.06^{a}$** |
| | LOTA dose | 4.14±0.31 | 4.05±0.22 | $3.73 \pm 0.08^{cd}$ | $3.55 \pm 0.09^{bc}$ | **$3.87 \pm 0.11^{BC}$** |
| | HOTA dose | 3.91±0.10 | 3.69±0.17 | $3.42 \pm 0.04^{d}$ | $3.06 \pm 0.06^{d}$ | **$3.52 \pm 0.09^{D}$** |
| | LOTA dose + yeast | 4.34±0.17 | 4.29±0.12 | $4.12 \pm 0.13^{ab}$ | $3.84 \pm 0.14^{b}$ | **$4.15 \pm 0.08^{AB}$** |
| | HOTA dose + yeast | 4.31±0.32 | 4.14±0.06 | $3.88 \pm 0.14^{bc}$ | $3.44 \pm 0.08^{bcd}$ | **$3.94 \pm 0.12^{BC}$** |
| | LOTA dose + whey | 4.22±0.18 | 4.20±0.18 | $4.02 \pm 0.20^{bc}$ | $3.65 \pm 0.25^{bc}$ | **$4.02 \pm 0.11^{BC}$** |
| | HOTA dose + whey | 4.18±0.12 | 3.98±0.25 | $3.70 \pm 0.03^{cd}$ | $3.42 \pm 0.10^{cd}$ | **$3.82 \pm 0.10^{C}$** |
| | Total Mean | **$4.21 \pm 0.08^{A}$** | **$4.10 \pm 0.07^{AB}$** | **$3.90 \pm 0.07^{B}$** | **$3.63 \pm 0.09^{C}$** | **3.96** |
| Albumin (g/dl) | Control | 3.10±0.11 | 3.16±0.21 | $3.06 \pm 0.10^{a}$ | $3.13 \pm 0.08^{a}$ | **$3.11 \pm 0.06^{A}$** |
| | LOTA dose | 3.03±0.23 | 2.87±0.03 | $2.73 \pm 0.06^{b}$ | $2.52 \pm 0.04^{c}$ | **$2.79 \pm 0.07^{B}$** |
| | HOTA dose | 2.95±0.04 | 2.76±0.14 | $2.65 \pm 0.08^{b}$ | $2.47 \pm 0.05^{c}$ | **$2.71 \pm 0.06^{B}$** |
| | LOTA dose + yeast | 3.09±0.25 | 2.97±0.13 | $2.81 \pm 0.14^{b}$ | $2.73 \pm 0.05^{b}$ | **$2.90 \pm 0.08^{B}$** |
| | HOTA dose + yeast | 3.04±0.33 | 2.87±0.09 | $2.75 \pm 0.06^{b}$ | $2.76 \pm 0.07^{b}$ | **$2.84 \pm 0.09^{B}$** |
| | LOTA dose + whey | 3.06±0.12 | 2.92±0.09 | $2.79 \pm 0.07^{b}$ | $2.73 \pm 0.06^{b}$ | **$2.87 \pm 0.05^{B}$** |
| | HOTA dose + whey | 3.00±0.04 | 2.81±0.06 | $2.67 \pm 0.04^{b}$ | $2.52 \pm 0.06^{c}$ | **$2.75 \pm 0.05^{B}$** |
| | Total Mean | **$3.04 \pm 0.06^{A}$** | **$2.91 \pm 0.05^{AB}$** | **$2.78 \pm 0.04^{BC}$** | **$2.69 \pm 0.04^{B}$** | **2.85** |
| Globulin (g/dl) | Control | 1.29±0.17 | 1.21±0.22 | 1.34±0.11 | $1.33 \pm 0.11^{a}$ | **$1.29 \pm 0.07^{A}$** |
| | LOTA dose | 1.11±0.38 | 1.18±0.22 | 0.99±0.12 | $1.03 \pm 0.12^{ab}$ | **$1.08 \pm 0.11^{A}$** |
| | HOTA dose | 0.96±0.10 | 0.92±0.26 | 0.77±0.11 | $0.59 \pm 0.07^{b}$ | **$0.81 \pm 0.08^{B}$** |
| | LOTA dose + yeast | 1.25±0.22 | 1.33±0.23 | 1.31±0.07 | $1.11 \pm 0.17^{ab}$ | **$1.25 \pm 0.09^{A}$** |
| | HOTA dose + yeast | 1.27±0.07 | 1.27±0.12 | 1.12±0.12 | $0.73 \pm 0.13^{b}$ | **$1.10 \pm 0.08^{A}$** |
| | LOTA dose + whey | 1.16±0.24 | 1.29±0.27 | 1.24±0.26 | $0.92 \pm 0.31^{ab}$ | **$1.15 \pm 0.13^{A}$** |
| | HOTA dose + whey | 1.18±0.15 | 1.17±0.21 | 1.03±0.03 | $0.89 \pm 0.10^{ab}$ | **$1.07 \pm 0.07^{A}$** |
| | Total Mean | **$1.17 \pm 0.07^{A}$** | **$1.19 \pm 0.08^{A}$** | **$1.12 \pm 0.06^{AB}$** | **$0.94 \pm 0.07^{B}$** | **1.11** |
| A/G Ratio | Control | 2.55±0.36 | 3.01±0.74 | 2.33±0.20 | 2.42±0.26 | **2.58±0.21** |
| | LOTA dose | 4.00±1.54 | 2.68±0.46 | 2.87±0.34 | 2.60±0.44 | **3.04±0.41** |
| | HOTA dose | 3.17±0.34 | 4.18±1.47 | 3.84±0.87 | 4.48±0.71 | **3.92±0.44** |
| | LOTA dose + yeast | 2.75±0.55 | 2.53±0.57 | 2.16±0.17 | 2.66±0.48 | **2.53±0.22** |
| | HOTA dose + yeast | 2.43±0.33 | 2.36±0.35 | 2.55±0.31 | 4.46±1.34 | **2.95±0.40** |
| | LOTA dose + whey | 3.00±0.58 | 2.63±0.62 | 2.67±0.68 | 4.50±1.54 | **3.20±0.47** |
| | HOTA dose + whey | 2.69±0.36 | 2.74±0.62 | 2.59±0.11 | 2.95±0.39 | **2.74±0.19** |

Values in the same item with different letters are significantly different.
LOTA dose (80 µg OTA/kg fish). HOTA dose (160 µg OTA/kg fish).
Yeast (0.5 g/kg diet). Whey (14% of diets).

**Table 7.3: Effect of Ochratoxin A (OTA), Yeast and Whey on the Glutamic-oxaloacetic Transaminase (GOT), Alkaline Phosphatase (ALP), Creatinine and Uric Acid of *O. niloticus* Through Out Experimental Period ($\bar{X}$ ± SE)**

| Items | Treatments | Week 2 | Week 4 | Week 6 | Week 8 | Total Mean |
|---|---|---|---|---|---|---|
| GOT (units/ml) | Control | 24.67±4.06 | 28.33±5.07 | 29.67±2.51$^{b}$ | 36.00±3.46$^{c}$ | 29.67±.07 |
| | LOTA dose | 26.33±5.49 | 30.83±4.80 | 33.33±0.29$^{ab}$ | 44.83±2.13$^{ab}$ | 33.33±2.39 |
| | HOTA dose | 28.00±1.15 | 34.33±2.67 | 35.78±1.61$^{a}$ | 49.00±2.08$^{a}$ | 35.78±2.06 |
| | LOTA dose + yeast | 21.50±3.62 | 26.33±4.70 | 29.61±0.46$^{b}$ | 38.67±2.40$^{bc}$ | 29.61±2.64 |
| | HOTA dose + yeast | 24.50±1.04 | 27.00±2.75 | 31.05±1.01$^{b}$ | 41.00±1.53$^{bc}$ | 31.06±2.13 |
| | LOTA dose + whey | 23.67±0.73 | 30.83±4.64 | 32.11±0.86$^{ab}$ | 41.83±1.92$^{abc}$ | 32.11±2.24 |
| | HOTA dose + whey | 24.67±4.42 | 30.33±0.88 | 32.78±0.24$^{ab}$ | 45.33±2.60$^{ab}$ | 32.78±2.44 |
| | Total Mean | 24.76±1.16$^{C}$ | 29.71±1.36$^{B}$ | 32.05±0.60$^{B}$ | 41.67±1.11$^{A}$ | 32.05 |
| ALP (IU/L) | Control | 21.60±2.18 | 17.62±2.14 | 18.58±1.49$^{b}$ | 18.06±1.48$^{c}$ | 18.97±0.92 |
| | LOTA dose | 20.43±0.75 | 19.52±3.42 | 21.98±0.40$^{ab}$ | 23.32±1.33$^{ab}$ | 21.31±0.92 |
| | HOTA dose | 23.19±0.60 | 20.54±1.44 | 23.63±0.54$^{a}$ | 25.10±1.58$^{a}$ | 22.32±0.89 |
| | LOTA dose + yeast | 20.48±0.44 | 18.49±0.49 | 21.79±0.88$^{ab}$ | 20.40±0.74$^{bc}$ | 20.29±0.45 |
| | HOTA dose + yeast | 22.13±3.22 | 18.14±3.26 | 21.51±1.58$^{ab}$ | 22.32±1.13$^{ab}$ | 21.02±1.18 |
| | LOTA dose + whey | 20.00±1.86 | 18.70±3.24 | 20.38±0.79$^{ab}$ | 20.45±1.14$^{bc}$ | 20.68±0.90 |
| | HOTA dose + whey | 21.86±2.64 | 19.62±0.97 | 23.07±1.95$^{a}$ | 23.47±1.29$^{ab}$ | 22.00±0.90 |
| | Total Mean | 21.38±0.66$^{A}$ | 18.95±0.79$^{B}$ | 21.56±0.52$^{A}$ | 21.87±0.63$^{A}$ | 20.94 |
| Creatinine (mg/dl) | Control | 0.78±0.03 | 0.62±0.11 | 1.59±0.14$^{c}$ | 1.76±0.33 | 1.31±0.21 |
| | LOTA dose | 1.10±0.25 | 1.61±0.62 | 2.10±0.04$^{bc}$ | 3.06±0.31 | 1.97±0.27 |
| | HOTA dose | 1.32±0.46 | 1.83±0.32 | 3.63±0.32$^{a}$ | 3.50±0.28 | 2.57±0.34 |
| | LOTA dose + yeast | 1.10±0.09 | 1.34±0.47 | 1.66±0.30$^{c}$ | 2.72±0.52 | 1.71±0.25 |
| | HOTA dose + yeast | 1.07±0.21 | 1.36±0.17 | 2.43±0.37$^{bc}$ | 3.02±0.14 | 1.97±0.26 |
| | LOTA dose + whey | 1.08±0.30 | 0.64±0.35 | 1.84±0.46$^{c}$ | 2.57±0.97 | 1.53±0.33 |
| | HOTA dose + whey | 0.92±0.39 | 1.10±0.27 | 2.80±0.08$^{ab}$ | 3.17±1.10 | 2.00±0.40 |
| | Total Mean | 1.05±0.10$^{C}$ | 1.22±0.15$^{C}$ | 2.29±0.18$^{B}$ | 2.90±0.22$^{A}$ | 1.87 |
| Uric Acid (mg/dl) | Control | 0.83±0.26 | 1.26±0.26 | 2.25±0.45 | 2.19±0.31$^{c}$ | 1.63±0.23 |
| | LOTA dose | 0.86±0.34 | 1.56±0.27 | 3.00±0.42 | 3.86±0.62$^{ab}$ | 2.32±0.40 |
| | HOTA dose | 2.05±0.47 | 2.45±0.53 | 3.55±0.59 | 4.14±0.43$^{a}$ | 3.05±0.33 |
| | LOTA dose + yeast | 0.93±0.23 | 1.29±0.27 | 3.04±0.41 | 2.98±0.17$^{abc}$ | 2.06±0.31 |
| | HOTA dose + yeast | 0.83±0.35 | 1.62±0.37 | 2.65±0.17 | 3.02±0.37$^{abc}$ | 2.03±0.29 |
| | LOTA dose + whey | 1.12±0.09 | 2.24±0.33 | 2.88±0.18 | 2.25±0.52$^{c}$ | 2.13±0.24 |
| | HOTA dose + whey | 1.51±0.41 | 2.13±0.48 | 2.73±0.21 | 2.51±0.33$^{bc}$ | 2.22±0.21 |
| | Total Mean | 1.16±0.14$^{C}$ | 1.79±0.15$^{B}$ | 2.87±0.15$^{A}$ | 2.99±0.21$^{A}$ | 2.20 |

Values in the same item having different letters are significantly different. LOTA dose (80 µg OTA/kg fish). HOTA dose (160 µg OTA/kg fish). Yeast (0.5 g/kg diet). Whey (14% of diets).

The results of creatinine and uric acid showed increase especially with HOTA dose than other treatments. Moreover, the addition of yeast and whey decreased creatinine and uric acid levels especially with LOTA dose.

The histopathological examination in the present study showed that LOTA dose after 8 weeks from treatment caused diffuse hydropic degeneration of hepatic cells, congestion of hepatic sinusoids and mild incidence of melanomacrophage centers (MMCs). Moreover, the posterior kidney showed mild acute cellular swelling and MMCs activationwere observed in kidney and spleen (Figs. 7.1, 7.2 and 7.3).

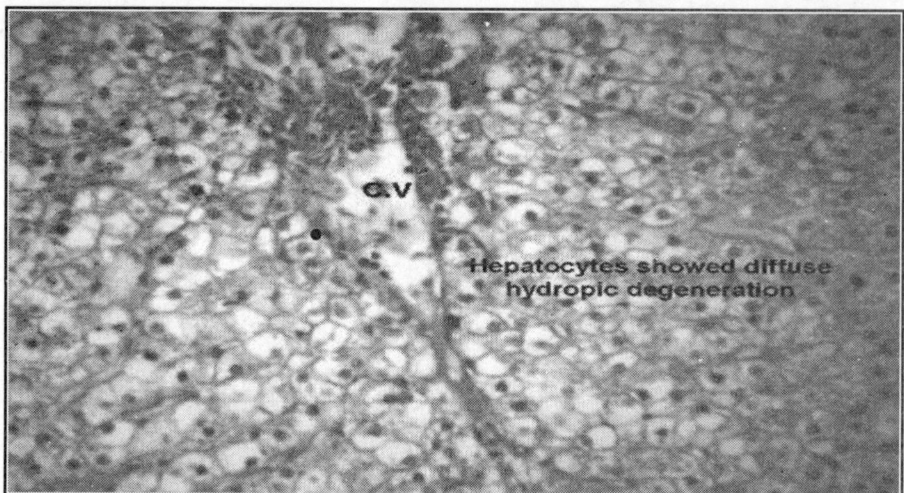


**Fig. 7.1: Liver of *O. niloticus* Exposed to LOTA Dose Showing Diffuse Hydropic Degeneration of Hepatic Cells. H&E. (X 250)**

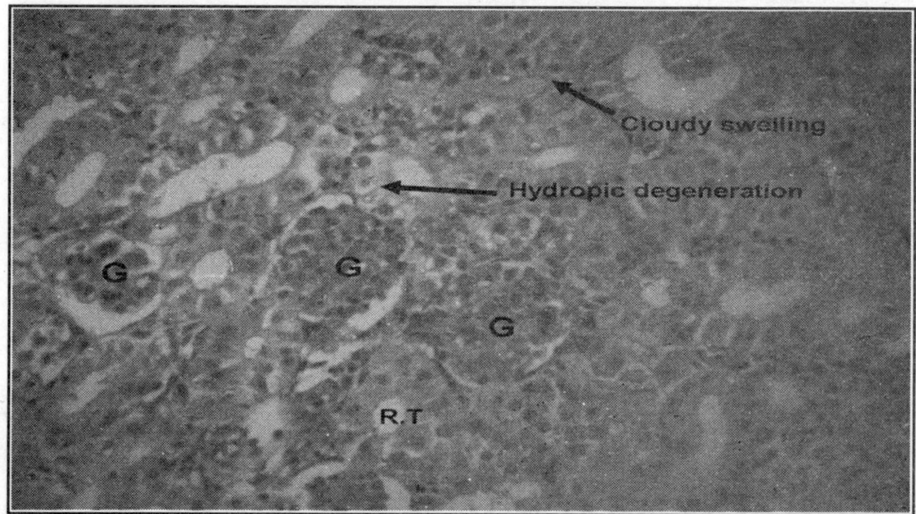


**Fig. 7.2: Kidney of *O. niloticus* Exposed to LOTA Dose Showing Mild Acute Cellular Swelling. H&E. (X 250)**

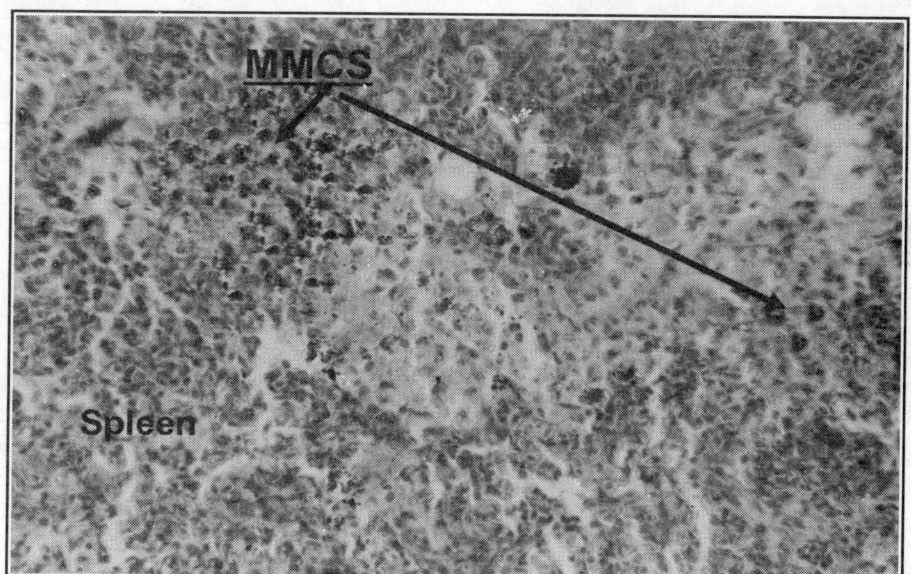


**Fig. 7.3: Spleen of *O. niloticus* Exposed to LOTA Dose Showing Activation of MMCS. H&E. (X 250)**

In case of HOTA dose diffuse advanced fatty changes appeared as Signet ring, atrophied of hepatic cells and activation of MMCs in pancreatic islets were recorded. In kidney, infiltration and activation of MMCs and acute tubular necrosis were recorded. Severe infiltration of MMCs to extent that total replaced of the splenic tissues were also noticed (Figs. 7.4, 7.5 and 7.6).

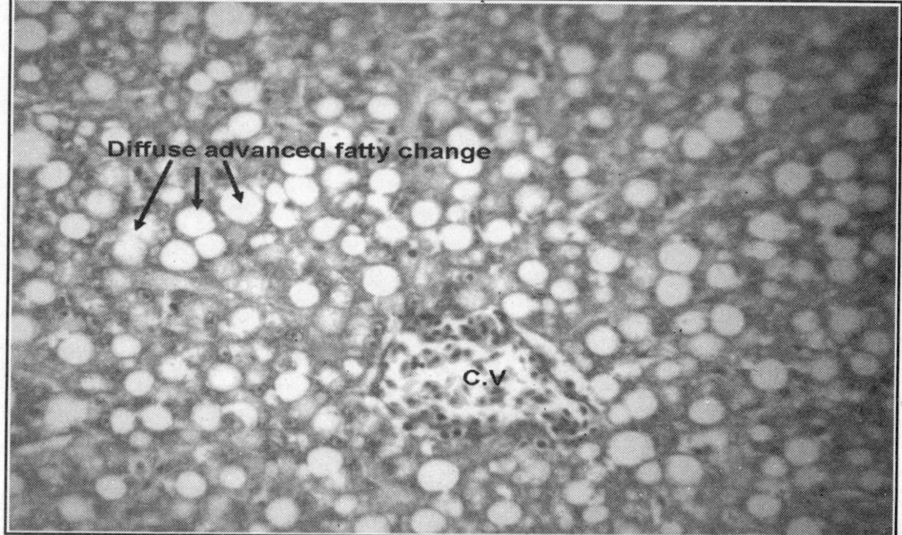


**Fig. 7.4: Liver of *O. niloticus* Exposed to HOTA Dose Showing Diffuse Advanced Fatty Changes Characterized by Hepatic Cells Appear as Signet Ring. H&E. (X 250)**

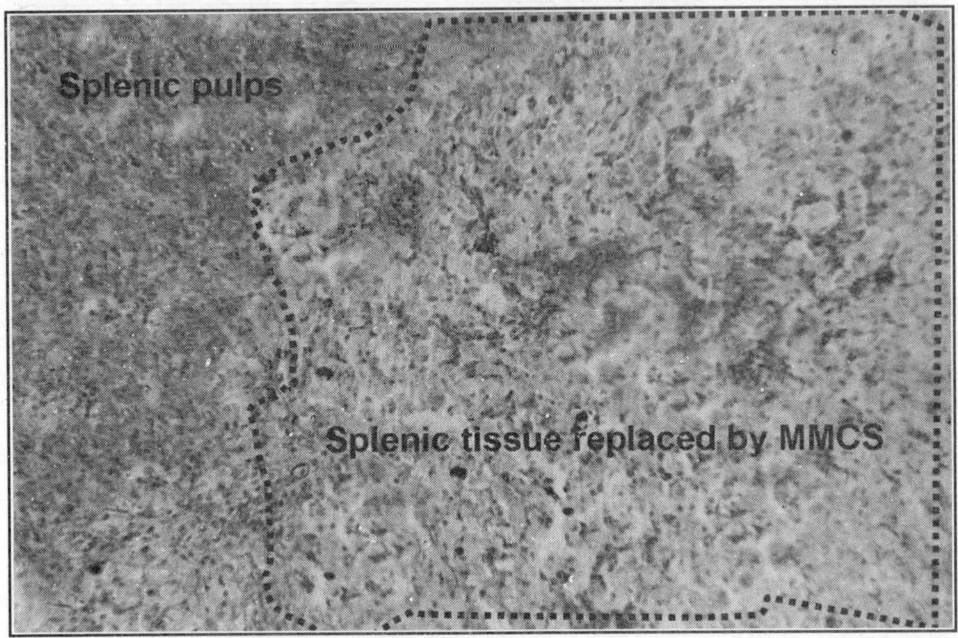


Fig. 7.5: Spleen of *O. niloticus* Exposed to HOTA Dose Showing Severe Infiltration of the Splenic Pulps with MMCS to Extent that Total Replacement of the Splenic Tissues. H&E. (X 160)

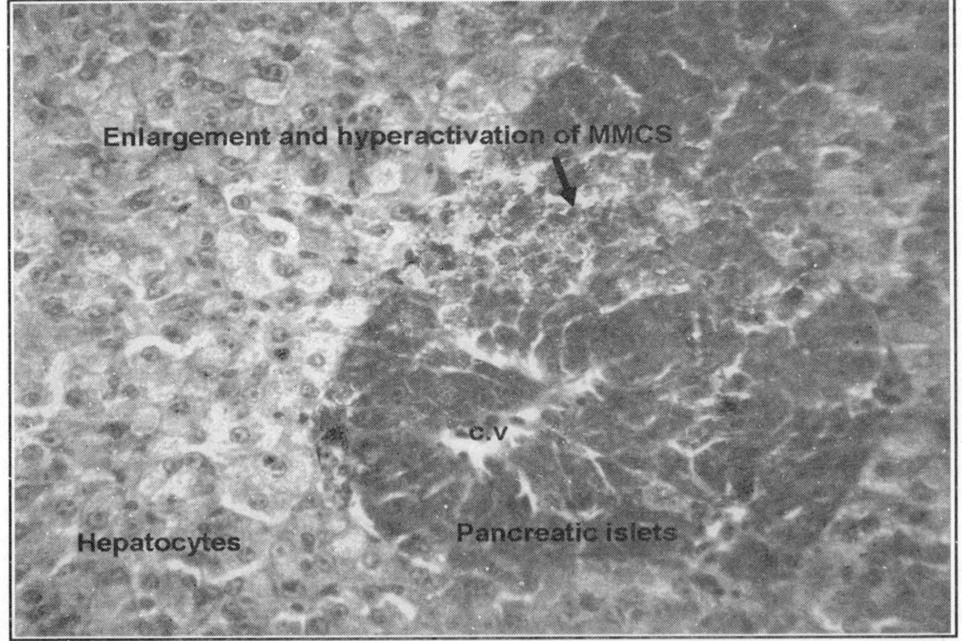


Fig. 7.6: Liver of *O. niloticus* Exposed to HOTA Dose Showing Severe Infiltration of MMCS in Pancreatic Islets. H&E. (X 250)

Regarding to addition of yeast to diets the drastic effects of OTA on hepatopancreas and kidneys in LOTA treatment were similar as control.

HOTA dose showed acute cloudy swelling, tubular necrosis and mild activation of MMCs. Also spleen in LOTA dose didn't affected but in HOTA dose spleen showed mild activation of MMCs (Figs. 7.7, 7.8 and 7.9).

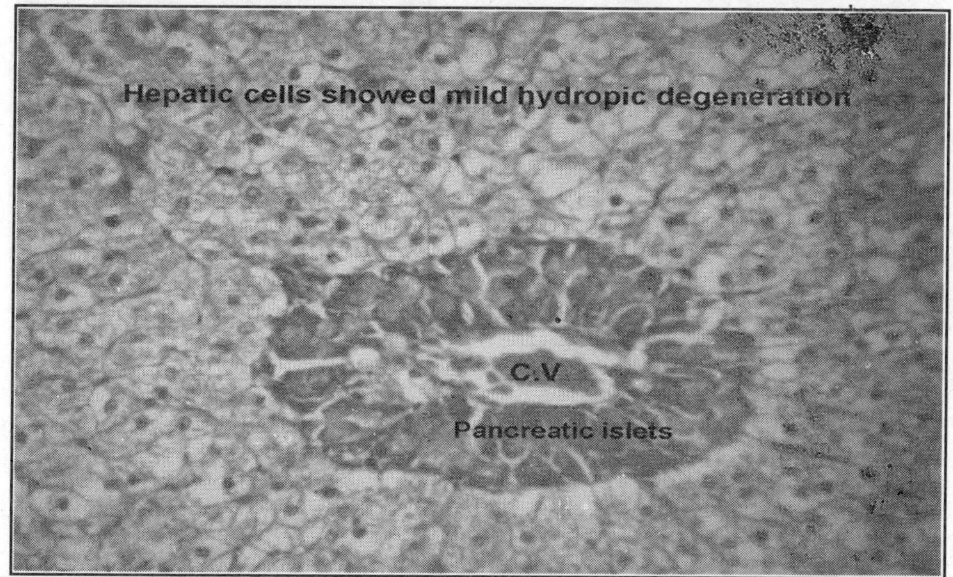


**Fig. 7.7: Liver of *O. niloticus* Exposed to HOTA Dose Plus Yeast Showing Mild Hydropic Degeneration of the Hepatic Cells. H&E. (X 250)**

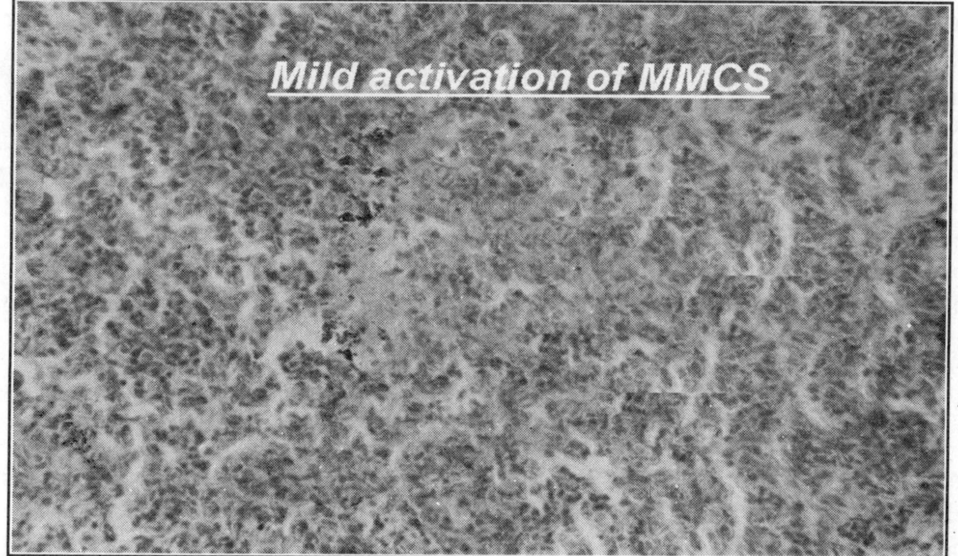


**Fig. 7.8: Spleen of *O. niloticus* Exposed to HOTA Dose Plus Yeast Showing Mild Activation of MMCS. H&E. (X 160)**

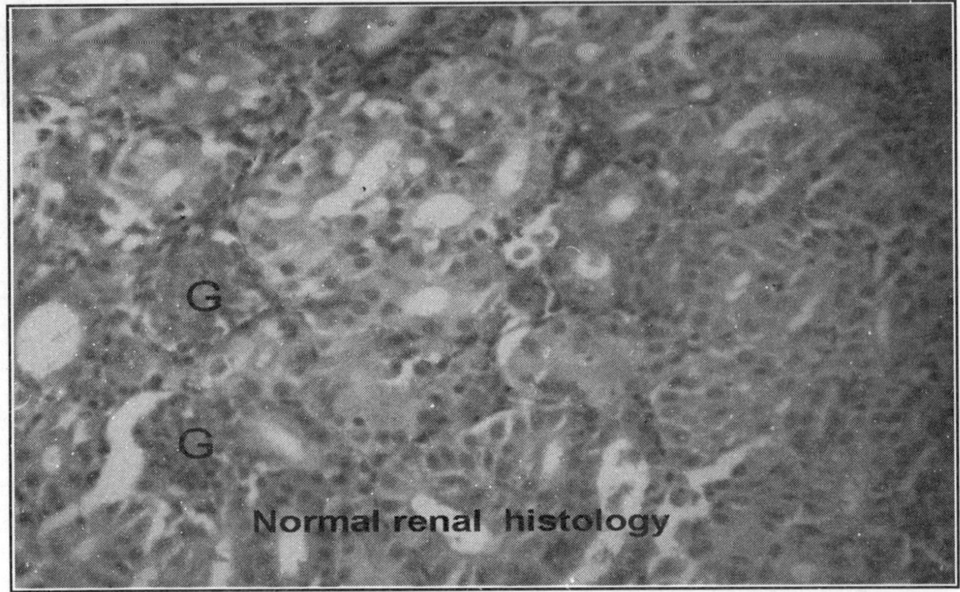


**Fig. 7.9: Kidney of *O. niloticus* Exposed to LOTA Dose Plus Yeast Showing Normal Renal Architecture and Histology. H&E. (X 250)**

Addition of whey to fish diets with OTA showed mild congestion and hydropic degeneration of liver cells in case of LOTA. Meanwhile, with HOTA dose the alteration appeared as mild fatty changes, focal lymphocytic aggregation, enlargement and hyper activation of MMCs. Kidney in LOTA dose showed slight acute cellular swelling of tubular epithelial lining with mild MMCs infiltration. The effect of HOTA dose with whey on posterior kidney appeared as focal tubular necrosis replaced by inflammatory cells. In spleen the alteration is activation of MMCs in both OTA doses but the severity increased with HOTA dose (*See Figs. 7.10, 7.11 and 7.12 on pages 105, 106*).

## DISCUSSION

The reduction of RBCs count which observed in the present study may be due to destruction of mature RBCs and inhibition of erythrocyte production due to reduction of haeme synthesis by ochratoxicosis. Also, the decrease in the RBCs may related to the elimination of RBCs from circulation as a result of ochratoxin – induced extravasations of the blood (Jordan *et al.*, 1977). Moreover, Shalaby (2004) found a significant reduction in RBCs of *O. niloticus* feed contaminated diet with OTA.

Decrease of WBCs count with LOTA and HOTA doses significantly than control group and reduced insignificantly than yeast and whey treatments all over the experimental period were noticed. The decrease of WBCs may be due to the immunosuppressive effects of OTA. Saad (2002) reported lymphopenia in case of acute and chronic exposure of *O. niloticus* to OTA.

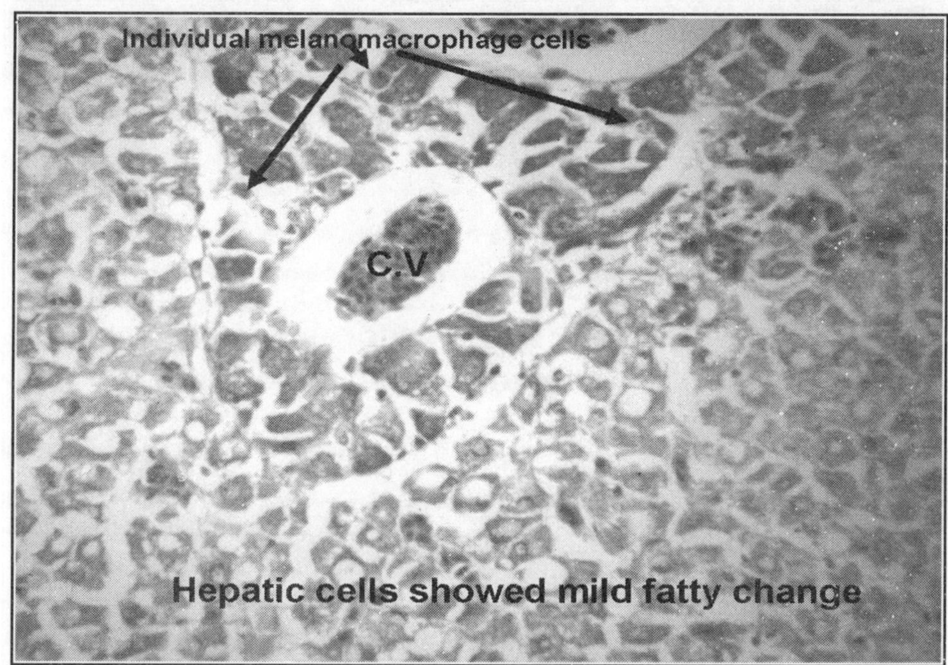


Fig. 7.10: Liver of *O. niloticus* Exposed to HOTA Dose Plus Whey Showing Mild Fatty Change of Hepatic Cells Beside Individual Infiltration of MMC Plus in Pancreatic Islets. H&E. (X 250)

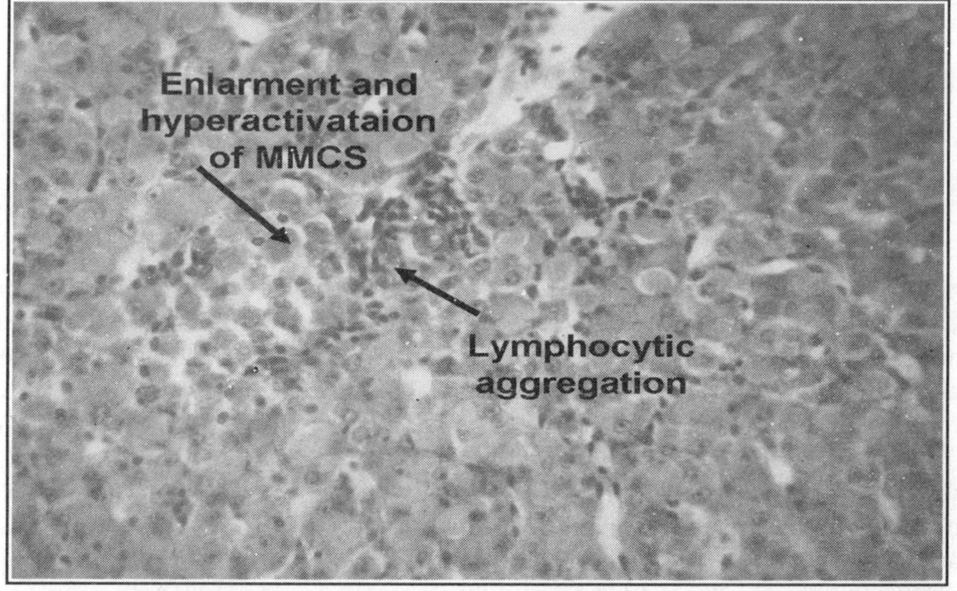


Fig. 7.11: Hepatopancreas of *O. niloticus* Exposed to HOTA Dose Plus Whey Showing Focal Lymphocytic Aggregation and Enlargement and Hyperactivation of MMCS. H&E. (X 250)

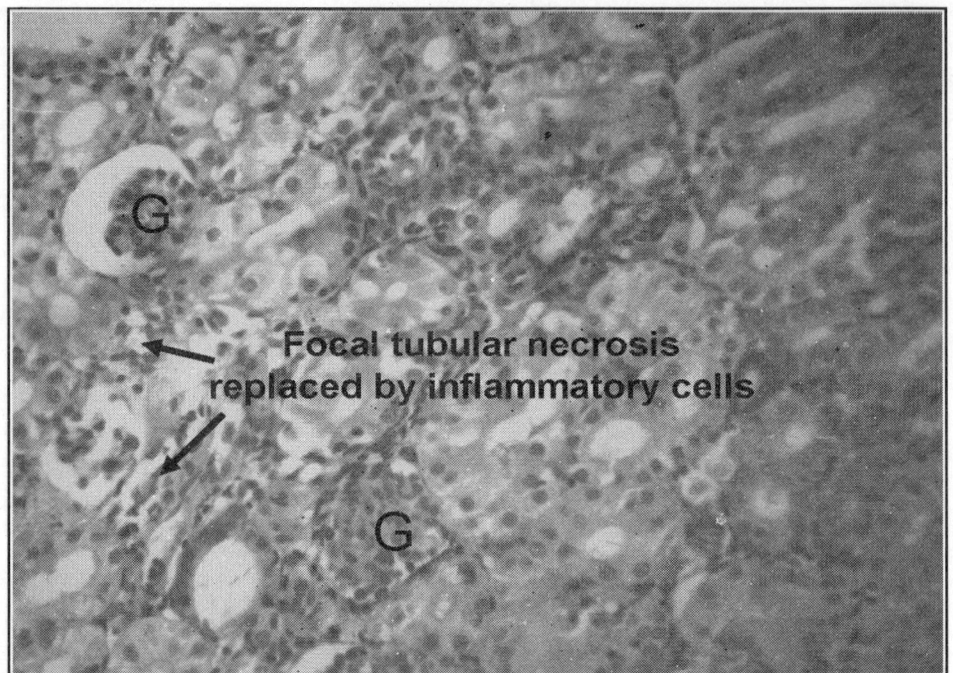


**Fig. 7.12: Posterior Kidney of *O. niloticus* Exposed to HOTA Dose Plus Whey Showing Focal Tubular Necrosis Replaced by Inflammatory Cells. H&E. (X 160)**

This change usually associated with acute stage of haemolytic anemia (Chang *et al.*, 1979) and destructive effects of OTA on spleen, kidney and liver (Smith and Hamilton, 1970). Moreover, Easa (1997) confirmed these results by recording depletion of hematopiotic elements due to the effects of OTA. The PA of HOTA dose reduced significantly than other treatments. Meanwhile, insignificant ($P$ <0.05) differences were observed among LOTA dose and detoxification treatments. Control showed the highest significant ($P$>0.05) PA value.

The phagocytic index differ significantly from the second week of treatment, where HOTA dose recorded the lowest significant ($P$>0.05) PI and showed insignificant ($P$ <0.05) differences with LOTA dose and HOTA dose plus whey all over the experiment. The addition of yeast ameliorate the drastic effect of OTA significant ($P$>0.05) on PI especially with LOTA dose. Meanwhile, slightly improve of PI observed with HOTA dose plus yeast and LOTA dose plus whey. Saad (2002) who found that OTA (10,000 ng/kg fish) decreased phagocytic activity and phagocytic index in *O. niloticus* after eight weeks of treatments. The decrease of PA and PI by OTA may be due to the stress effect of OTA on *O. niloticus* (Pickering, 1981). This lead to increase level of serum cortisol which leads to suppression of phagocytosis process (Khalil, 1998).

The increase of Phagocytic activity by addition of yeast may be attributed to enhancing the phagocytic and oxidative activities of kidney phagocytic cells Sakai et,al (2001). The significant effects of OTA, yeast and whey on total protein observed at week six to eight and showed significant ($P<0.05$) decrease of total protein with both LOTA and HOTA doses treatments. Meanwhile, the addition of yeast increased total protein values with both LOTA (significant $P<0.05$) and HOTA doses. Whey addition increased total protein but not significantly ($P <0.05$) with both LOTA and HOTA doses.

In general, OTA disruptive total protein level in *O. niloticus* and addition of yeast and whey improved total protein level especially with HOTA dose. Moreover, total protein levels decreased significant ($P<0.05$) with term of exposure.

OTA and detoxification treatments showed significant ($P <0.05$) decrease of albumin value (hypoalbuminemia) than control group. Although LOTA and HOTA doses decreased albumin level significant ($P<0.05$) than control, yeast treatments and whey with LOTA dose. The results showed insignificant ($P <0.05$) decrease of globulin with LOTA and HOTA doses and significant ($P <0.05$) increase with yeast and whey until sixth week. Meanwhile, at eighth week globulin decrease significant ($P <0.05$) with LOTA and HOTA dose. The reduction of plasma total protein may be due to liver damage caused by OTA where all plasma protein synthesis usually occurs in liver except gamma globulins which are produced by lymphocytes (Coles, 1986 and Khalil, 1998). This reduction may be interpreted to the inhibitory effect of OTA to protein synthesis (Ringot *et al.*, 2006).

The hypoproteinemia and hypoalbuminemia my be attributed to three main causes: hepatic insufficiency, renal loss (protein-losing nephropathy), and gastrointestinal loss (protein-losing enteropathy) Carlye-Rose, (2002). Moreover, OTA found to be hepatotoxic (Gagliano *et al.* 2006), nephrotoxic (Saad, 2002), and increase the permeability of gastrointestinal tract (McLaughlin *et al.*, 2004) which interpreted the decrease of total protein and albumin with OTA treatments in the present study.

Globulin is the building source of antibody where called immunoglobulin (White, 1986). So globulin used as immune indicator and the decrease of its level in the present study with OTA treatments revealed the immunosuppressive effects of OTA. Elkafory (2006) reported increase in fish serum proteins (total protein, albumin, globulin and A/G ratio) received yeast with diet.

Antibody titer reduced significantly with HOTA dose than control group. Insignificant ($P <0.05$) differences were observed among other treatments and control group. In eighth week (the forth week after vaccination) a significantly ($P >0.05$) decreased of antibody titration was observed with LOTA and HOTA doses compared to other treatments.

However, the addition of yeast and whey to the diet increase significantly antibody titration especially with HOTA dose.

Regarding to the overcome of detoxification agents to OTA on antibody titer where significantly increase of antibody titer was observed with yeast supplementation. Yoshida *et al.* (1995) showed that *Saccharomyces cerevisiae* was a source of nucleic acids and â-1,3-glucans which have been recognized to effectively enhance immune functions of African catfish. Also, Anderson *et al.* (1995) reported that Baker's yeast, *S. cerevisiae*, contains various immunostimulating compounds such as â-glucans, nucleic acids and mannan oligosaccharides. Moreover, Glucan treatment in fish enhanced the expression of interleukin 1 and complement activity Engstad *et al.* (1992).

In case of whey, which increase antibody titer may be due to whey act as source of biologically active molecules. Several of which are known to impact on the immune system (Knowles and Gill 2002). The biological components of whey protein, including lactoferrin, beta-lactoglobulin, alpha-lactalbumin, glycomacropeptide, and immunoglobulins, demonstrate a range of immune-enhancing properties (Horton, 1997).

Also, whey protein concentrates found to be enhanced humoral immunity, with significantly elevated serum and intestinal tract antibody responses to orally administered antigens (Rutherfurd-Markwick, *et al.*, 2005). The significant differences of GOT observed at the sixth week of treatment where GOT values with LOTA and HOTA doses increased significantly than control and yeast supplementation treatments. Alkaline phosphatase showed significantly ($P<0.05$) different at sixth week where control group decreased significantly than other treatments. The increase of serum transaminases may reflect myocardial and hepatic toxicity leading to extensive liberation of the enzymes in to blood circulation (Fuchs *et al.*, 1986). These results agreed with Saad (2002) who found significant increase of serum aspartat aminotransferase and alkaline phosphatase with OTA treatment on *O. niloticus*.

The increase of liver function enzymes in case of LOTA and HOTA doses may be due to the toxic effect of toxin in liver cells. Moreover the liver used to be the site of detoxification of the OTA to 4(*R*)-and 4(*S*) - hydroxyochratoxin A (Stormer and Pederson, 1980). In the same time the level of liver enzymes in case of OTA plus yeast were less than OTA only. This may be indicated that yeast decreased the toxic effect of OTA on liver and in the same time increase liver function.

The increase of creatinine and uric acid in serum of ochratoxicosis fish my be attributed to renal disturbance associated with damage of proximal tubules and thickening of the glomerular basement membrane caused by OTA which lead to reduce the ability of kidney to produce concentrated urine (Marquadret, 1996). Moreover, kidney is the main target organ of OTA genotoxicity, where induced DNA single-strand breaks and DNA adducts in kidney (Pfohl-Leszkowicz,et.al, 1993). Saad (2002) found that in case of OTA on acute and chronic toxicity in *O. niloticus* causes severe destruction of the proximal tubules of the posterior kidney and hydropic degeneration of the tubular epithelium.

Creatinine is a protein produced by muscle and released into the blood hence removed by the kidney and the increase of creatinine levels indicated to decrease of kidney function (Zotti *et al.*, 2008). The histopathological alteration which confirmed in case of LOTA and HOTA in the form of activation of melanomacrophage centers in liver and spleen atrophied of hepatic cells, severe fatty changes, and cellular degeneration of kidneys could be attributed to the toxic effects of OTA (Saad 2006). Similar results obtained by Manning *et al.*, (2003) in case of catfish fed dietary concentrations of 2.00 to 8.00 mg OTA/kg which revealed increase incidence and activation of MMCs centers in hepatopancreatic tissue and posterior kidney.

Orrenius and Bellomo (1986) demonstrated that lipid perox idation which caused by OTA may be an early event in hepatotoxicity, which results in structural changes in the cell membrane and allow an influx of cellular calcium to cause changes in metabolic activity within the cell and ultimately cause cell necrosis. Also the activation of the MMCs considered as indicative on the degree of the tissue damage (Roberts, 2001).

Regarding to addition of yeast to diets of ochratoxicosis fish elimenate the drastic effects of OTA on hepatopancreas. Also spleen in LOTA dose didn't affected but in HOTA dose spleen showed mild activation of MMCs.

Addition of whey to toxicated fish diets affects the histological findings as follow; Hepatopancreas in LOTA dose are congestion and hydropic degeneration. Meanwhile, with HOTA dose the alteration appeared as mild fatty changes, focal lymphocytic aggregation, enlargement and hyper activation MMCs. Posterior kidney in LOTA dose showed acute cellular swelling of tubular epithelial lining with mild MMCs infeltiration. The effect of HOTA dose on posterior kidney appeared as focal tubular necrosis replaced by inflammatory cells. In spleen the alteration is activation of MMCs in both OTA doses but severity increased with HOTA dose.

The histopathological examination results concluded that yeast more effective than whey in minimize the destructive effect of ochratoxin in the most affected organs (hepatopancreas, kidney and spleen) especially at the LOTA dose.

Moreover, yeast reduce the presence of potentially pathogenic bacteria by competitive exclusion and causes intestinal microbial balance of the host organism and confer various beneficial effects include immunostimulation and enhance disease resistance (Gatlin *et al.*, 2006).

The detoxification effect of yeast on OTA may be revealed to the ability of yeasts to secrete an enzyme related to carboxypeptidases which convert

OTA to OTá (non toxic form) (Péteri *et al.*, 2007) by the cleavage of the peptide bond between isocoumarin and phenylalanine in OTA moiety (Marquardt, 1996). Furthermore, yeast cell wall was an effective adsorbent for OTA (Ringot *et al.*, 2007) which may reduce OTA absorption from the fish gastro intestinal tract and excluded with feces.

Molnar *et al.* (2004) found that yeast strain of the genus *Trichosporon* from the hindgut of the termite, refers to important characteristics to detoxify mycotoxins such as OTA. Since, fish gastric microorganisms able to transform mycotoxin to non toxic form in various environmental conditions (Guan *et al.*, 2009). Moreover, yeast showed antagonistic effects to OTA production and growth of OTA producing fungi (Petersson *et al.*, 1998 and Masoud & Kaltoft, 2006).

In conclusion, OTA proved to produce drastic effects on physiological and pathological levels of *O. niloticus*. Meanwhile, active yeast and Sweet whey were successed to neutralize the drastic toxic effects of OTA.

## REFERENCES

1. Abdel-Tawwab, M., Abdel-Rahman, A.M. and Ismael N.E.M. (2008a). Evaluation of Commercial Live Bakers' Yeast, *Saccharomyces cerevisiae* as a Growth and Immunity Promoter for Fry Nile Tilapia, *Oreochromis niloticus* (L.) challenged *in situ* with *Aeromonas hydrophila*. Aquaculture, 280: 185-189.
2. Abdel-Tawwab, M., Mousa, M.A.A. and Mohammed, M.A. (2008b). Effect of Yeast Supplementation on the Growth Performance and Resistance of Galilee Tilapia *Sarotherodon galilaeus* (L.) to Environmental Copper Toxicity. 8th International Symposium on Tilapia in Aquaculture, 459-474.
3. Abdel-Wahhab, M.A., Hassan, A.M., Aly, S.E. and Mahrous, K.F. (2005). Adsorption of Sterigmatocystin by Montmorillonite and Inhibition of its Genotoxicity in the Nile Tilapia (*Oreochromis niloticus*). Mutation Research, 582: 20-27.
4. Anderson, D.P. and Siwicki, A.K. (1995). Basic Haematology and Serology for Fish Health Programmes. In: Diseases in Asian aquaculture II, M. Shariff, J.R. Arthur and R.P. Subasinghe (Eds). Fish Health Section, Asian Fisheries Society, Manila, Philippines, pp. 185-202.
5. Anderson, D.P., Siwicki, A.K. and Rumsey, G.L. (1995). Injection or Immersion Delivery of Selected Immunostimulants to Trout Demonstrate Enhancement of Nonspecific Defense Mechanisms and Protective Immunity. In: Shariff, M., Arthur, J.R., Subasinghe, R.P. (Eds.), Diseasesin Asian Aquaculture: II. Fish Health Section. Asian Fisheries Society, Manila. 413-426.
6. Badran, A. F. (1990). The Role of Adjuvants in the Immune Response of the Fish. Zagazeg Veterinary Medicine Journal. 18: 126-136.
7. Carlye-Rose, D.V.M. (2002). Evaluation of Hypoalbuminemia. HCVMA Newsletter, February. 1-2.
8. Chang, C.F., Huff W.E. and Hamilton. P.B. (1979). Aleucocytopenia Induced in Chickens by Dietary Ochratoxin-A. Poultry Science. 58: 555-558.

9. Coles, E.H. (1986). Veterinary Clinical Pathology. 2[nd] Ed. W.B. Saunders Company, Philadelphia and London.

10. Culling, C.F. (1983). Handbook of Histopathologic and Histochemical Staining. 3[rd] Ed., Buterworth, London.

11. Duncan, D. B. (1955). Multible Range and Multible F test. Biometric, 11: 1-42.

12. Easa, A.A.M. (1997). Effect of *Aspergillus Ochraceus* Mould and its Metabolites on some Cultured Fresh Water Fishes in Egypt. M.V. Sc. Faculty of Veterinary Medicine. Cairo University.

13. Elaroussi, M.A., Mohamed, F.R., El Barkouky, E.M., Atta, A.M., Abdou, A.M. and Hatab, M.H. (2006). Experimental Ochratoxicosis in Broiler Chickens. Avian Pathology, 35(4): 263-269.

14. Elkafoury. M.A. (2006). Comparative Studies Between *Oreochromas niloticus* and Monosex Tilapia from Immunological and Pathological Aspect of View. M.V. SC. Faculty of Veterinary Medicine. Alexandria University.

15. Engstad, R.E., Robertsen, B. and Frivold, E. (1992). Yeast Glucan Induces Increase in Activity of Lysozyme and Complemente Mediated Haemolytic Activity in Atlantic Salmon Blood. Fish Shellfish Immunol, 2: 287-97.

16. Fuchs, R., Appelgren, L.E. and Hult, K. (1986). Distribution of 14 C-ochratoxin A in the Rainbow Trout (*Salmogaidneri*). Acta Pharmacologica et Toxicologica, 59: 220-227.

17. Fuchs, S., Sontag, G., Stidl, R., Ehrlich, V., Kundi, M. and Knasmüller, S. (2008). Detoxification of Patulin and Ochratoxin A, Two Abundant Mycotoxins, by Lactic Acid Bacteria. Food and Chemical Toxicology, 46 (4): 1398-1407.

18. Gatlin III, D.M., Li, P., Wang, X., Burr, G.S., Castille F. and Lawrence, A.L. (2006). Potencial Application of Prebiotics in Aquaculture. En: Editores: L. Elizabeth Cruz Suarez, Denis Ricque Marie, Mireya Tapia Salazar, Martha G. Neito Lopez, David A. Villarreal Cavazos, Ana C. Puello Cruzy Armando Garcia Ortega. Avances en Nutricion Acuicola VIII. VIII Simposium International de Nutricion Acuicola. 15-17 Noviembre. Universidad Autonoma de Nuevo Leon, Monterrey, Nuevo Leon, Mexico. ISBN 970-694-333-5.

19. Guan, S., He, J., Young, J.C., Zhu, H., Li, X., Ji, C. and Zhou T. (2009). Transformation of Trichothecene Mycotoxins by Microorganisms from Fish Digesta. Aquaculture, 290: 290-295.

20. Hesser, E.F. (1960). Methods for Routine Fish Haematology. Progressive Fish Culturist, 22: 164-171.

21. Hichey, C.R. (1976). Fish Haematology, its Used and Significance. New York Fish com. J., 33: 170-175.

22. Horton, B. (1997). The Whey Processing Industry. Into the 21[st] Century. In: Proceedings of the Second International Whey Conference, Chicago, USA, 27-29 October. International Dairy Federation. pp. 12-25.

23. Jordan, M., Rzehak, K. and Maryanska, A. (1977). The Effect of Two Pesticides; Miedzian 50 and Gtsagard 50, on the Development of Tadpoles of *Rana temporaia*. Bulletin of Environmental Contamination, 17: 349-354.

24. Kawahara, E., Ueda T. and Nomura. S. (1991). *In vitro* Phagocytic Activity of White-spotted Shark Cells After Injection with *Aermonas salmonicida* Extracellular Products. Gyobyo Kenkyu, Japan, 26: 213-214.

25. Kermanshahi, H. and Rostami, H. (2006). Influence of Supplemental Dried Whey on Broiler Performance and Cecal Flora. International of Journal Poultry Science, 5: 538-543.
26. Khalil, R.H. (1998). Effect of Bayluscide on Some Cultured Fresh Water Fish *Oreochromis niloticus*. Ph.D. Thesis, Faculty of Veterinary Medicine. Alexandria University.
27. Knowles, G. and Gill, H.S. (2002). Immune Modulation by Dairy Ingredients: Potential for Improving Health. In: Shortt C, O'Brien J, Editors. Functional Dairy Products. Boca Raton 7 CRC Press; pp. 125-54.
28. Madhyastha, M.S., Marquardt, R.R. and Frohlich, A.A. (1992). Hydrolysis of Ochratoxin A by the Microbial Activity of Digesta in the Gastrointestinal Tract. Archives of Environmental Contamination and Toxicology, 23: 468-472.
29. Manning, B.B., Ulloa, R.M., Li, M.H., Robinson, E.H. and Rottinghaus, G.E. (2003). Ochratoxin A Fed to Channel Catfish (*Ictalurus punctatus*) Causes Reduced Growth and Lesions of Hepatopancreatic Tissue. Aquaculture, 219: 739-750.
30. Manning, B.B., Terhune, J.S., Li, M.H., Robinson, E.H., Wise, D.J. and Rottinghau, G.E. (2005). Exposure to Feedborne Mycotoxins T-2 Toxin or Ochratoxin A Causes Increased Mortality of Channel Catfish Challenged with *Edwardsiella ictaluri*. Journal of Aquatic Animal Health. 17: 147-152.
31. Marquardt, R.R. (1996). Effects of Molds and Their Toxins on Livestock Performance: A Western Canadian Perspective. Animal Feed Science and Technology, 70: 3968-3988.
32. Masoud, W. and Kaltoft, C.H. (2006). The Effects of Yeasts Involved in the Fermentation of Coffea Arabica in East Africa on Growth and Ochratoxin A (OTA) Production by *Aspergillus ochraceus*. International Journal of Food Microbiology, 106: 229- 234.
33. McLaughlin, J., Padfield, P.J., Burt, J.P.H. and O'Neill, C.A. (2004). Ochratoxin A Increases Permeability Through Tight Junctions by Removal of Specific Claudin Isoforms. American Journal of Cell Physiology, 287: C1412–C1417.
34. Molnar, O., Schatzmayr, G., Fuchs, E. and Prillinger H. (2004). *Trichosporon mycotoxinivorans sp.* nov., A New Yeast Species Useful in Biological Detoxification of Various Mycotoxins. Systematic and Applied Microbiology, 27: 661-671.
35. Naghton, P.J., Mikkelsen, L.L. and Jensen, B.B. (2001). Effects of Non Digestible Oligosaccharides on *salmonella typhimuium* and Non Pathogenic Escherichia *in vitro*. Journal of Applied and Environmental Microbiology, August pp. 3391-3395.
36. Nurmi, E.V. and Rantal (1973). New Aspects of Salmonella Infection in Broiler Production. Nature, 241: 210-211.
37. Orrenius, S., and Bellomo, G. (1986). Toxicological Implications of Perturbation of $Ca_2$+ Homeostasis in Hepatocytes. In: W.Y. Cheung (Ed.) Calcium and Cell Function. p 185. Academic Press, Orlando, FL.
38. Péteri, Z., Téren, J., Vágvölgyi, C. and Varga, J. (2007). Ochratoxin Degradation and Adsorption Caused by Astaxanthin-producing Yeasts. Food Microbiology, 24: 205-210.

39. Petersson, S., Hansen, M.W., Axberg, K., Hult, K. and Schnurer, J. (1998). Ochratoxin A Accumulation in Cultures of *Penicillium verrucosum* with the Antagonistic Yeast *Pichia anomala* and *Saccharomyces cerevisiae*. Mycological Research, 102 (8): 1003-1008.

40. Pfohl-Leszkowicz, A., Grosse, Y., Kane, A., Creppy, E.E. and Dirheimer, G. (1993b). Differential DNA Adducts Formation and Disappearance in Three Mouse Tissues after Treatment with the Mycotoxin Ochratoxin A. Mutation Research, 289: 265-273.

41. Pickering, A.D. (1981). Stress and Fish. Academic Press, Londo, New York. P. 149-152.

42. Reyes-Becerril, M., Tovar-Ramírez, D., Ascencio-Valle, F., Civera-Cerecedo, R., Gracia-López, V. and Barbosa-Solomieu, V. (2008). Effects of Dietary Live Yeast *Debaryomyces hansenii* on the Immune and Antioxidant System in Juvenile Leopard Grouper Mycteroperca Rosacea Exposed to Stress. Aquaculture, 280: 39-44.

43. Ringot D., Chango A., Schneider Y. and Larondelle Y. (2006). Toxicokinetics and Toxicodynamics of Ochratoxin A, an Update. Chemico-Biological Interactions 159: 18-46.

44. Ringot, D., Lerzy, B., Chaplain, K., Bonhoure, J., Auclair, E. and Larondelle, Y. (2007). *In vitro* Biosorption of Ochratoxin A on the Yeast Industry By-products: Comparison of Isotherm Models. Bioresource Technology. 98: 1812-1821.

45. Roberts, R.J. (2001). Fish Pathology. Third Rdition. Harcourt Publishers Limited 2001.

46. Rutherfurd-Markwick, K.J., Johnson, D., Cross, M.L. and Gill, H.S. (2005). Modified Milk Powder Supplemented with Immunostimulating Whey Protein Concentrate (IMUCARE) Enhances Immune Function in Mice. Nutrition Research. 25: 192-203.

47. Saad, T.T. (2002). Some Studies on the Effects of Ochratoxin-A on Cultured *Oreochromis niloticus* and Carp Species. M.V.SC. Faculty of Veterinary Medicine. Alexandria University.

48. Safinaz, G. M. I. (2001). Effect of Phenol on the Immune Response of Tilapia Fish and Susceptibility to Disease. Ph.D. Thesis Faculty of Veterinary Medicine Suez Canal University, Egypt.

49. Sakai, M., Yoshida, T., Atsuta, S. and Kobayashi, M. (1984). Enhancement of Resistance to Vibriosis in Rainbow Trout, *Oncorhynchus mykiss* (walaum), by Oral Administration of *Clostridium butyricum* Bacterin. Journal of Fish Diseases, 18: 187-190.

50. Sakai, M., Taniguchi, K., Mamoto, K., Ogawa, H. and Tabata, M. (2001). Immunostimulant Effects of Nucleotide Isolated from Yeast RNA on Carp, *Cyprinus carpio* L. Journal of Fish Disease, 24: 433-438.

51. Shalaby, A.M.E. (2004). The Opposing Effect of Ascorbic Acid (vitamin C) on Ochratoxin Toxicity in Nile Tilapia (*Oreochromis niloticus*). In: Proceedings of the 6th International Symposium on Tilapia in Aquaculture (R.B. Remedios, G.C. Mair and K. Fitzsimmons, eds), pp. 209-221.

52. Smith, J.W. and Hamilton, P.B. (1970). Aflatoxicosis in the Broiler Chicken. Poultry Science. 49: 207-215.

53. Soliman, M.K. (1996). Principals of Fish Disease. Effect of Stress on Immune System of Fish. Faculty of Veterinary Medicine. alexandria University, pp. 12-23.
54. Sreemannarayana, O., Frohlich, A.A., Vitti, T.G., Marquardt R.R. and Abramson, D. (1988). Studies of the Tolerence and Disposition of Ochratoxin A in Young Calves. Journal of Animal Science, 88: 1703.
55. Stormer, F.C. and Pederson, J.I. (1980). Formation of (4R)- and (4S)-hydroxyochratoxin A from Ochratoxin A by Rat Liver Microsomes. Applied and Environmental Microbiology, 39: 971-975.
56. Tellez, C.E., Dean, C.E., Corrier. D.E., Deloach, J.R., Jaeger, L. and Hargis, B.M. (1993). Effect of Dietary Lactose on Cecal Morphology, pH, Organic Acid and *Salmonella Enteritidis* Organ Invasion in Leghorn Chicks. Poultry Science, 72: 636- 642.
57. Trucksess, M.W. and Pohland, A.E. (2001). Mycotoxin Protocols, in: J.M. Walker (Ed.), Methods in Molecular Biology, Volume 157, Humana Press, New Jersey.
58. Wang, G.H., Xue, C.Y., Chen, F., Ma, Y.L., Zhang, X.B., Bi, Y.Z. and Cao, Y.C. (2009). Effects of Combinations of Ochratoxin A and T-2 Toxin on Immune Function of Yellow-feathered Broiler Chickens. Poultry Science, 88: 504-10.
59. White, D.G. (1986). Evaluation of a Rapid, Specific Test for Detecting Colostral IgG in the Neonatal Calf. Veterinary Record, 118: 68-70.
60. Yoshida, T., Kruger, R. and Inglis. V. (1995). Augmentation of Non-specific Protection in African Catfish, *Clarias gariepinus* (Burchell) by the Long-term Oral Administration of Immunostimulants. Journal of Fish Disease, 18: 195-198.
61. Zotti, F.D., Visonà, E., Massignani, D., Abaterusso, C., Lupo, A. and Gambaro, G. (2008). General Practitioners' Serum Creatinine Recording Styles. Journal of Nephrology, 21(1): 106-109.

8

# Bacterial Isolation and Characterization of Narmada River Flowing from Omkareshwar to Badwạni (M.P), India

**Shailendra Sharma, *India*; Taniya Sengupta, *India*; Kapil Sunar, *India***

**ABSTRACT**

A study was conducted with the objectives to isolate and identify the bacterial population in the water of the Narmada River. Samples were collected from six stations. The confluences of Narmada form the major outlets of domestic sewage and industrial effluents into the water. The presence of large numbers of Gram negative bacteria within the water is a matter of concern. The Bacteria which have been identified are the indicators of pollution in the water. A correlation was also developed to determine the change in temperature and pH of the water due to presence of huge number of bacterial population. The present finding indicates the urgency of detailed investigations on the aspects, especially with reference to pathogenic organisms. The paper discusses these aspects in detail.

*Keywords:* Narmada River, Bacterial flora, Biochemical identification, Correlation Coefficient.

## INTRODUCTION

River is very rich in bacteria because of the large quantity of dissolved organic matter present in water. Bacterial population is one of the major problems with respect to fresh water pollution. Due to the effect of temperature on the rate of a chemical reaction, one would predict that all bacteria would continue grow at lower pace as the temperature is reduced, until the system freezes. Bacterial number ranges from a few too many millions in a millimetre of water depending upon the source and the level of contamination. Inshore water of Narmada particularly the regions from Omkareshwar to Barwani are the examples of highly degraded environment because of anthropogenic perturbations.

Religious faiths and social practices add to pollution to river water. Carcasses of cattle and other animals are disposed in the river. Dead bodies are cremated on the river banks. Partially burnt bodies are also flung into the river. These practices pollute the river water and adversely affect the water quality. Mass bathing in the river during religious festival is another environmentally harmful practice.

It is known that the pathogens that gain entrance into bodies of water arrive there via intestinal discharges of humans and other animals. Furthermore, certain bacterial species designated as Coliforms are normal inhabitant of the large intestine of humans and other animals and are consequently present in faces. Thus the presence of any of these bacterial species in water is evidence of faecal pollution of human or animal origin. If these organisms are present in water the way is also open for intestinal pathogens to gain entrance, scince they too occur in faeces.

The coliform group of bacteria includes all the aerobic and facultative anaerobic, Gram negative, non sporulating bacilli that produces acid and gas from the fermentation of lactose. The classical species of this group are *Escherichia Coli* and *Enterobacter aerogens*. The relationship of these organisms to others oh the enteric group - *Salmonella, Shigella, Klebsiella, Proteus, Serratia and other genera* - all of which are Gram negative non sporulating bacilli and are normal inhabitant of the intestinal tract of human and other animals. These species bear a very close resemblance to each other in their morphological and cultural characteristics. Consequently, it is necessary to resort to biochemical tests for differentiation.

The Narmada is a river in central India and the fifth largest river in the Indian subcontinent. It forms the traditional boundary between North India and South India and flows westwards over a length of 1,312 km (815.2 mi) before draining through the Gulf of Cambey (Khambat) into the Arabian Sea, 30 km (18.6 mi) west of Bharuch city of Gujarat.[1] It is one of only three major rivers in peninsular India that runs from east to west (largest west flowing river) along with the Tapti River and the Mahi River. It flows through the states of Madhya Pradesh (1,077 km (669.2 mi)), Maharashtra, (74 km (46.0 mi)) – (35 km (21.7 mi)) border between Madhya Pradesh and Maharashtra and (39 km (24.2 mi) border between Madhya Pradesh and Gujarat and in Gujarat (161 km (100.0 mi)). The Narmada basin, hemmed between Vindya and Satpuda ranges, extends over an area of 98,796 km$^2$ (38,145.3 sq mi) and lies between east longitudes 72 degrees 32′ to 81 degrees 45′ and north latitudes 21 degrees 20′ to 23 degrees 45′ lying on the northern extremity of the Deccan Plateau. The basin covers large areas in the states of Madhya Pradesh (86%), Gujarat (14%) and a comparatively smaller area (2%) in Maharashtra. In the river course of 1,312 km (815.2 mi) explained above, there are 41 triburaries, out of which 22 are from the Satpuda range and the rest on the right bank are from the Vindhya range.

The present paper deals with the pathogenic bacteria load of the river water collected from six stations namely Omkareshwar, Moretakka, Mandleshwar, Maheshwar, Khalghat and Badwani. According to Zinged (1999), excess organic loading, often associated with the release of untreated or partially treated domestic waste water is largely responsible for this degradation. Some bacteria such as *Pseudomonas, Vibrio and Salmonella* Species are responsible for many of diseases caused to fish and humans. Bacteria are usually considered not as the source, but as the major consumers of dissolved organic matter.

Key (1935) estimated that 15 per cent of the organic matter in sea water could be used by bacteria. Some bacteria are pathogenic though there are a large number of them, which are useful in medicine and industry. Mostly, Gram negative bacteria are responsible for patho-physiology or endotoxic shocks. Inshore bacteria fulfil the most valuable role of breakdown to the vast amount of sewage and other solids. In the present study, an attempt was made to study the bacterial flora present in Narmada River.

## MATERIAL AND METHODS

The water samples were collected in the year 2010 from six stations Omkareshwar, Moretakka, Mandleshwar, Maheshwar, Khalghat and Badwani.

The Narmada river is considered as the life line of Madhya Pradesh. The catchment area of the riverexists in the States of Madhya Pradesh (86.18%),Gujarat (11.6%), Maharashtra (1.5%), and Chattisgarh (0.72%). During its course, the river drops from an elevation of 1051 m to sea level, and flows through narrow gorges in the head reaches. The basin is bounded on the north by the Vindhya ranges, on the east by the Maikal range, on the south by the Satpura ranges and on the west by the Arabian Sea.

Deep black soil covers the major portion of the basin. The river has 41 tributaries, of which 22 are on the left bank and 19 are on the right bank. The Barna, Tawa, Kolar, and Sukta dams have been constructedon the tributaries. The Bargi is constructed on the mainstream, while the Indirasagar, Omkareshwar, Maheshwar and Sardar Sarovar dams are under construction.

## SAMPLING STATIONS

### OMKARESHWAR

Omkareshwar is a famous place of pilgrimage, situated 77 km from Indore in Khandwa District, Madhya Pradesh. Shaped like the holy Hindu Symbol 'OM' this sacred island, on the conflux of the river Narmada and

Kaveri is visited by pilgrims from all over the country to seek blessing at the temple of Shri Omkar Mandhata. Millions of the pilgrims of both local & foreigners visit the place every year. It's Latitude (DMS) 22° 15′, 1″N and Longitude (DMS) 76° 8″, 48″E.

## MORETAKKA

This place is situated in West Nimar (Khargon), Madhya Pradesh, India, its geographical coordinates are 22° 14′ 0″ North, 76° 3′ 0″ East and its original name (with diacritics) is Mortakka.

## MANDLESHWAR

Mandleshwar is a town and a Nagar Panchayat in Khargone district of Madhya Pradesh. It is a town of historical and religious importance situated on the bank of Narmada river, 8 km east of Maheshwar, and 99 km south of Indore. Mandleshwar in Central India is on the bank of the Narmada River at a narrow point wherein the monsoon the stream often rises 60 feet above its normal level becoming a roaring torrent. It has an average elevation of 153 metres (501 feet). It's latitude (DMS) 22°10″, 60″N and Longitude (DMS) 75°40′, 0″E.

## MAHESHWAR

Maheshwar is a small town in Khargone district of Madhya Pradesh state in central India. It is located 91 km away from Indore, the commercial capital of the state. The town lies on the north bank of the Narmada River. It's latitude 22°10′, 60″N and longitude 75°34′60″E.

## KHALGHAT

Khalghat is a town and a municipality in Dhar district in the state of Madhya Pradesh. It has an average elevation of 150 metres (495 feet). It is located on the banks of Narmada River and National Highway 3 Agra-Indore-Dhule-Mumbai. Its latitude 21° 06′N and longitude 75°27′E.

## BARWANI

Barwani, also known as Siddh Nagar is a city and a municipality in Barwani District in the state of Madhya Pradesh, India. The place is also famous for Chool Giri, Jain pilgrimage centre of Bawangaja. The town is situated near the left bank of the Narmada river. The great Narmada river flows through Barwani (Just 5 km from city). Barwani is located150 km away from Indore. Before Independence Barwani was known as 'The Paris of Nimar' It's latitude (DMS) 22°10″, 60″N and longitude (DMS) 74°54″, 0″E.

Temperature was recorded at the sampling sites with a mercury filled Celsius thermometer. pH was recorded by pH meter and samples were brought to laboratory in sterilized bottles for further process.

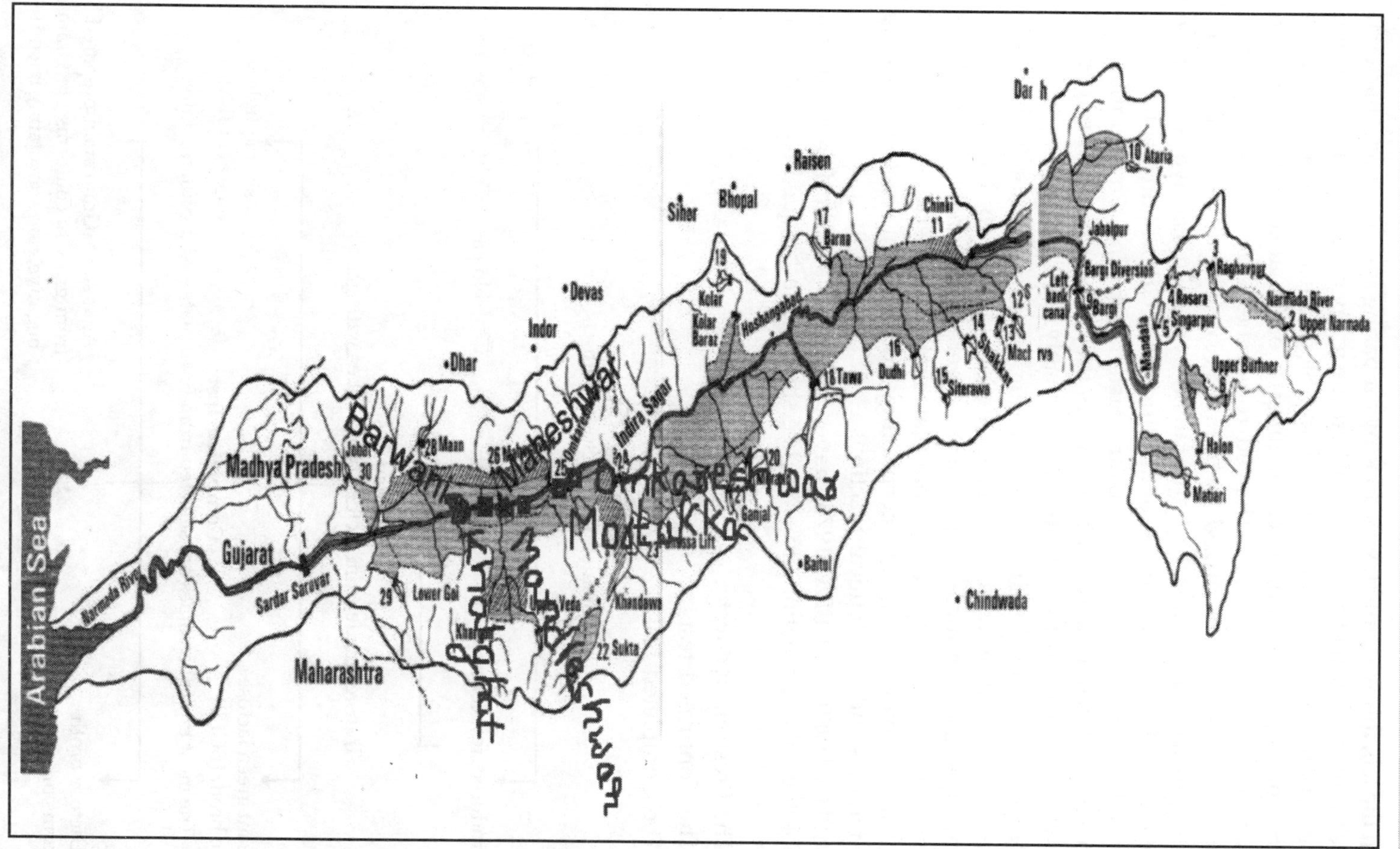


The Sampling Stations of Narmada

In the lab, the experiment was done by preparing an "unknown" bacterial sample for biochemical identification. There are many methods for identifying bacteria. Traditionally an observational and biochemical approach has been used. Simply looking at (and even smelling) a bacterial colony growing on an agar plate can give an experienced researcher clues to a bacterium's identity. Bacteria are categorized as "Gram Positive" or "Gram Negative" according to whether or not they are stained by a chemical dye, a common biochemical technique. (The basis for the differential Gram Stain is a difference in cell wall construction.). Which sugars bacteria ferment, which antibiotics they have resistance to and which enzymes they produce are all important identifying characteristics that can be reasonably easily tested?

Nutrient agar (HiMedia) was used for the enumeration of bacteria. Further microbial tests were conducted for identification of bacteria. Gram staining was also conducted. The bacteria were enumerated on sterilized nutrient agar by standard dilution pour plate method. Bacteria were identified from isolated colonies through morphology and staining reactions, culture characteristics and biochemical reactions.

APHA (1980) and EPA (1978) have developed standard methods for microbiological examination of water. The standard technique involves three successive steps:

1. The Presumptive test
2. The Confirmed test
3. The Completed test.

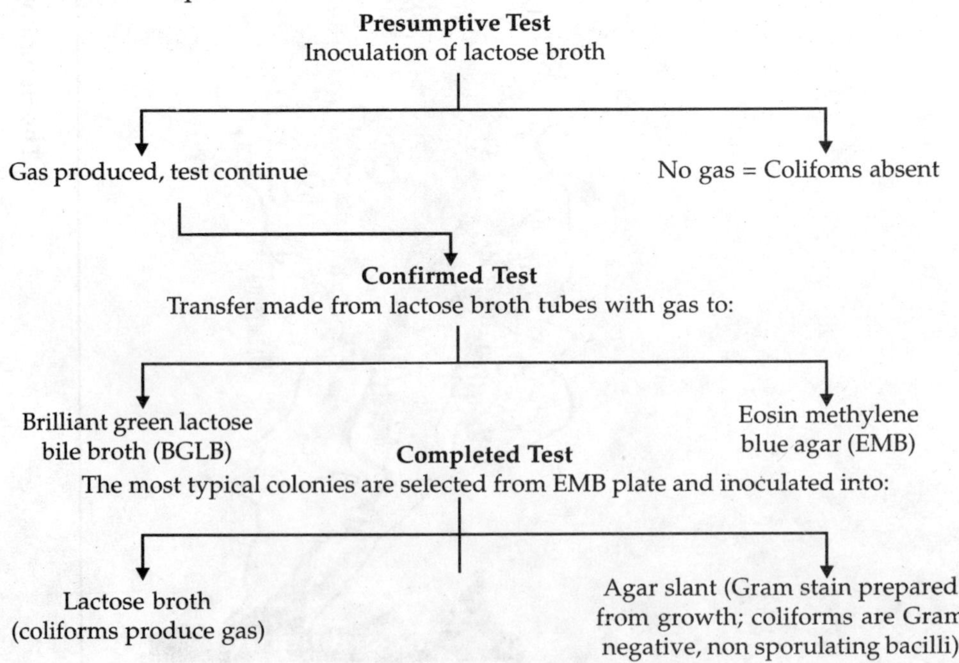

## Biochemical Tests

IMViC: A battery of biochemical tests known as IMViC are used in the clinical lab to distinguish between enteric microorganisms. The acronym IMViC stands for indole, methyl red, VogesProskauer and citrate. The "i" in the acronym is added for pronunciation purposes.

Tryptone broth/Indole test ("I"): Used to demonstrate the ability of a bacterium to produce the enzyme tryptophanase. This enzyme acts on the amino acid to produce "indole".

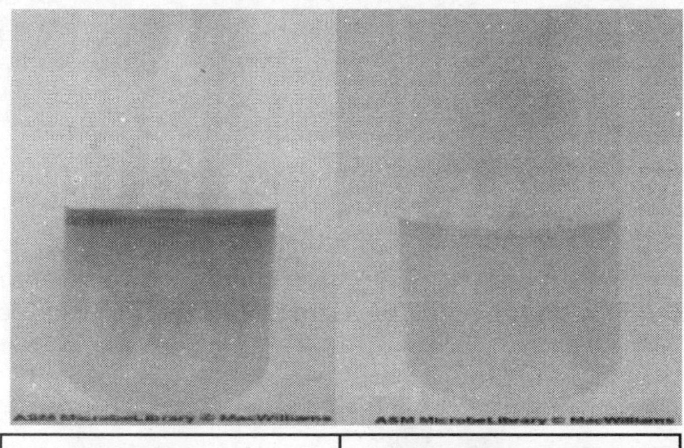

| Tryptone broth/indole – positive result | Tryptone broth/indole – negative result |
|---|---|

Methyl Red ("M") – an indicator of low pH (red below pH of 4.4) – used to show the mixed acid fermentation ability of bacteria.

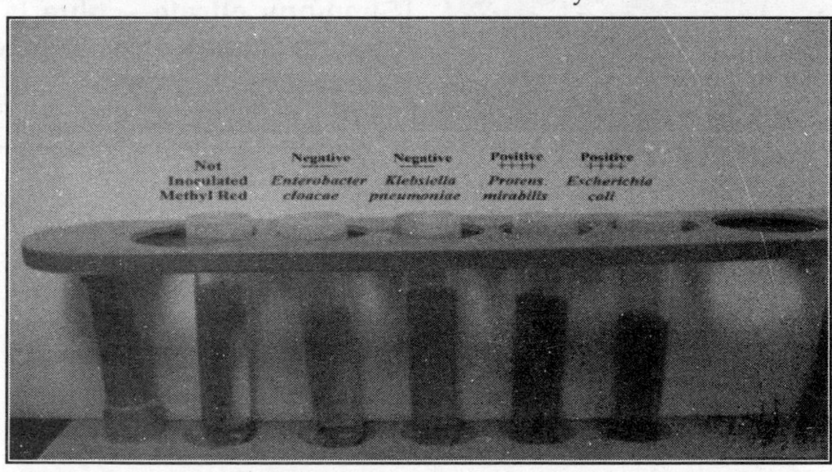

VP -Voges-Proskauer Test ("Vi") – used to show bacterial production of acetoin, also known as 2,3-butanediol.

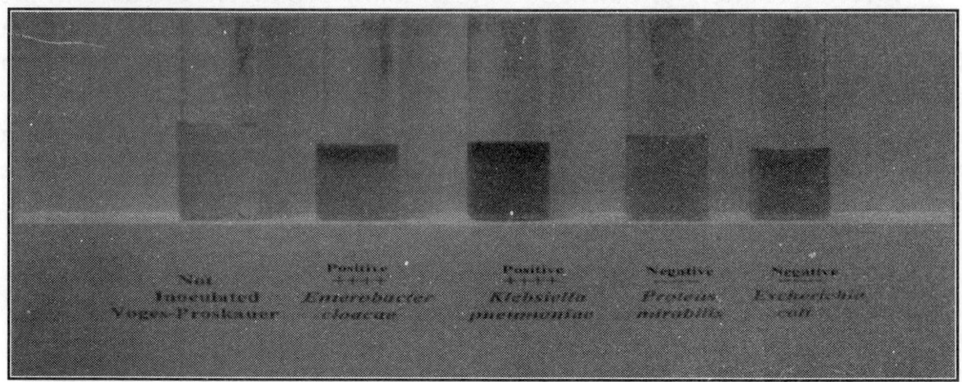


Simmons citrate slant ("C") – Simmons citrate agar tests for the ability of a gram-negative organism to import citrate for use as the sole carbon and energy source. Only bacteria that can utilize citrate as the sole carbon and energy source will be able to grow on the Simmons citrate medium, thus a citrate-negative test culture will be virtually indistinguishable from an uninoculated slant.

**Simmons citrate – blue is a positive citrate test, while green is negative/no growth**

U -Urea broth: demonstrates the ability of a bacterium to produce the enzyme urease, capable of hydrolyzing urea. Phenol red indicator is added (fuchsia above pH 8.4) to show rise in pH due to accumulation of ammonia.

The parameter such as temperature and pH were estimated following standard methods, APHA (2002).

Correlation was estimated by Karl Pearson's correlation method. When relationship between variables is of quantitative nature, the appropriate statistical tool for discovering and measuring the relationship as well as expressing it in brief formula is known as correlation. Correlation analysis helps us in determining the degree of relationship between two variables it doesn't tell us anything about cause and effect relationship. If both variables are changing in the same direction i.e. both are increasing or both are decreasing then they have a positive correlation between them. If they vary in opposite directions they posses negative correlation for calculation purpose formula for coefficient of correlation (Karl pearson's method) used is:

$$r = \frac{n\Sigma(dx.dy) - \Sigma dx \Sigma dy}{\sqrt{(n\Sigma dx^2 - (\Sigma dx)^2)(n\Sigma dy^2 - (\Sigma dy)^2)}}$$

The coefficient of correlation measures the degree of relationship between two sets of figures.

For interpretation purpose

1. r = 1 is considered to be prefect positive correlation.
2. 0 < r < 0.39 is considered to be low positive correlation.
3. 0.40 < r < 0.69 is considered to be moderate positive correlation.
4. 0.70 < r < 0.99 is considered to be high positive correlation.
5. -0.39 < r < -0.1 is considered to be low negative correlation.
6. -0.69 < r < -0.40 is considered to be moderate negative correlation.

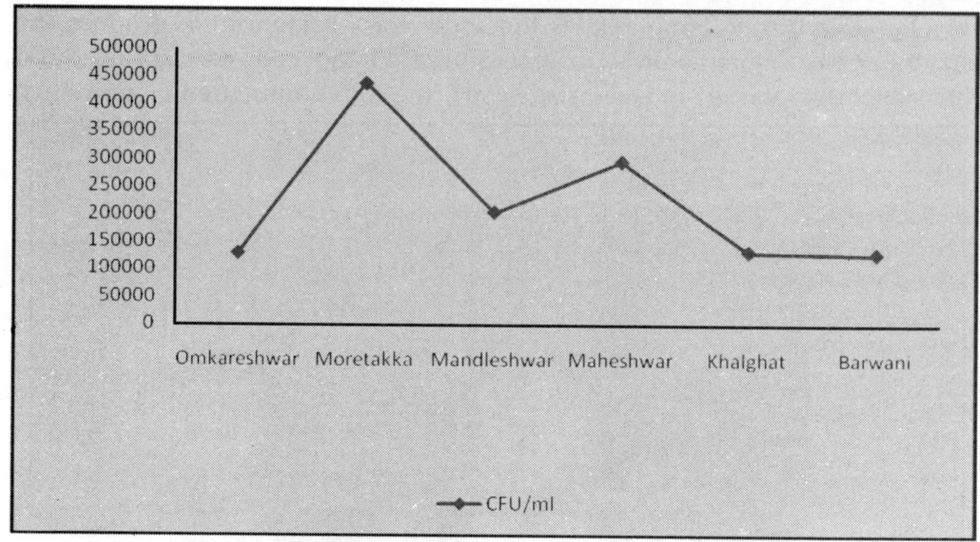


**Graph 8.1: Bacterial population in Narmada River**

**Acidic- Yellow Colour**
**Alkaline- Red Colour**
**Black- $H_2S$ Production**

## Characters of Bacteria of Narmada River

### 1. *Escherichia coli*

Gram-negative, rod-shaped bacterium that is commonly found in the lower intestine of warm-blooded organisms (endotherms). Most *E. coli* strains are harmless, but some serotypes can cause serious food poisoning in humans, and are occasionally responsible for product recalls due to food contamination. The harmless strains are part of the normal flora of the gut, and can benefit their hosts by producing vitamin K2, and by preventing the establishment of pathogenic bacteria within the intestine.

*E. coli* and related bacteria constitute about 0.1 per cent of gut flora, and fecal-oral transmission is the major route through which pathogenic strains of the bacterium cause disease. Cells are able to survive outside the body for a limited amount of time, which makes them ideal indicator organisms to test environmental samples for fecal contamination. There is, however, a growing body of research that has examined environmentally persistent *E. coli* which can survive for extended periods of time outside of the host.

### 2. *Klebsiella*

Non-motile, Gram-negative, oxidase-negative, rod-shaped bacteria with a prominent polysaccharide-based capsule. It is named after the German microbiologist Edwin Klebs (1834-1913). Frequent human pathogens, *Klebsiella*

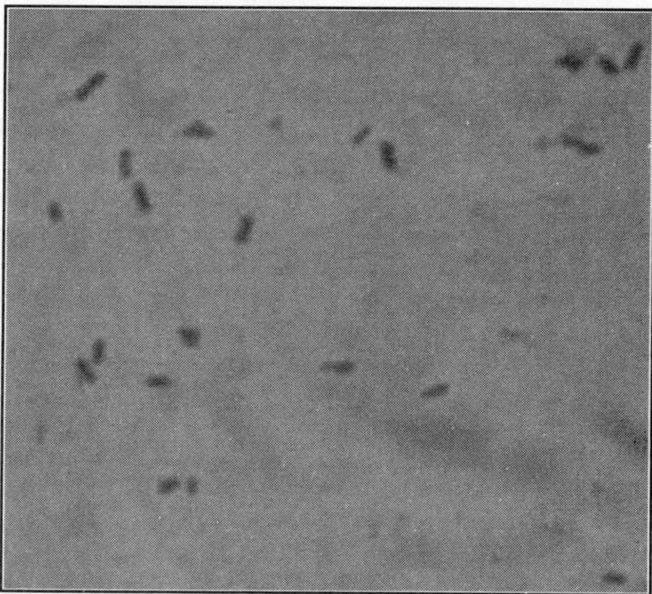

**Fig 8.1: Gram staining of *E.coli***

organisms can lead to a wide range of disease states, notably pneumonia, urinary tract infections, septicemia, and soft tissue infections. *Klebsiella* species are ubiquitous in nature.

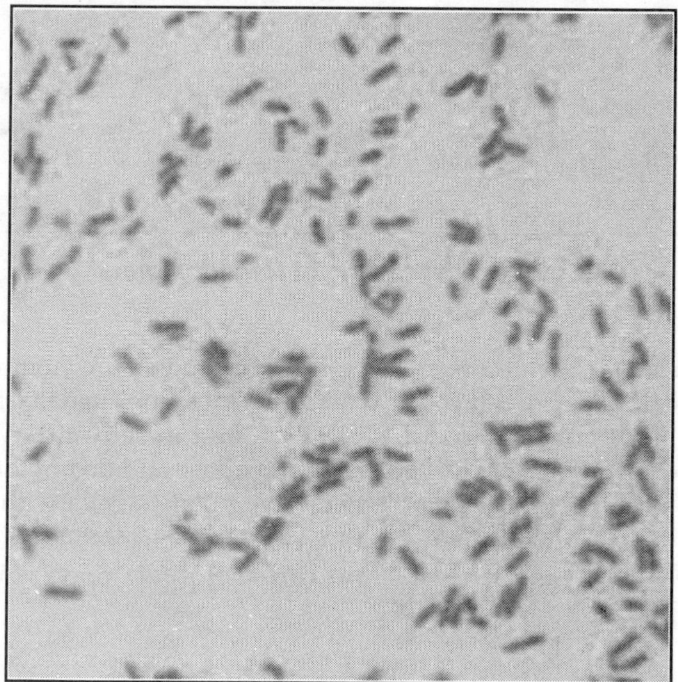

**Fig. 8.2: Gram Staining of *Klebsiella***

### 3. *Pseudomonas*

Rod shaped, Gram-negative, motile, aerobic, non spore forming with oxidase and catalase positive bacteria. *Pseudomonas* has the ability to metabolise a variety of diverse nutrients. Combined with the ability to form biofilms, they are thus able to survive in a variety of unexpected places. For example, they have been found in areas where pharmaceuticals are prepared. A simple carbon source, such as soap residue or cap liner-adhesives is a suitable place for them to thrive. Other unlikely places where they have been found include antiseptics, such as quaternary ammonium compounds, and bottled mineral water.

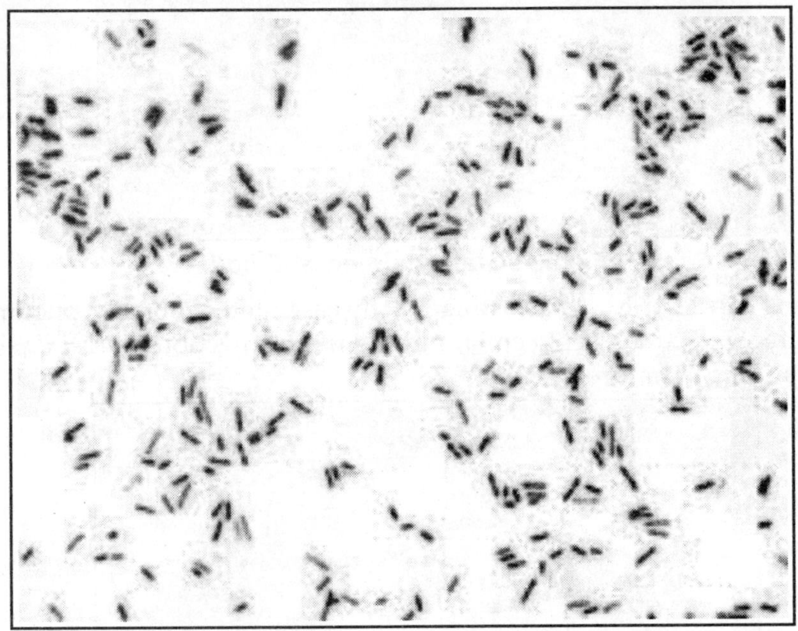

**Fig. 8.3: Gram Staining of *Pseudomonas***

### 4. *Vibro*

Gram-negative bacteria possessing a curved rod shape (comma shape), several species of which can cause foodborne infection, usually associated with eating undercooked seafood. Typically found in saltwater, Vibrio spp. are facultative anaerobes that test positive for oxidase and do not form spores. All members of the genus are motile and have polar flagella with sheaths.

Several species of Vibrio are pathogens. Most disease-causing strains are associated with gastroenteritis, but can also infect open wounds and cause septicemia.

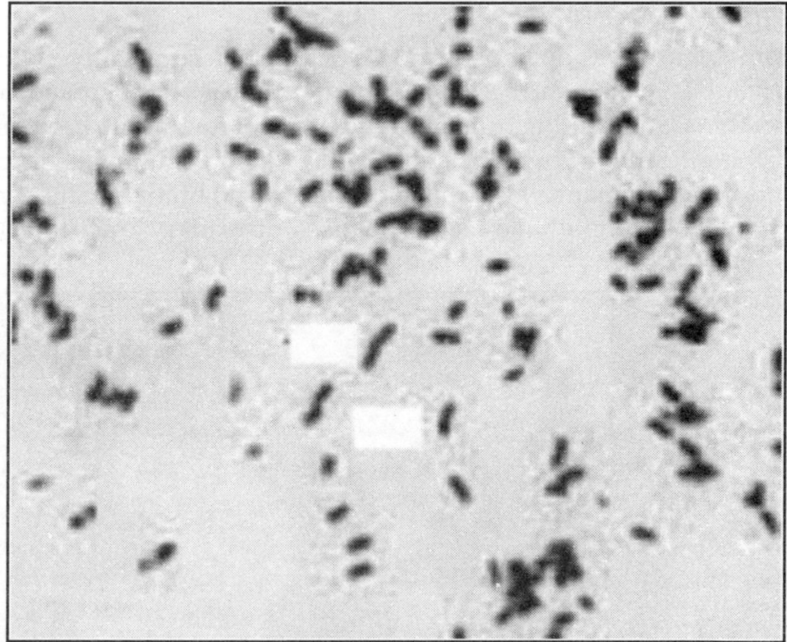

Fig. 8.4: Gram Staining of *Vibro*

## 5. *Enterobacter*

Gram-negative, rod-shaped, motile with oxidase negative bacterium. *Enterobacter* species grow best at 30°C rather than 37°C. They occur mainly in water, sewage, soil, meat, plants and vegetables. Some species also occur in human and animal faeces, and some can be opportunistic human pathogens.

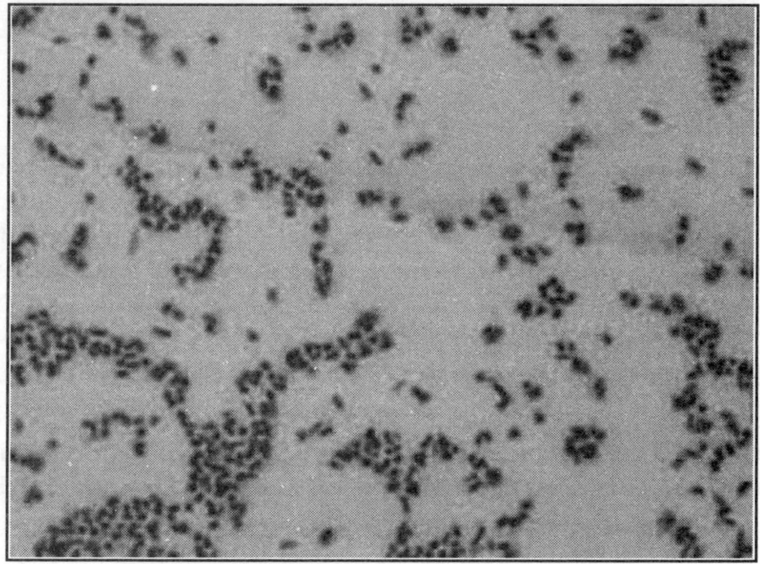

Fig. 8.5: Gram Staining of *Enterobacter*

### 6. *Proteus*

Gram-negative, rod-shaped, motile with oxidase negative bacterium. These organisms can swarm on agar media; that is, they spread over the plates in a thin film resulting from periodic cycles of migration. Proteus strains occur in the intestine of humans and a wide variety of animals, in polluted water and in the soil, and they can be opportunistic human pathogens. Like *E. Coli*, proteus is one of the leading causes of urinary tract infections in human.

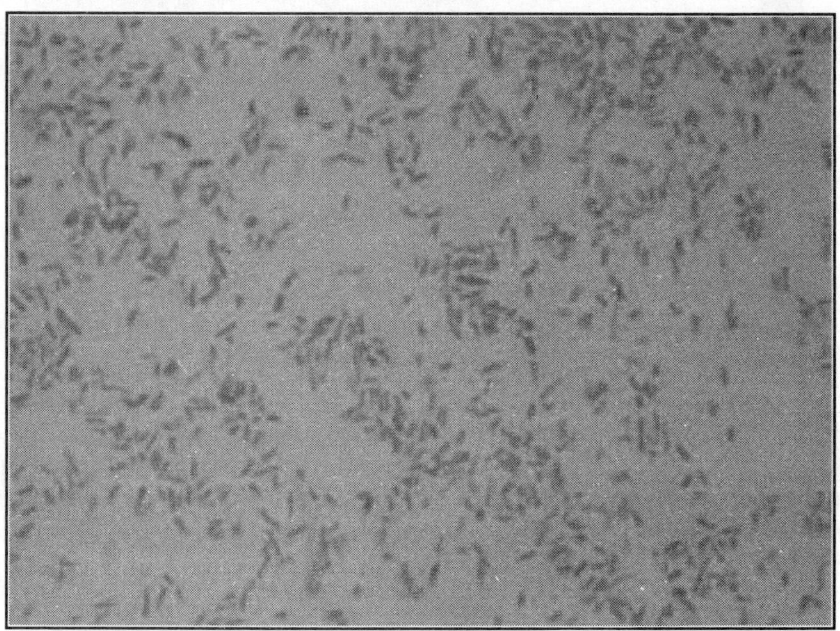

**Fig. 8.6: Gram Staining of *Proteus***

### 7. *Salmonella*

Gram-negative, rod-shaped, motile with oxidase negative bacterium. This is a group of organisms that are closely related to one another and probably should be considered as a single species. All strains are pathogenic for humans, causing enteric fever such as typhoid and paratyphoid, gastroenteritis and septicaemia; many strains also infect animals. Over 2,000 antigenic types of salmonella occur.

## RESULTS AND DISCUSSIONS

The data on the hydrological parameters are given in Table 8.1. The temperature of water does not show much variation. It only varies from 30°C to 33°C and pH remained between 7.91 and 8.65. Data on total bacterial count of the water samples are presented in Table 8.2.

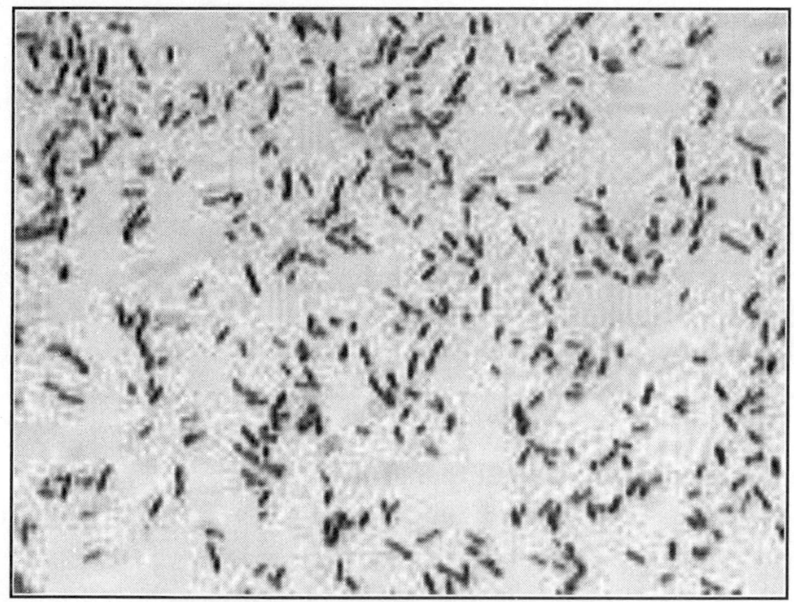

Fig. 8.7: Gram Staining of *Salmonella*

**Table 8.1: Temperature and pH of the Water**

| Sr. No. | Stations | Temperature(°C) | pH |
|---|---|---|---|
| 1. | Omkareshwar | 31 | 8.18 |
| 2. | Moretakka | 33 | 8.09 |
| 3. | Mandleshwar | 32 | 7.91 |
| 4. | Maheshwar | 33 | 8.22 |
| 5. | Khalghat | 30 | 8.65 |
| 6. | Barwani | 31 | 8.18 |

**Table 8.2: Bacterial Population (CFU/ml) in Narmada River**

| Sr. No. | Stations | CFU/ml |
|---|---|---|
| 1. | Omkareshwar | 129000 |
| 2. | Moretakka | 438000 |
| 3. | Mandleshwar | 204000 |
| 4. | Maheshwar | 296000 |
| 5. | Khalghat | 132000 |
| 6. | Barwani | 128000 |

**Table 8.3(a): Result of Biochemical Test**

| Sr. No. | Genera | Name of Test | | | | | |
|---|---|---|---|---|---|---|---|
| | | Indole | Methyl Red | Voges-Proskauer | Citrate Utilization | Urease Production | $H_2S$ Production |
| 1. | *Escherchia* | + | + | – | – | – | – |
| 2. | *Klebsiella* | – | – | + | + | + | – |
| 3. | *Pseudomonas* | – | – | – | + | – | – |
| 4. | *Vibrio* | – | – | – | + | + | – |
| 5. | *Enterobacter* | – | – | + | + | + | + |
| 6. | *Proteus* | + | + | – | – | + | + |
| 7. | *Salmonella* | – | + | – | – | – | + |

**Table 8.3(b): Results of TSI Slant**

| Sr. No. | Genera | Reaction | | Gas Production | $H_2S$ Production |
|---|---|---|---|---|---|
| | | On Slant | In Butt | | |
| 1. | *Escherchia* | Acidic | Acidic | + | – |
| 2. | *Klebsiella* | Acidic | Acidic | + | – |
| 3. | *Pseudomonas* | Alkaline | Alkaline | – | – |
| 4. | *Vibrio* | Acidic | Acidic | – | – |
| 5. | *Enterobacter* | Alkaline | Black | – | + |
| 6. | *Proteus* | Alkaline | Black | – | + |
| 7. | *Salmonella* | Alkaline | Acidic | – | + |

Moretakka shows the highest bacterial count among all six selected stations having 438000 cfu/ml and the lowest number was 128000 cfu/ml in the Badwani station. Purushothaman (1994) had estimated 389 to 5352 cfu/ml in sea water on the coast of Thiruvanthapuram. In this case, there has been a factor which adversely affected the bacteria, the effluents from adjoining industrial establishments. Added to this is the large quantity of sewage and other effluents brought through numerous creeks into the water, Zingde (1999), which provide ample nutrition for the heterotrophic bacterial population.

Table 8.4 gives the type of bacterial genera isolated from different sampling stations. Escherichia and Enterobacter are the most common bacterial genera found in all the stations under the study area. Next is pseudomonas which was found in all of the stations except Khalghat. Vibro was isolated from Omkareshwar, Mandleshwar, Maheshwar and Badwani it was absent in two stations moretakka and Khalghat. Whereas Klebsiella was isolated from water flowing from Moretakka, Khalghat and Badwani. Fecal coliform Salmonella was present only in the water of Maheshwar and Mandleshwar receiving a huge amount of domestic and municipal sewage. Proteus was only seem to present in Moretakka. These evidences provide us an aim to determine the difference in the type of pollutant adding in the River water in different Sampling Stations and also the factors which are favouring and inhibiting the growth of the particular type of the bacterial genera.

**Table 8.4: Bacterial Genera Isolated from Narmada River**

| Sr. No. | Genera | Stations | | | | | |
|---|---|---|---|---|---|---|---|
| | | Omkareshwar | Moretakka | Mandleshwar | Maheshwar | Khalghat | Badwani |
| 1. | *Escherichia* | √ | √ | √ | √ | √ | √ |
| 2. | *Klebsiella* | × | √ | × | × | √ | √ |
| 3. | *Pseudomonas* | √ | √ | √ | √ | × | √ |
| 4. | *Vibrio* | √ | × | √ | √ | × | √ |
| 5. | *Enterobacter* | √ | √ | √ | √ | √ | √ |
| 6. | *Proteus* | × | √ | × | × | × | × |
| 7. | *Salmonella* | × | × | √ | √ | × | × |

Correlation from Table 8.5 between bacterial population and temperature was positive whereas between pH and total bacterial count gives negative correlation.

**Table 8.5: Correlation Between Total Bacterial Count and Physio-chemical Parameters**

| | Temperature | pH | Total Bacterial Count |
|---|---|---|---|
| Temperature | 01 | -0.630 | +0.886 |
| pH | -0.630 | 01 | -0.351 |
| Total Bacterial count | +0.886 | -0.351 | 01 |

The present study indicates extremely high levels of bacterial populations in the Narmada River indicating adverse effects of pollution and deterioration of the environment through the organic and inorganic pollutant that enter the water. The presence of large number of Gram negative bacteria in the water is a matter of concern. The present findings indicate the urgency of detailed investigations on these aspects, especially with reference to the pathogenic organisms in this region. The results also indicate that with rise in bacterial population temperature of water increases whereas pH of water decreases i.e. bacterial population shows positive correlation with temperature and negative correlation with pH With increase in Bacterial population the pH of water becomes more acidic.

*Escherichia coli* are the most common coliform which have been isolated from all the stations under study area. It shows that the domestic pollution from the catchment villages and cities flow into the river by various means. Other coliforms and Gram negative bacteria also give the indication for the same.

## REFERENCES


APHA (1980) Standard Methods for the Examination of Water and Wastewater, 15th ed., American Public Health Association, New York. An Extensive Compendium of Physical, Chemical and Biological "Standard Methods" for the Examination of Water. APHA (2002) Standard Methods for the Examination of Water and Wastewater. 19th edn. American Public Health Association, Washington. D.C.

Environmental Protection Agency (1978) Microbiological Methods for Monitoring the Environment, Water and Wastes U.S. Environmental Protection Agency, Washington. A Manual of Laboratory Procedures.

Feng P, Weagant S, Grant, M. (2002). "Enumeration of *Escherichia coli* and the Coliform Bacteria". Bacteriological Analytical Manual (8th ed.). FDA/Center for Food Safety & Applied Nutrition. http://www.cfsan.fda.gov/~ebam/bam-4.html. Retrieved 2007.

Ganguly, T., Kumar, B., Sen, A. K. and Bhunia, A.B. (1999): Assessment of Water Quality of Damodar River Through Comparative Analysis of Bioindicators and Physico Chemical Determinations. J. Env. & Poll. Vol. 6 (2 & 3):189-196.

Ishii, S and Sadowsky, M.J. (2008) *Escherichia coli* in the Environment: Implications for Water Quality and Human Health. Microbes and Environments Vol. 23: 101-108.

Kumar,A., Bisht, B.S., Joshi, V.D., Singh, A.K. and Talwar A. (2010) Physical, Chemical and Bacteriological Study of Water from Rivers of Uttarakhand. J. Hum Ecol.,Vol. 32 (3): 169-173.

Key, W.W., Phipps, B.M., Ishiguro, E.E. and Trust, T.J. (1985) Porphyrin Binding by the Surface Array Virulence Protein of *Aeromonas salmonicida*. J. Bacteriol., 164: 1332-1336.

Patralek, L.N. (1992) Bacterial Density in Ganges at Bhagalpur, Bihar. J. Eco. Biol. Vol 3(2): 102-105.

Pelczar,M.J., Chan, E.C.S., Krieg, N.L. (2011) Microbiology, TATA McGraw Hill, 40th Edition. 271-273. ISBN 0-07-049234-4.

Purushothaman, C.S. (1994) Studies on Phosphate Solubilising and Phosphatase Producing Bacteria in Veli Lake. Ph.D. Thesis, University of Kerala, Thiruvanthapuram, 175 pp.

Palleroni, Norberto J. (2010). "The Pseudomonas Story". Environmental Microbiology, Vol. 12 (6): 1377-1383.

Roy, P.N. (2002): Studies on Hydrological Status of Stream in Santel Pargans (South Bihar) with Special Reference to Pollution. Indian J. Environ. & Ecoplan. Vol. 3(1): 127-130.

Sharma, R., Sharma, M.S., Sharma,V. and Malara, H. (2008) Study of Limnology and Microbiology of Udaipur Lakes. 12th World Lake Conference. 1504-1508.

Singh, A.K (2002) Quality Assessment of Surface and Sub-surface Water of Damodar River Basin, India J. Environ. HLTH 1 Vol. 44 (1): 41-49.

Unni, K.S. (1997) Ecology of Narmada River, Ashish Publishing House New Delhi Vol. 371, 8 pp.

Verghese Susan P. Singh Monika and MishraAnjali (2005) An Assessment of Water Quality of River Yamuna during Mansoon at Agra City" Indina J. Env. Prot. Vol. 25 (10): 893-898.

Zingde, M.D. (1999) Marine Pollution – What are we heading for? In: Somayajulu, B.L.K. (ed.), Ocean Science: Trends and Future Directions. Ind National Sc Academy, New Delhi, 229-246.

9

# Studies on Vibrio Infection in Cultured Freshwater Fish

Safinaz G.M. Ismail, *Egypt*; W.D.Saleh, *Egypt*; Monạ Zaki, *Egypt*

***ABSTRACT***

During the course of this study 10 isolates were isolated from *M.capito* collected from several farms in Behera province. The morphological and biochemical characters of isolated bacteria were proved to be belong to *V.anguillarum* (2 isolates), *V.ordalii* (6 isolates) and *V. parahaemolyticus* (2 isolatea).The isolation of the 3 Vibrio sp. from internal organs of naturally infected *M.capito* indicated that isolates are able to induce infection in *M.capito*. The examined *M.capito* showed signs of septicemia in the form of hemorrhagic patches on the caudal peduncle area and base of the fins, superficial ulcers, ascites and congestion of internal organs. Up on injection of *V.ordalii* in eels both the clinical signs and postmortem lesions were more severe than that observed in naturally infected *M.capito*. The histopathological changes were severe hyperplasia of secondary gill lamellae, hepatocyts necrosis, activation of melanomacrophage centers and bacterial colonization in the ellipsoid of the spleen. The vaccinated eels respond positively to the injected *V.ordalii* bacterin with relative level of protection of 100 per cent. To the best knowledge of the authors it is the first time to isolate *V.ordalii* from *M.capito* in Egypt. Moreover, isolation of *V. parahaemolyticus* is an alarm not only as fish pathogen but also as human hazard.

*Keywords:* Vibrio; Infection; Freshwater Fish.

## INTRODUCTION

One of the main factors affecting fish production and efficiency is the fish diseases and especially that resulted from bacterial diseases which are responsible for heavy mortality among wild and cultured fish (Saad., 2002). Vibrio species are gram negative bacteria affected all type of fish of either marine or freshwater fish allover the world in the different areas of Asia, America, Australia, Africa and Europe. (Toranzo and Barja., 1993 and Austin and Austin., 1999). Genus Vibrio comprises more than 45 species, most of which are which are widely distributed in the marine environment. Bacteria of this genus constitute the dominant intestinal microbiota of a wide range of marine fish (Sakata et al., 1980; Onarheim and Raa. (1990).

Fish affected by Vibriosis suffered from severe congestion at the base of the fins, erosion of the fins, excessive mucoid secretion on gills, severe congestion of gills, hemorrhagic ulcerations, linear hemorrhages over different parts of the body and severe congestion or hemorrhagic protrusion of the anal opening (Toranzo et al., 2005). Morovere, the most important postmortem lesions were congestion of internal organ and distention of gall bladder (Xio et al., 2005 and Reader et al., 2007)

In Egypt, production of fish has significantly increased during the last ten years, due to the improvement in culture techniques specially in *Oreochromis niloticus* farming. However, disease outbreaks have bean reported with economic losses:

The outbreaks of Vibriosis were common problems among cultured marine and freshwater fish which have occurred at various stages of cultured and caused serious economic losses (Rasheed.,1989 a).

Vibrio spp. has been isolated from freshwater environment and isolation rates increased with increase environmental temperature and organic pollution (Rhades et al., 1986 and Reham, Ali (2009).

The aim of this study was isolation and identification of *V. ordalii* that affect cultured *M.capito* and clarify the pathogenicity in cultured eel) *Anguilla Anguilla*).

## MATERIALS AND METHODS

### Naturally Infected Fish

A total number of 80 *Mugil capito* (50± 5 mg)were collected moribund and alive from a private fish farm in Behera Province. Fish were subjected to clinical and microbiological examinations according to Austin and Austin., (1987) and Schaperculaus et al., (1992). Isolation of Vibrio spp. was achieved from ulcers, liver, kidneys and spleen of naturally infected *M. capito* alive and freshly dead.

### Experimental Fish

A total of 130 apparently healthy eel *(Anguilla anguilla)* with an average weight of 40± 5 gm were obtained from natural sources in Behera province.

They were Kept in glass aquaria provided with aerated dechlorinated tap water and kept at temperature of 22 ± 1 C. with continuous aeration according to Innes (1966). The fish were fed on commercial diet containing 40 per cent crude protein at the level of 5 per cent of body weight according to Eurell et al., (1978). They were used for evaluation of the pathogenicity of isolated Vibrio Spp. Ten eels were random collected and submitted for bacteriological examination to verify the absence of *Vibrio ordalii*.

Primary isolation was don from internal organ of examined *M.capeto* according to Eleonor., et al (1997), on Tryptcase soya agar (TSA).

**Isolation and Identification of the Isolated Bacteria**

Primary isolation was done on trypticase soya agar (TSA) supplied with different concentrations of sodium chloride (1.5-8%) according to Eleonor et al (1997), incubated for 24 hours at 30C. The recovered suspected colonies were picked up and purified for further identification according to culture, morphological and biochemical characterization.

Morphological characters, colonial and growth feature on TSA as well as biochemical were used for identification of isolated bacteria according to Berge's(1982) and Whitman. (2004).

Moreover the API.20E system (Analytab products, Plainview New York) was also used for biochemical characteristics of all suspicious isolates.

**Detection of the Pathogen City of Isolated Bacteria in eel *(Anguilla anguilla).***

**Medial Lethal dose 50 ($LD_{50}$)**

Medial lethal dose 50 ($LD_{50}$) for the isolate (N 10) was estimated in *A. anguilla* according to Reed and Muench (1938). Graded doses ranged from $10^{-1}$ to $10^{-7}$ CFU/ml was used. A total number of 80 apparently healthy eels (40+ 5 gm) were grouped into 8 groups (10 eels/group). The first seven groups were injected intra peritoneal (I.P.) with one ml of specified bacterial concentrations. The eight groups was injected I.P with one ml of sterile saline and served as control. Mortalities were recorded for 7 days post injection. Freshly dead fish were submitted for bacterial isolation and re-isolation and identification of tested bacteria was done to verify specificity of mortality.

**Experimental Infection**

A total of 40 eels (40 + 5 g) was allotted to four equal groups. Fish of the first three groups were injected I. m with 0.2 ml of 0.5 dose of $LD_{50}$ according to Shehate et al., (1988). The fourth group was injected with 0.2 ml of sterile saline and served as control. Infected and control groups were kept under daily observation for two weeks. Both clinical sings and mortalities were recorded.

All freshly dead eels were submitted to bacterial isolation and *V. ordalii* isolated was re-identified to verify the specificity of mortality.

Histopathological and ultra changes were carried out from organs of experimentally infected eels according to Culling, (1983).

Evaluation of potency of prepared vaccine against *V.ordalli* were done according to the method described by Sakai et al., (1984) and Badran and Eissa, (1991). The formalin inactivated bacterin were mixed with an equal volume of 0.85 per cent sterile saline and adjusted to Macfarland's No.5 (approximately $6 \times 10^8$ cells/ml).

Twenty eels were injected with 0.2 ml bacterin/fish (IP). Twenty eels was also injected with 0.2 ml (IP) sterile saline control. After 2 weeks the injected eels received booster dose from bacterin (Same dose) and control group injected with 0.2 ml sterile saline.

Blood collection was carried out after 28 days post injection for serum collection. The antibody titer was evaluated by microagglutination test according to Badran and Eissa (1991).

After 28 days both infected and control groups were injected with 0.2 ml of virulent isolate of *V. ordalii* previously adjusted to $6 \times 10^8$ cfu/ ml.

Clinical signs and mortality were observed for one week. The potency of bacterin was examined by calculating the relative level of protection (RLP) by the following formula:

RLP = % 1- mortality of vaccinated eels × 100/% mortality of control

According to Newman and Majnarich, (1982).

All groups of eels in this study were anesthetized with a solution containing 1 gm of benzocaine (ethyl aminobenzoate) in 10 ml ethanol prior to injection.

## RESULTS

### Results of Clinical Examination of Naturally Infected Fish

The clinical signs in *Mugil capito*, were hemorrhagic patches on the caudal peduncle area and base of fins as well as superficial *hemorrhagic ulcers at the abdominal wall* (*See fig. 9.1 on next page*). The postmortem changes in *Mugil capito* were characterized by deep seated muscle lesions, enlargement and congestion of the spleen which became cherry red in colour and losses its sharp edges. Moreover, ascites and corneal opacity were also noticed in some examined fish (*See fig. 9.2 on next page*)

### Isolation and Identification of Vibrio Species

Attempts to isolate Vibrio spp. from different organs (kidneys, liver and spleen) of naturally infected *M. capito* gave ten isolates that grow on trypticase soya agar with different concentration from NaCl (1.5% to 8%). The colonies appeared after 24 hrs post – incubated at 30C.*Colonies* were of medium size (2-3 mm in diameter) and creamy in color. They proved to be Gram – negative, motile rods and gave presumptive identification of Vibrio species.

**Fig. 9.1:** ***Mugil capito*** **Naturally Infected with** ***Vibrio ordalii*** **Showing Hemorrhagic Patches on the Caudal Peducle and Base of Fins**

**Fig. 9.2:** ***Mugil capito*** **Naturally Infected with** ***Vibrio ordalii*** **Showing Congestion and Enlargement of Spleen**

## Biochemical Characterization of Isolates

The biochemical and growth characteristics of the isolates using traditional tests indicated that all the isolates were positive for oxidase and motility tests. Variable results were obtained in case of lysine decarboxylase, arginine dihydrolase and ornithine decarboxylase. Moreover, all isolates gave positive results in case of sucrose fermentation except isolate No. 9 and 10. The other tested sugars gave variable results. Further biochemical characterization of 10 isolates, was carried out by using the API 20E system. All tested isolates were positive for sodium pyruvaate (VP) (except N9 and N10), gelatin liquefaction and tryptophane (except N9 and N10) Negative results were obtained for tryptophane (IND) (except N9 and N10), sodium thiosulphate (H2S) and orthonitrophenyl galactoside (except isolates N1 and N2). Variable results were observed for arginine | (ADH), lysine (LDC), ornithine (ODC), sodium citrate (Cit) and urea (URE).

Concerning the results of sugar fermentation by using API20E system, the tested isolates gave positive results for glucose, mannitol, sucrose, sorbitol and rhamnose except (N2).Variable results were noticed in case of other sugars

According to both morphological and biochemical characters of Vibrio species, the tested isolates were identified as *V.anguillarum* (2 isolates), *V.ordalii* (6 isolates) and *V.parahaemolyticus* (2 isolates).

## Pathogenicity Assay

Due to the unique isolation *of V.ordalii* for the first time in Egypt according to the best knowledge of the authors, the most virulent one which proved by developing rapid and severe clinical and MP lesions was used for further experimental studies in *Anguilla Anguilla*.

The results of determination of the virulence of selected *V. ordalii* isolate by calculation of the lethal concentration 50 (LD50) showed that the LD50 of *V. ordalii* was $10^{2.4}$ bacterial cells/ml.

## Experimental Infection with *V.ordalii*

This experiment was done to determine the nature of experimental infection of selected *V.ordalii* isolate in eel (*A. Anguilla*).

After 2 day post injection, the eels became sluggish and the escape reflex was too weak. The clinical signs were characterization by server hemorrhages over the body, in some cases these hemorrhages covered the whole body surface and congestion of the head region (*See Figs. 9.3 and 9.4 on next page*). Haemorrhagic ulcers were recognized at the body surface of infected eel.

The postmortem lesions were in the form of server congestion of the liver which some times became edematous. Enlargement of spleen which became cherry red and loss its sharp edges in addition to severe congestion of the kidneys and inflammation of the intestine (*See fig. 9.5 on page 141*). Fifteen eels were died during the course of experiment.

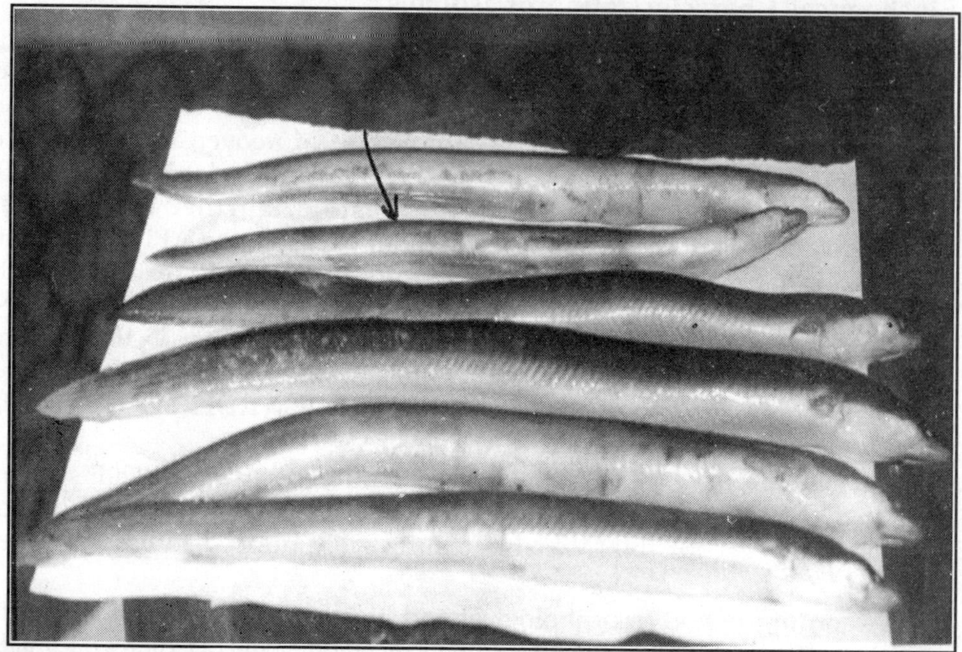

**Fig. 9.3: Eel (*Anguilla Anguilla*) Experimentally Infected with *Vibrio.ordalii* Showing Severe Hemorrhages Over the Body**

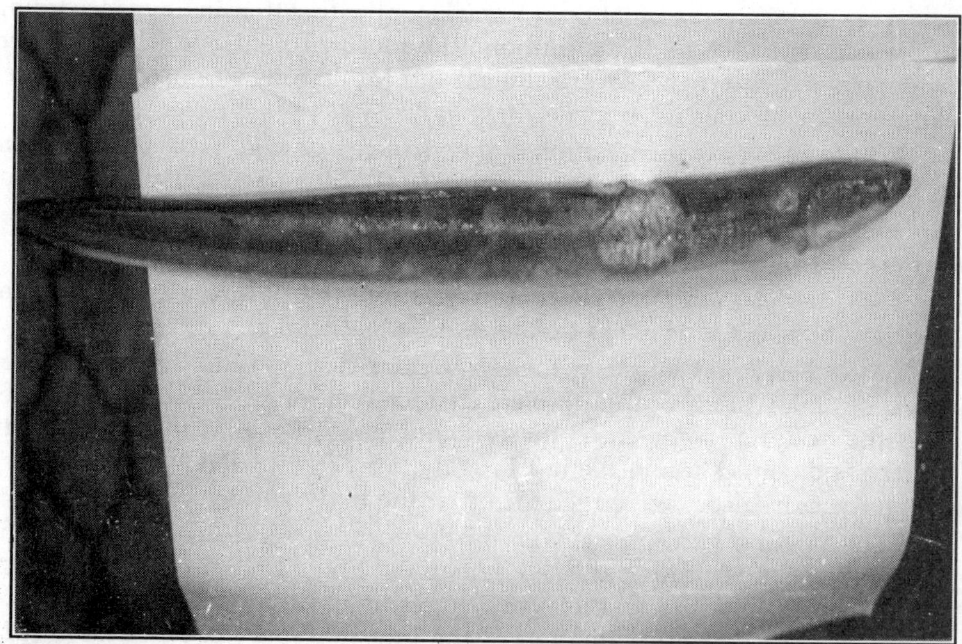

**Fig. 9.4: Eel (*Anguilla Anguilla*) Experimentally Infected with *Vibrio.ordalii* Showing Deep Hemorrhagic Ulcer**

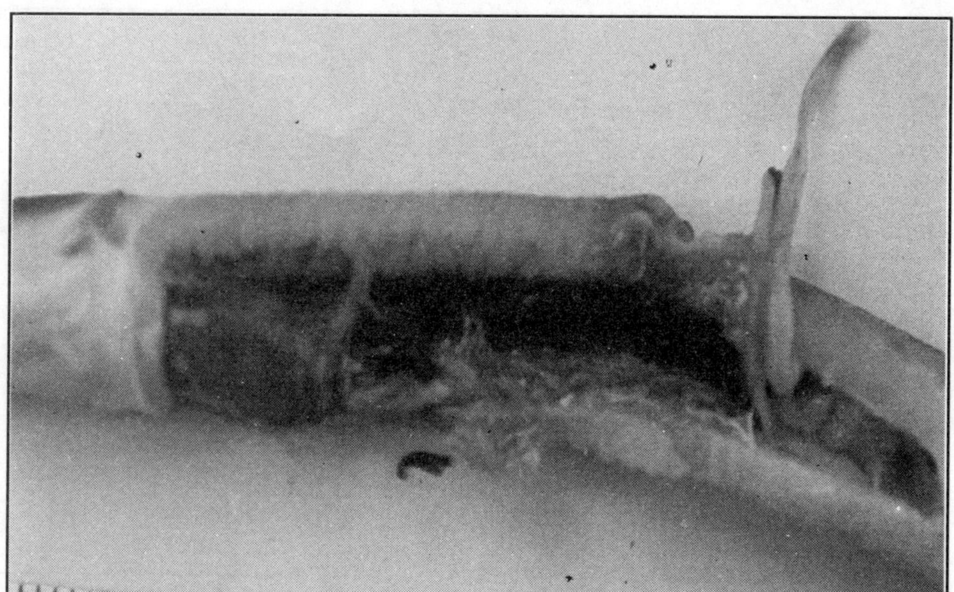

**Fig. 9.5: Eel *(Anguilla Anguilla)* Experimentally Infected with *Vibrio.ordalii* Showing Congestion of Internal Organs**

## Evaluation of Antibody Titers of *Vibrio ordalii* in eel

The antibody response in *A anguilla* infected with *V.ordalii* was detected 28 days post-injection of bacterin. The detected antibody titer was $2^5$.

The injected *A.anguilla* were firstly examined to verify their freedom from Vibrio species infection and proved to be free. The results revealed that fish vaccinated with prepared bacterin gave complete protection when challenged with $10^4$ cells·/ml of live bacteria, were the relative protection level reached 100 per cent.

The re-isolation of injected bacteria was positive in case of freshly dead infected eel.

## Histopathological Changes

Histopathological sections from different organs of injected eels with *V. ordalii* revealed the following results.

### Gills

The major histopathological changes were characterized by severe hyperplasia and filamental thickening adhesion with mononuclear cell infiltration (*See fig. 9.6 on next page*). There were also thrombus formation in the bronchial artery. There was also slight oedema and diffuse lymphocytic infiltration in the gill arch and epithelial hyperplasia at the base of the secondary lamellae.

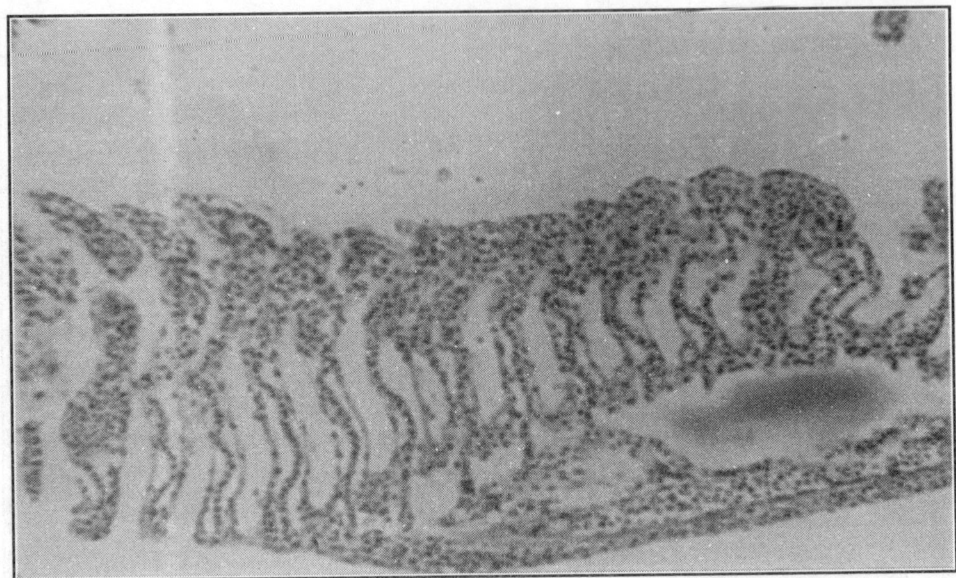

**Fig. 9.6: Gills of eel Experimentally Infected with *Vibrio. ordalii* Showing Severe Lamellar Hyperplasia with Filamental Adhesion. (H&E.X160)**

## Liver

The lesion in the liver were characterized by extensive areas of oedematous, vacuolated and atrophied hepatocytes. There were hepatocytic cell necrosis in between swollen cells and normal hepatocytes (Fig. 9.7), as well as thrombus formation.

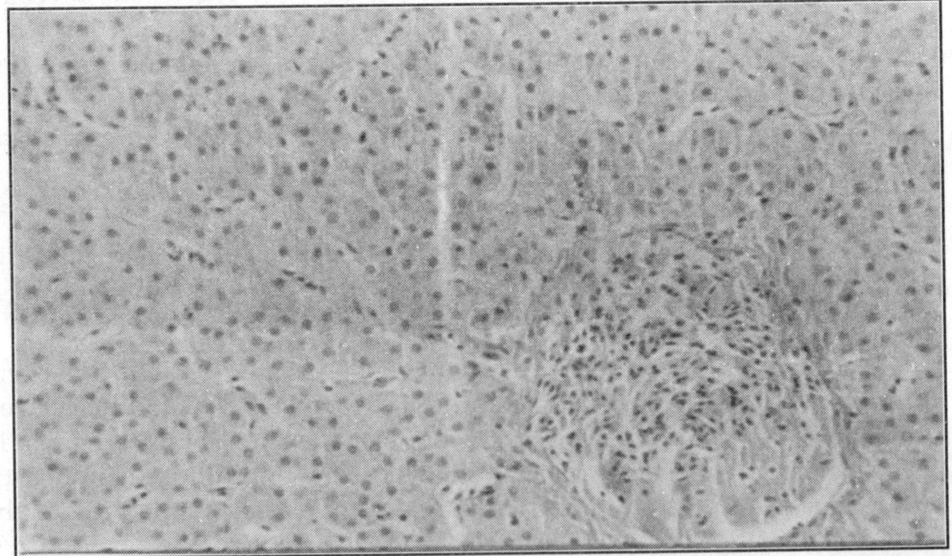

**Fig. 9.7: Liver of eel Experimentally Infected with *Vibrio.ordalii* Showing Thrombus Formation. (H&E.X160)**

## Kidneys

The kidneys showed hyper activation of the melanomacrophage centers. The melanomacrophge centers were seen around and within the tunica media of the long arterioles. The interstitial tissues of the kidney showed depletion and cell necrosis (*Fig. 9.8*).

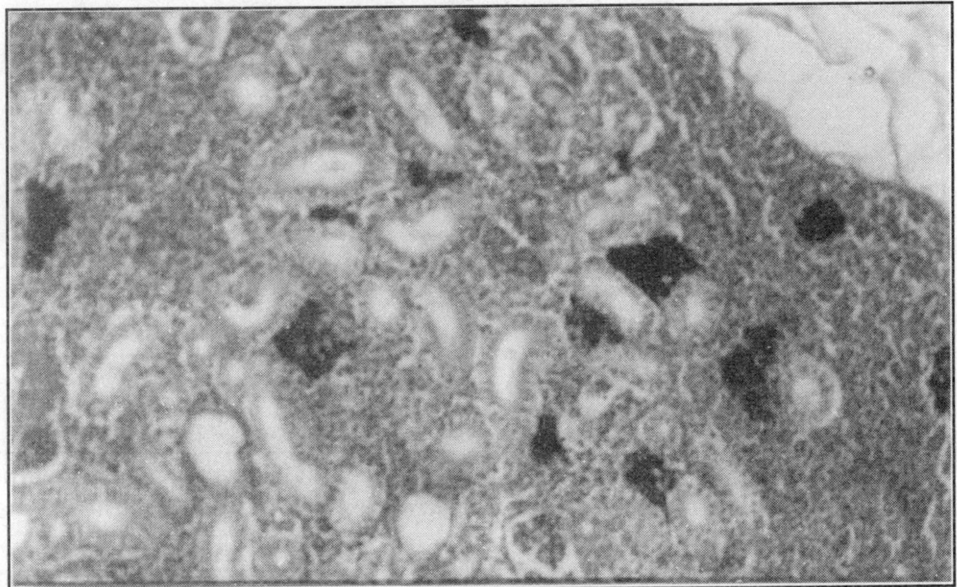

**Fig. 9.8: Kidneys of eel Experimentally Infected with *Vibrio.ordalii* Showing Hyper Activation of the Melanomacrophage Centres. (H&E.X160)**

## Skin and Underlying Musculature

The skin showed excessive melanosis in the dermis with multifocal slight dermal oedema (*See fig. 9.9 on next page*). Leucocytic infiltration of muscle was observed. Oedema and extensive haemorrhages as leucocyte infiltration were noted between muscle fibers as well as muscle necrosis.

## Spleen

In most samples, the spleen was extensively colonized by *V. ordalii* Bacteria accumulated mainly in the ellipsoide. The spleen was hyperaemic and the number of macrophages and neutrophils increased considerably in the periellipsoidal area and red pulp. These macrophages were hypertrophied and contained phagocytosed erythrocytes, bacteria, melanin granules and cell debris.

## Ultra Changes

The ultra changes in liver of eel previously injected with *V.ordalii* were pronounced and clear. Electron micrograph of liver in case of infected eel revealed vacuolation of hepatocyte with server glycogen deposition (*See Fig. 9.10 on next page*). Moreover, server endoplasmic dilatation and server glycogen deposition were observed.

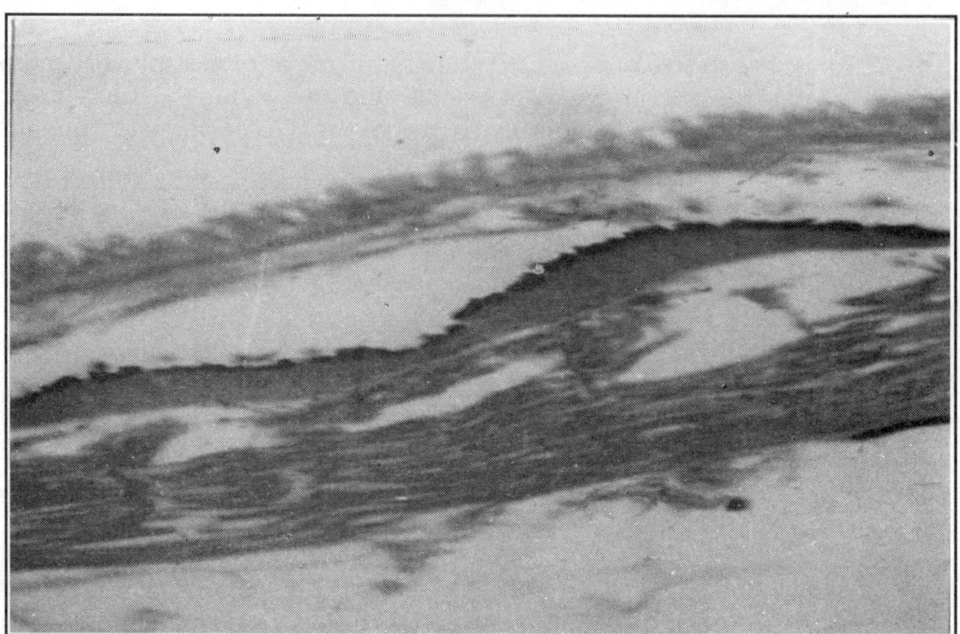

Fig. 9.9: Skin of eel Experimentally Infected with *Vibrio ordalii* Showing Excessive Melanosis in the Dermis with Multifocal Slight Dermal Oedema.(H&E.X250)

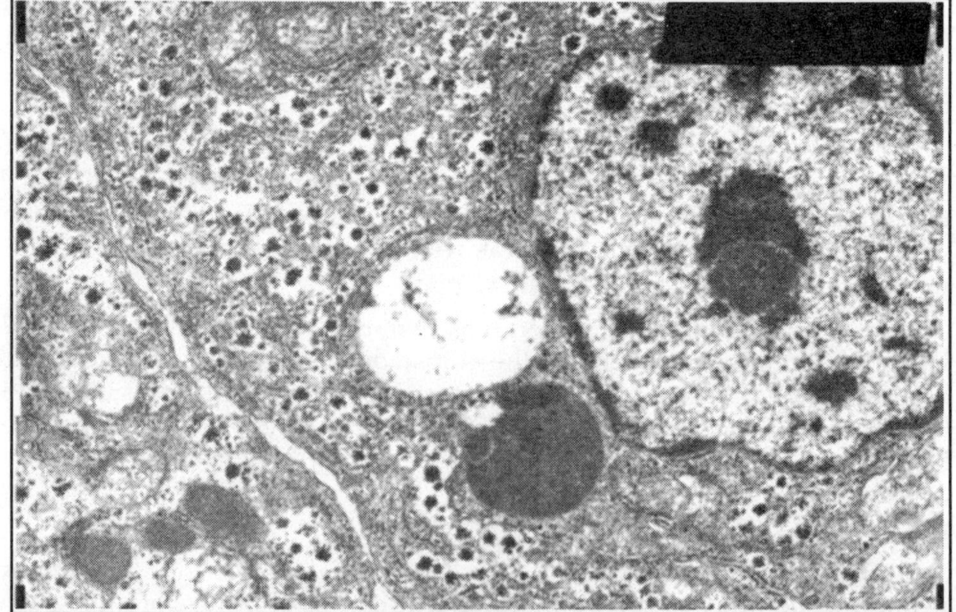

Fig. 9.10: Electron Micrograph of Liver of eel Experimentally Infected with *Vibrio.ordalii* Showing Valuation of Hepatocytes with Severe Glycogen Deposition. (x10000)

## DISCUSSION

The Vibrio, *V. alginolyticus, V. anguillarum, V. ordalii* are fish pathogens. All are associated with acute bacterial septicemia or chronic focal lesions in infected fish. Generally, Vibriosis in fish accompanies with some other stress or physical trauma but some strains, especially of *V.anguillarum, V.ordalii* and *V*. salmonicida appear to be highly infectious primary pathogens (Robert et al., 1975).

During the course of this study 10 isolates from several outbreaks of Vibriosis among cultured *Mugil capito* were isolated. The isolates were submitted to complete morphological, cultural and biochemical examination by using both tube biochemical method and AP120E system.

The morphological and biochemical characters of isolated bacteria were proved to belong to *V.anguillarum* (2 isolates), *V.ordalii* (6 isolates) and *V. Parahaemolyticus* (2 isolates). The identification of the previously mentioned Vibrio species were based on the data published by Grisez et al. (1991) and the criteria of the manufacturer of AP 120E system. Moreover, the negative results of arginine dihydrolase, reduction of $NO_2$, Voges-Proskauer production and utilization of both arabinose and sorbitol distinguished *V. ordalii* from *V. anguillarum*.

Also, the positive results of lysine decarboxylase, ornithine decarboxylase, citrate simmons and indole and negative results of Vp and utilization of sucrose and melibiose distinguished the *V. parahaemolyticus* from *V.ordalii* and *V. anguillarum* (Austin and Austin, 1987, Grisez et al. 1991 and Saeed, 1995).

The isolation of both *V. anguillarum* and *V.ordalii* from internal organs of naturally infected *Mugil capito* (namely spleen, kidneys and liver) indicated that both Vibrio species are pathogen and able to induce infection in *Mugil capito*. Moreover, the isolation of Vibrio species from internal organs may be attributed to the ability of bacteria to produce septicemia as well as bacteriaemia.

Chart and trust (1984) and Davease et at. (1985) reported that *V. anguillarum* and *V. ordalii* were well known to be the primary pathogens to fish. While, Austin and Austin (1987) pointed out that seven Vibrio fish pathogens as follows: *V. alginolyticus, V. anguillarum, V. carchariae, V. cholerae, V. damsela and V. ordalii*. While, Noel et al. (1996), Benediktsdottir et al. (1998) and Akhlaghi (1999) had reported isolation of different types of Vibrio (namely, *V.anguillarum, V. alginolyticus, V. carchariae, V. cholera, V. damsela, V. ordalii, V salmonicida, V. parahaemolyticum* and *V. vulnificys* biotype 2) from different internal organs such as liver, spleen kidneys, muscular lesions of different infected fish species-. Moreover, Ransom et al. (1984) reported that *V. ordalii* induced pathogenesis in fish not particularly different from that of

*V. anguillarum* but generally less server. They also added that the infection by *V. ordalii* may be occurred via ascending infection from the posterior gut or through the skin.

The isolation of the two isolates which were identified as *V. parahaemolyticus* is very interesting since the *V. parahaemolyticus* has been reported to be implicated in fish disease and human infection as fish food poisoning. Moreover, *V. parahaemolyticus* has been reported to be isolated from human disease situation (Austin and Austin, 1987).

Daniels et al. (2000) reported an outbreak of *V. parahaemolyticus* serotype $O_{3:}$ $K_6$ infection in the United States. The same authors added that, the consumers should understand that raw or undercooked fish infected with *V. parahaemolyticus* can cause illness in from of gastroenteritis.

It is worthy to mention that, the less information about the susceptibility of eel to *V. ordalii* directed us to study the pathogenicity of this species in eels.

The result of $LD_{50}$ proved that *V ordalii* (No. 10) used in the present study was highly virulent for eel. $LD_{50}$ being estimated to be $10^{2.4}$ CFU/ fish.

Nordmo et al., (1997) recorded that $LD_{50}$ of *V. ordalii* was $10^6$ CFU/L fish in Atlantic salmon. The difference in the $LD_{50}$ value in this study may be attributed to the difference in fish species, bacterial strain and environmental conditions.

The extensively colonization of *V.ordalii* in spleen ellipsoide directed us to believe that the spleen is the predilection sit for *V.ordalii* and organ of choice for isolation of the bacteria.

The histopathological changes due to infection of *V.ordalii* varied and recognized in different organs. These changes may be attributed to the extensive bacterial multiplication and the secretion of cytotoxin, haemolysin and protease by *V.ordalii* (Santos, et al 1991, kumar et al,. 2006 and Reham 2009) Ultra structurally, the lesions in liver were not specific and frequently in the liver of fish exposed to toxic agents (Ghadially, 1988), The same conclusion was reported by Lamas et al., (1994) in case of Rainbow trout experimentally infected with *V. anguillarum*.

The Relative level of protection (RLP) of vaccinated eel was 100 per cent.This result proved that eel was respond positively to the formalized killed bacterin which prepared from *V. ordalii* isolated from *M. capito* in Egypt. *V. ordalii* isolated from *M.capito* succeeded to produce system infection in eel upon experimental infection.

The experimentally injected eels showed sings of septicemia in the form of sever hemorrhage of the body, hemorrhagic ulcers and congestion of internal organs. The recorded signs may by due to toxins produced by injected bacteria Nordmo et al., (1997) and Reham (2009).

## REFERENCES

Akhlaghi, M.(1999): Passive Immunization of Fish Against Vibriosis, Comparison of Intrperitoneal, Oral and Immersion Routes. Aquaculture, 180: 191-205. Ramsted, A. (1997): Experimental Infection with *Vibrio salmonicida* in Atlantic salmon (*Salmo salar* L.) an Evolution of Three Different Challenge Methods. Aquaculture, 158: 23-32.

Austin,B.and Austin, D. (1999): Bacterial Fish Pathogens: Disease in Farmed and Wild Fish. John Wiley and Sons Chichester.

Badran and Eissa. (1991) Studies on Bacteria Diseases Among Cultured Fresh Water Fish (*O.niloticus)* in Relation to the Incidence of Bacteria Pathogens at Ismailia Governorates. J. Egypt. Vet. Med. ASS.

Benediktsdottir, E.;Heigason, S.and sigurjonsdottir, H.(1998): Vibrio spp. Isolated from Salmonids with Shallow Skin Lesions and Reared at Low Temperature. J.Fish Dis., 21: 19-28.

Bergey,S,R.W.(1982): Somonella and Edwardsiella tarda in gulla faces a Source of Contamination in Fish Processing Plants. Appl. Microbiol.24(3): 501-3.

Chart, H. and Trust, J.J. (1984): Characterization of the Surface Antigen of Marine Fish Pathogens Vibrio Anguillarum and Vibrio ordalii. Canadian J.Microbiol., 30: 703-710.

Culling, C.F(1993): Handbook of Histopathologic and Histochemical Stanining 3rd Ed., Buterworth London.

Daniels, N.A.; Ray, B.; Easton, A.; Marano, N.; Kahn, E.; Mcshan, A.L. Del Rosario, L.; Badwin, T., Kingsley, M.A.; Puhr, N.P.; Wells, J.G and Angulo, F.J. (2000): Emergences of a New Vibrio Parahaemolyticus Serotype in Raw Oysters. A Prevention Quandary. Jama, 284(12): 1541-1545.

Devesa, S.; Toranzo, A.E. and Baria, J.L.(1985): First Report of Vibriosis in Turbot (Scophthalmus maximus) Cultyred in North Western Spain. In: Fish and Shellfish Pathology (ed.Ellis, A.E.) pp. 131-139. Academic Press London.

Eleonor, V.; Alapide Tendencia, Loudes, A. and Dureza, (1997): Isolation of vibrio Species from Penaeus Monodon (Fabricius) with Red Disease Syndrome. Aquculture, 154: 107-114.

Ghadially, F.N (1988): Ultrastructural Pathology of the Cell and matrix.3 rd Ed. Butterworth, London, 1340 p.

Grisez,L.; Ceusters, R.; Ollevier (1991): The Use of API 20E for the Identification of Vibrio Anguillarum and V.ordalii.J.Fish Dis., 14: 359- 365.

Kumar, S.R.; Parameswaran, V.; Ahmed, V.P.I.; Mustag S.Sand Hameed, As.

Lamas, J.; Santo,Y.; Bruno, D.; Alicia, E.Toronzo and Anadon, Ramon (1994): Comparison of Pathological Changes Caused by Vibrio Anguillarum and its Extracellular Products in Rainbow Trout (Onchorhynchus mykiss). Fish Pathology Dis., 29(2): 79-89.

Kumar, S.R., Parameswaran, V., Ahmed, V.P., Muataq, S.S., and Hameeed, A.S. (2006): Protective Efficiency of DNA Vaccinationin Asian Seabass Against Vibrio Anguillarum. Fish & Shellfish Immunology 1-11.

Neman, S.G. and Majnarich J.J. (1982): Direct Immersion Vaccination of Juvenile Rainbow Trout, Salmo gairdneri Richardison, and Juvenile Coho Salmon, Onchorhynchus kisutch (walbaum), with Yersinia Ruckeri Bacterin. Journal of Fish Diseases. 5, 339-341.

Noel, T., Nicolas, J.L; Boulo, V.; Mialhe, E. and Roch, P.H (1996): Development of Acolony – Blot ELISA Assay Using Monoclonal Antibodies to Identify Vibrio PI Responspible for "Brown Ring Diseases" in the Clam Taps Philippinarum. Aquaculture. 146: 171-178.

Nordmo, R.; Sevatdal, S. Onarheim and Raa J. (1990): Charactrization and Possible Biological Significance of an Autochthonous Flora in the Intestinal Mucosa of Sea Fish. In Microbiology in Poecilotherms ed. Lessel, R. pp. 197-201.

Onarhim, A.M. and Raa, J (1990): Characteristics and Possible Biological Significance of an Autochthonous Flora in the Intestinal Mucosa of Sea-water Fish. In Microbiology in Picilotherma ed. Lesel, R. pp. 197-201 Amsterdam Alsevier Science.

Ransom, D.P.; Lannon, C.N.; Rehovec, J.S.and Fryer, J.L (1984): Comparison of Histopathology Caused by Vibrio Anguillarum and Vordalii in Three Species of Pacifice Salmon. J. Fish Dis., 7: 107-115.

Rasheed,V. (1989): Vibriosis Outbreak Among Cultured Sea Bream Brood Stock in Kuwait. Aquaculutre, 76: 189-197.

Reed,L.Jand Meunch, H. (1938): A Simple Method of Estimating Fifty per cent and Points. Am. J. Hyg., 27: 493-494.

Reham, A. Abd Elaziz (2009): Some Studies on Vibriosis on Cultured Fish. M.V.Sc. This is Dept. of Avian and Aquatic Animal Med. Fac. of Vet. Med. Alex. Univ. Egypt.

Ades L., and Ogg, H.(1986): Isolation of non- Vibrio Cholera Serovar from Surface Water in Western Colorado. Appl. Env. Microbiol., 51: 1216-1219.

Robertes,R.J.(1975): Melanin Containing Cells of Teleost Fish and Their Relation to Disease. In the Pathology of Fish. Ed.By. W.E.Ribrlin and G.Migoki, pp. 399-423. Univ.Wisconsin Press Madison.

Roaeder, I.L., Paulson, S.M., and Willassen, N.P.(2007): Effect of Fish Skin Mucouson the Soluble Protein of Vibrio Salmoniscida Analysis by 2-D gel electrophorisis. Microb. Pathogen 42: 36-45.

Saad, T. (2002): Some Studies on the Effects of Ochratoxin on Cultured O. niloticus and Carp spp. M.V.Sc. Thisis. Dept. of Avian and Aquatic Animal Med. Fac. of Vet. Med. Alex. Univ. Egypt.

Saeed, M.O. (1995): Association of Vibrio harveyi with Mortalities in Cultured Marine Fish in Kuwait. Aquaculture, 136: 21-29.

Sakai,M.; Aoki, T.; Kiato, T.; Rohovec, J.S. and Fryer J.L (1984): Comparison of the Cellular Immune Response of Fish Vaccinated by Immersion and Injection of *Vibrio anguillaruim*. Bull. of the Japanese Soc. of Sci. Fisheries, 50(7): 1187-1192.

Santos Y.; Lallier, R.; Bandin, I.; Lamas, J. and Toranzo, A.e. (1991): Susceptibility of Turbot (*Scophthalmus maximus*), Coho salmon (*Oncorhynchus kisutch*) and Rainbow Trout (*O.mykiss*) to Strains of *V.anguillarum* and Their Exotoxins. J.Appl.ichthyol., 160-167.

Sakata, T., Okabayashi, J and Kaimato.D. (1980): Variation in the Intestinal Microflora of Tilapia Reared in Fresh and Sea Water. Bulletin of the Japanease Soc. Of Sci Fisheries. 46: 313-317.

Schaperclaus, H.S.(1992): Blood Changes in Brook Trout Induced by Infection with Numerous Salmonicida. J.Wild Dis. Jan. 12(1): 77-82.

Toranzo, A.E and Barja,J.J (1993) : Virulence Factors of Bacteria Pathogenic for Cold Water Fish. Annu. Rev. Fish Diseases 3, 5-36.

Toranzo, A.E., Colwell, R.R and Hetrick F.M. (2005): Characterization of Plasmid in Bacterial Fish Pathogen. Infect. Immun. 39 (1): 184-192.

Whitmann, J.G. (2004): Intergenic Sequences and Gene Order (N-M-G) of Spring Viremia of Carp Virus. In: B.w.J.Mahy and D.Kolakofsky (Eds).The Biology of Negative Strand Viruses. Elsevier, Amsterdam, pp. 221-226.

Xio.,Q. Carson, J.Huang and J.Z.Liao: (2005): Pathological and Pathogenic Study on Vibriosis in eels. Chines J.of Vet. Sci. 19:3, 258-260.

(2006): Protective Efficiency of DNA Vaccination in Asian Seabass (*Lates calcarifer*) Against *Vibrio anguillarm*. Fish & Shellfish Immunology xx(2006): 1-11.

10

# Efficiency of Water Hyacinth (*Eichhornia crassipes*) in Remediation of Sewage Water Pollutants

**Faisal Abbas,** ***India***

***ABSTRACT***

Increasing urbanization, industrialization and over population is one of the leading causes of environmental degradation and pollution which posses threat to human and other organisms. Sensitive aquatic macrophytic species have serve as indicators and those resistances to pollution as accumulators. *Eichhornia crassipes,* an aquatic macrophyte has tremendous capacity to remove the pollutant from the water and also to grow and multiply rapidly in sewage containing aquatic environment. The aquatic plant water hyacinth is a powerful tool for mediating pollution from aquatic environment.

In present study, the nutrient removal capacity of *Eichhornia crassipes* is not as good as pollutant removal capacity. Removal of $Ca^{++}$, $Mg^{++}$ and $PO_4^-$ was very less in compare to removal of BOD, COD and turbidity. In the present study, BOD was removed 60 per cent, 67 per cent and 75 per cent in 10 day, 15 day and 20 day with dilution. But without diluted condition maximum 45 per cent removal at $10^{th}$ day was observed and COD was removed 56 per cent to 80 per cent in diluted condition, but in without diluted condition maximum 48 per cent removal at $10^{th}$ day.

*Key words:* Eichhornia crassipes, phytoremediation, sewage water, pollutants.

## INTRODUCTION

Water hyacinth (*Eichhornia crassipes*) treatment systems are generally known in tropical areas. The system with water hyacinth can operate at higher loading rates. Their end-use products can be utilized for mulch and organic fertilizer. Dry water hyacinth petioles can be woven into baskets and purse (Polprasert, 1996). Domestic wastewater or sewage is prime concern for its disposal in our country as its generate in huge quantity. The disposal and treatment has become a challenge for the municipalities in India. Many of the municipalities in growing cities neither have proper disposal system nor have any treatment facility due to higher cost. In such a situation domestic wastewater is diverted in to low lying area in to aquatic bodies like ponds and lakes, where it is posing a serious threat to the water quality.

Increasing urbanization, industrialization and over population is one of the leading causes of environmental degradation and pollution (Singh et al., 2012). Waste-water is the combination of liquid or water-carried wastes originating in the sanitary conveniences of dwellings, commercial or industrial facilities and institutions, in addition to any ground water, surface water and storm water that may be present. Untreated wastewater generally contains high levels of organic material, numerous pathogenic microorganisms, as well as nutrients and toxic compounds (Dixit et al., 2011). Among water plants, water hyacinth is found to be most effective in reducing BOD, COD, removal of nitrogen, phosphorus, suspended solids, heavy metals and the like from waste water (Gupta and Sujatha, 1996). Water hyacinth (*Eichhornia crassipes*) is common wetland weed (Warries and Saroja, 2008).

Water hyacinth (*Eichhornia crassipes*) tops the list of most dreaded aquatic weeds and now spread to around the globe. This is one of the fastest growing plants known to man. Prior to 1975, this weed was considered an uncontrollable curse covering water bodies and thus rendering them unsuitable for navigation and other purposes. The research later on turned this prolific pest to a potential provider. The production of high quality vegetable protein, vitamins, minerals, fertilizer, chemicals and energy (in the form of biogas) from hyacinth has reduced its nuisance value and made it a potential provider. Figure 10.5 (*See Fig. on page 160*) showing the picture of water hyacinth.

### Classification of *Eichhornia crassipes*

Kingdom-Plantae

Divison - Magnoliophyta

Class - Lipiopsida

Sub Class - Liliidae

Familty - Pontederiaceae

Genus - *Eichhornia*

Species - *Crassipes*

## History of *Eichhornia crassipes*

The area of origin of *Eichhornia crassipes* is South America, Venezuela in particular. It was first officially recognized as a serious hydrophyte on June 4, 1897 with the passage of a congressional act to investigate the effect of water hyacinth of obstruction of navigation in Louisaana and Florida (Dal fosse, 1977). It has now spread to over 50 countries around the earth. (Chawla, 1986). Water hyacinth *(Eichhornia crassipes)* was introduced to India form Brazil in 1896. Now covered nearly 5,00,000 acres under its domain in every state. In Bihar State of India alone, an area of nearly 2,33,333 acres in covered with his dreaded aquatic weed. Among the ten widely spread noxious weed in India, water hyacinth tops the list (Sharma, 1971; Haque *et al.*, 1980).

It has been successfully resisted all attempts of eradicating it by chemical, biological, mechanical or hybrid means. It is one of the most productive plants in the world (Gao-Lei, 2004). *E. crassipes* forms dense monocultures that can threaten local native species diversity and change the physical and chemical aquatic environment, thus altering ecosystem structure and function by disrupting food chains and nutrient cycling. The large, dense monoculture formed by this species covers lakes and rivers, blocking waterways and interfering with the water transport of agriculture products, tourism activities, water power and irrigation of agricultural fields. Dense mats of water hyacinth can lower dissolved oxygen levels in water bodies leading to reduction of aquatic fish production. Water hyacinth is very efficient in taking up Calcium, Magnesium, Sulfur, Ferric, Manganese, Aluminum, Boron, Copper, Molybdenum, Zinc, Nitrogen, Phosphorus and potassium favoring its growth over other aquatic species (Dandelot *et al.*,2008). When this macrophyte (water hyacinth) dies, sinks and decomposes, the water becomes more eutrophic due to the large release of nutrients (Gao-Lei, 2004). Water quality deteriorated, clean drinking water can be threatened and human health impacted.

Phytoremediation is the process of recovery of hazardous substances from soil and wastewater by using plants. Aquatic macrophytes such as species of *Salvina, Lemna, Azolla, Eichhornia, Sedeges* and even tree species are also known to tolerate, uptake and even accumulate heavy metals and other toxicants in their cell. Water hyacinth, *Eichhornia crassipes* is already being used to clean up wastewater in small-scale sewage treatment plants. This plant utilizes vast amount of many extreme nutrients and pollutants, which are poisonous to humans in these amounts. The water hyacinth has been shown to reduce nitrogen and phosphates, as well as biochemical oxygen demands of sewage water and other industrial effluents.

The aim objective of this study was to evaluate the effect of water hyacinth on sewage water treatment by Phytoremediation for parameters like pH, DO, Free $CO_2$, BOD, COD, Phosphorus, Hardness, Calcium, Magnesium and Turbidity.

## MATERIALS AND METHODS

Water hyacinth, *Eichhornia crassipes* were collected from a natural fresh water pond at Jwalapur, Hardwar. For each experiment, healthy *Eichhornia crassipes* were selected with equal fresh weights (approximately 250 gm). Each experiment was conducted under green house and laboratory conditions with glass aquarium of eight-litre capacity. The following treatments were employed with five-litre sewage. The present study based on two experiments a first experiment was conducted from 24 January 2003 to 13 February 2003 and a second experiment was conducted from 21 February to 13 March 2003. Sewage samples were collected from Jagjitpur sewage pumping station and Aryanagar sewage pumping station for experiment-1 and experiment-2 respectively.

There were two groups of the test aquaria. Control aquaria were also divided into two groups. There were three aquaria in each group. Water loss due to evaporation and evapo-transpiration were compensated daily by adding distilled water in first group of test and control experiments. These were control (with diluted condition) and test (with diluted condition). There was no compensation of water loss in second group. These were control (without diluted condition) and test (without diluted condition). The different sets of control and test experiments were conducted for period of 10 days, 15 days and 20 days, respectively.

## RESULTS AND DISCUSSION

Water hyacinth growth rate was influenced by nutrient composition of water and can tolerate a wide range of pH. Mehra et al. (1999) have mentioned that below pH 3.0 upto 9.0, the protoplasm and root of most vascular plants were severely damaged. In the present study, the pH values measured in the range of 6.9 to 7.9 during the experiments. In the test (without diluted condition) pH did not observed less than 7.6, it was observed at $15^{th}$ day. The pH value was decreased by water hyacinth in first 15 days and in next 5 days there was no reduction in the test without diluted condition.

In both (test and control) types of sewage samples $CO_2$ gas then reacts with water to produce $H_2CO_3$ acid which decrease the pH of water. Reduction with the diluted condition was observed due to the effect of less pH of distilled water. EL Glendy et al. (2002) found that pH is increased by hyacinth after conducting three experiments on landfill leachate for treatment. The values of pH were increased from 7.2 to 7.5, from 8.1 to 8.4 and from 8.1 to 8.6 in his first, second and third experiment respectively. The root system of water hyacinth growing in wastewater, saturated substrate must obtain oxygen from their aerial organ through photosynthesis and transport internal mechanisms. Oxygen leaks from the roots into the water enhancing dissolved oxygen level.

In the present study, dissolved oxygen decrease 5 times to 11 times by water hyacinth. Reddy and De Busk (1984) have been reported that aquatic macrophytes have the remarkable ability of transporting atmospheric oxygen to wastewater through their leaves, stems and roots. Oxygen concentration of sewage increase 10 folds in treatments with Pennywort, as compare to those without plants. Water hyacinth has been found to make reduction in free carbon dioxide. In the present study, free carbon dioxide was removed 35 per cent to 75 per cent by water hyacinth.

Biological and chemical oxygen demand is reliable markers of pollution load in any aquatic ecosystem. In aquatic macrophyte base treatment system bacteria as an energy source and for cell synthesis utilize BOD. These bacteria inhabit microenvironments in the sediment. The plant root zone and may also be dispersed throughout the water column. In the present study, BOD was removed 60 per cent, 67 per cent and 75 per cent in 10 day, 15 day and 20 day with dilution. But without diluted condition maximum 45 per cent removal at 10$^{th}$ day was observed. Abbasi and Ramaswami (1999) have also been reported that introduction of hyacinth to a pilot-plant treating sugar refinery wastewater resulted in the removal of BOD by 43.5 per cent in 7 day. Use of water hyacinth in the tertiary treatment of natural rubber processing effluent removal of 85 per cent BOD was achieved with a Hydraulic Retention Time of 10 days. Patra and Santra (1999) reported 57 per cent of BOD removal from paper mill effluent in 21 days.

Water hyacinth removes COD by oxygen transportation. Perdomo et al. (1999) reported that *Eichhornian crassipes* removes 93 per cent of COD from septic tank in 1 month. Oxygen transfer by water hyacinth into the root-zone plays a significant role in supporting aerobic bacteria in the root-zone and subsequent degradation of wastewater carbon. In the present study, COD was removed 56 per cent to 80 per cent in diluted condition, but in without diluted condition maximum 48 per cent removal at 10$^{th}$ day. Patra and Santra (1999) reported 38 per cent of COD removal from paper effluent in 21 days. Trivedy and Pattanshetty (2002) have found that 26 per cent of COD was removed in 4 days from dairy waste by water hyacinth.

Phosphorous in freshwater exists in either a particulate phase or a dissolved phase. The dissolved phase includes inorganic phosphorous (soluble orthophosphate form), organic phosphorous excreted by organisms and macromolecular colloidal phosphorous. The primary treatment removes only 10 per cent of the phosphorous in waste stream; secondary treatment removes only 30 per cent.

In the present study, phosphate phosphorous was removed from 52 per cent to 64 per cent with dilution. But maximum 39 per cent removal was found at 10$^{th}$ day in without dilution condition. Tripathi et al. (1991) reported 36.3 per cent to 70.2 per cent of phosphates can be removed by macrophytes (water hyacinth, lemna) from tropical fresh water pond. Boyd (1970) has reported that aquatic floating plants systems involves a variety of mechanisms to remove nutrients. Phosphate are mainly absorbed by the roots of the water hyacinth and oxidation of the organic matter is carried out by the microbial population associated to the oxygenated areas of the roots of water hyacinth. Dolan et al. (1981) reported that phosphorous can be removed from the wastewater by plant uptake, microbial assimilation precipitation with cations and adsorption by clay and organic matter. Nogales et al. (1994) told that the uptake of phosphorous can also be stimulated by the presence of other micronutrients.

During the study, hardness is removed from 30 per cent to 42 per cent in test without dilution condition. Calcium and magnesium are positively change ions. The roots of water hyacinth are negatively charged. So negatively charged root acts as a magnet to the positively charged ions of calcium and magnesium. Trivedy and Khomane (1985) have reported 32 per cent of calcium and 31 per cent of magnesium from metal industry waste in 39 days.

Organic and inorganic solids suspended in the sewage effluents cause turbidity conditions. In the present study, turbidity was removed 63 per cent to 82 per cent in diluted conditions. The maximum removal of turbidity was calculated 53 per cent at $10^{th}$ day without dilution conditions. Sinha and Sinha (1969) has been reported that water hyacinth removes 97 per cent turbidity from sugar refinery. When fresh water ponds plants (after acclimatization) applied in polluted sewage water, it removes pollutant and nutrient very fast, but activity of hyacinth is reduced with time.

Sewage treatment with out water hyacinth (control) is very slow. Results at $10^{th}$ and $15^{th}$ day were not significant. 20-day results have some significance. The minimization of pollutants and nutrients in control of both experiment 1 and experiment 2 was depended on mainly timer factor. 20 days removal in control is less than 10 days removal in test. Patra and Santra (1999) reported there was no significant change in pollutants after 21 days. Generally 10 days retention period is suggested.

It is very expensive to treat such low volumes by conventional technology because according to the economics of scale, lower the quantity of waste to have treated by any technology, higher is the cost of treatment per litre. This is one of the reasons why most villages and small town in developing countries don't have any sewage treatment facility. This leads to wide spread water and soil pollution and frequent outbreaks of water born diseases. Against the background, the emerging technology of using aquatic macrophytes especially water hyacinth, which enable cost effective treatment of sewage, assumes greater significance and promise.

**Table 10.1: Changes in Physico-chemical Parameters of Sewage Water (Jagjitpur Sewage Plant) by Water Hyacinth (with Diluted Condition) in Test Experiment**

| Sample Parameters | Initial Value | Value | | | Percentage of Decrease/Increase | | |
|---|---|---|---|---|---|---|---|
| | | 10th day | 15th day | 20th day | 10th day | 15th day | 20th day |
| Volume (litre) | 5.0 | 5.0 | 5.0 | 5.0 | 0 | 0 | 0 |
| pH | 8.5 | 7.5 | 7.2 | 7.0 | 13 | 16 | 18 |
| DO (mg/l) | 0.7 | 6.9 | 7.3 | 7.9 | 9.1** | 10.4** | 11.2** |
| Free $CO_2$ (mg/l) | 8.9 | 3.6 | 3.0 | 2.3 | 60 | 67 | 75 |
| BOD (mg/l) | 114 | 49.3 | 39.6 | 33.5 | 58 | 66 | 72 |
| COD (mg/l) | 196 | 86.4 | 64.8 | 50.7 | 56 | 68 | 75 |
| Phosphorous (mg/l) | 4.84 | 2.32 | 1.96 | 1.75 | 53 | 60 | 64 |
| Hardness (mg/l) | 396 | 280 | 262 | 254 | 30 | 34 | 36 |
| Calcium (mg/l) | 92.9 | 66.4 | 62.1 | 60.3 | 30 | 34 | 36 |
| Magnesium (mg/l) | 90.5 | 28.3 | 26.1 | 25.3 | 30 | 34 | 36 |
| Turbidity (JTU) | 320 | 105 | 80 | 65 | 68 | 75 | 80 |

** *Enhancement in times*

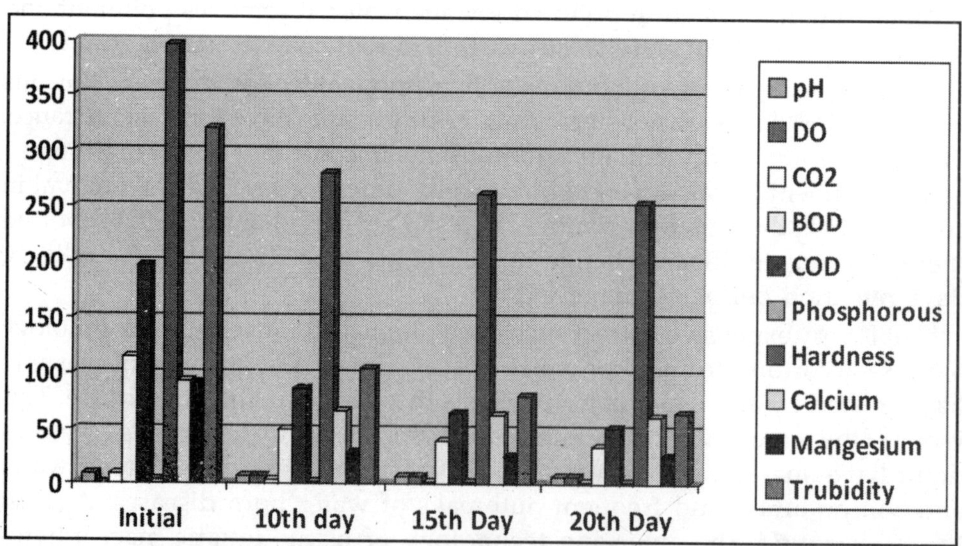


**Fig. 10.1: Showing the Changes in Physico-chemical Parameters of Sewage Water (Jagjitpur Sewage Plant) by Water Hyacinth (with Diluted Condition) in Test Experiment**

**Table 10.2: Changes in Physico-chemical Parameters of Sewage Water (Jagjitpur Sewage Plant) by Water Hyacinth (with Diluted Condition) in Control Experiment**

| Sample Parameters | Initial Value | Value | | | Percentage of Decrease/Increase | | |
|---|---|---|---|---|---|---|---|
| | | 10th day | 15th day | 20th day | 10th day | 15th day | 20th day |
| Volume (litre) | 5.0 | 5.0 | 5.0 | 5.0 | 0 | 0 | 0 |
| pH | 8.5 | 8.0 | 7.8 | 7.5 | 6 | 9 | 12 |
| DO (mg/l) | 0.7 | 2.2 | 2.9 | 3.7 | 3.1** | 4.1** | 5.2** |
| Free $CO_2$ (mg/l) | 8.9 | 6.0 | 5.1 | 4.3 | 33 | 43 | 52 |
| BOD (mg/l) | 114 | 89.3 | 80.2 | 72.2 | 22 | 30 | 37 |
| COD (mg/l) | 196 | 155.6 | 138.4 | 129.6 | 21 | 30 | 34 |
| Phosphorous (mg/l) | 4.84 | 3.93 | 3.52 | 3.26 | 19 | 28 | 33 |
| Hardness (mg/l) | 396 | 362 | 347 | 340 | 9 | 13 | 15 |
| Calcium (mg/l) | 92.9 | 84.2 | 81.7 | 78.4 | 9 | 13 | 15 |
| Magnesium (mg/l) | 90.5 | 36.8 | 35.7 | 34.4 | 9 | 13 | 15 |
| Turbidity (JTU) | 320 | 182 | 145 | 120 | 44 | 55 | 63 |

** *Enhancement in times*

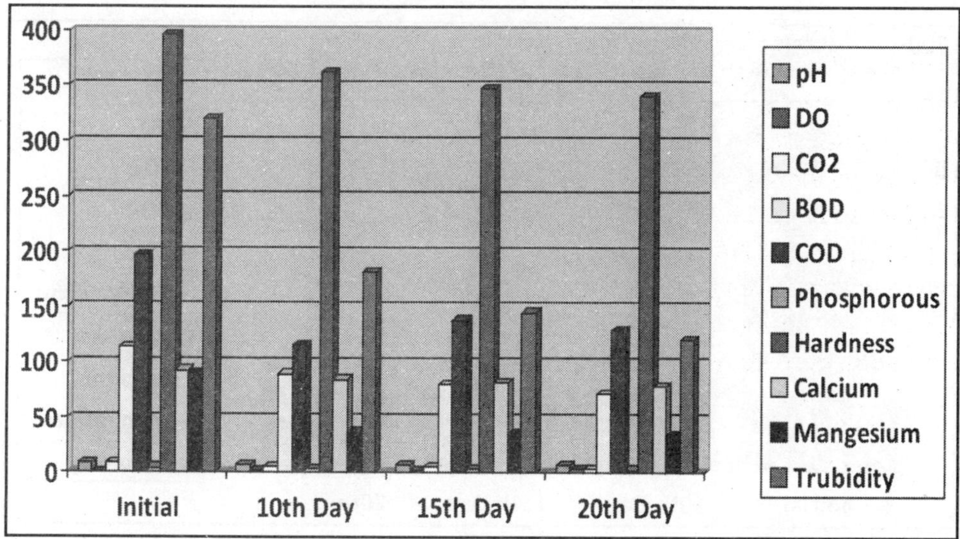


**Fig. 10.2: Showing the Changes in Physico-chemical Parameters of Sewage Water (Jagjitpur Sewage Plant) by Water Hyacinth (with Diluted Condition) in Control Experiment**

**Table 10.3: Changes in Physico-chemical Parameters of Sewage Water (Jagjitpur Sewage Plant) by Water Hyacinth (without Diluted Condition) in Test Experiment**

| Sample Parameters | Initial Value | Value | | | Percentage of Decrease/Increase | | |
|---|---|---|---|---|---|---|---|
| | | 10th day | 15th day | 20th day | 10th day | 15th day | 20th day |
| Volume (litre) | 5.0 | 3.74 | 2.84 | 1.83 | 27 | 43 | 64 |
| pH | 8.5 | 7.9 | 7.6 | 7.6 | 8 | 11 | 11 |
| DO (mg/l) | 0.7 | 5.8 | 6.9 | 7.6 | 8.2** | 9.8** | 10.8** |
| Free $CO_2$ (mg/l) | 8.9 | 5.2 | 4.6 | 4.1 | 42 | 48 | 54 |
| BOD (mg/l) | 114 | 63.0 | 67.0 | 82.0 | 45 | 42 | 29 |
| COD (mg/l) | 196 | 113.6 | 107.2 | 120.8 | 43 | 46 | 39 |
| Phosphorous (mg/l) | 4.84 | 2.97 | 3.13 | 3.94 | 39 | 36 | 19 |
| Hardness (mg/l) | 396 | 374 | 458 | 685 | 6 | 15* | 72* |
| Calcium (mg/l) | 92.9 | 87.7 | 107.4 | 154.7 | 6 | 15* | 72* |
| Magnesium (mg/l) | 40.5 | 38.2 | 46.8 | 69.6 | 6 | 15* | 72* |
| Turbidity (JTU) | 320 | 145 | 130 | 160 | 55 | 60 | 50 |

* *Percentage of increase*

** *Enhancement in times*

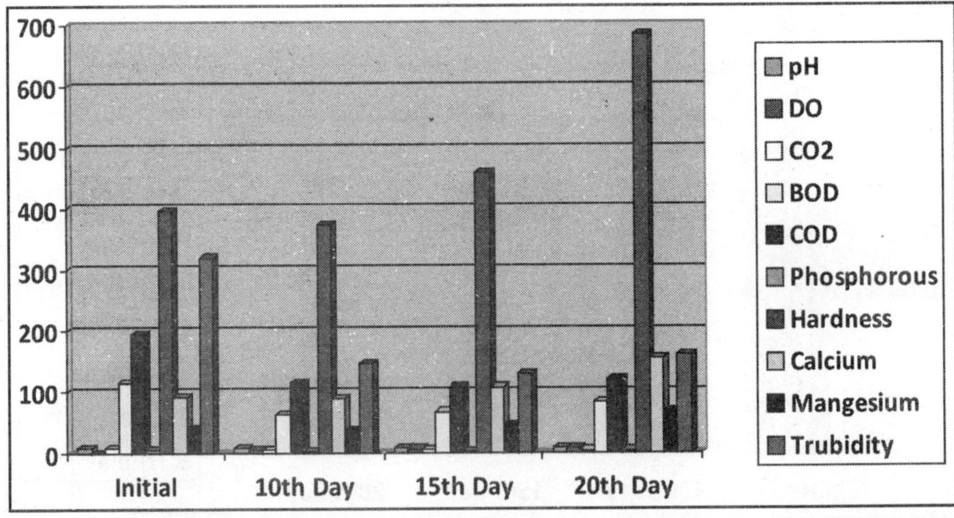


**Fig. 10.3: Showing Changes in Physico-chemical Parameters of Sewage Water (Jagjitpur Sewage Plant) by Water Hyacinth (without Diluted Condition) in Test Experiment**

**Table 10.4: Changes in Physico-chemical Parameters of Sewage Water (Jagjitpur Sewage Plant) by Water Hyacinth (without Diluted Condition) in Control Experiment**

| Sample Parameters | Initial Value | Value | | | Percentage of Decrease/Increase | | |
|---|---|---|---|---|---|---|---|
| | | 10th day | 15th day | 20th day | 10th day | 15th day | 20th day |
| Volume (litre) | 5.0 | 4.42 | 4.00 | 3.56 | 12 | 20 | 29 |
| pH | 8.5 | 8.3 | 8.2 | 8.1 | 3 | 4 | 5 |
| DO (mg/l) | 0.7 | 1.4 | 1.7 | 2.2 | 2** | 1.4** | 3.1** |
| Free $CO_2$ (mg/l) | 8.9 | 6.7 | 6.1 | 5.4 | 25 | 32 | 40 |
| BOD (mg/l) | 114 | 101 | 99 | 97 | 12 | 14 | 15 |
| COD (mg/l) | 196 | 178.4 | 171.2 | 163.2 | 9 | 13 | 17 |
| Phosphorous (mg/l) | 4.84 | 4.37 | 4.13 | 3.96 | 10 | 15 | 19 |
| Hardness (mg/l) | 396 | 409 | 433 | 477 | 3* | 9* | 20* |
| Calcium (mg/l) | 92.9 | 95.9 | 101.4 | 110.8 | 3* | 9* | 20* |
| Magnesium (mg/l) | 40.5 | 418 | 44.2 | 48.7 | 3* | 9* | 20* |
| Turbidity (JTU) | 320 | 210 | 175 | 155 | 35 | 46 | 52 |

* *Percentage of increase*

** *Enhancement in times*

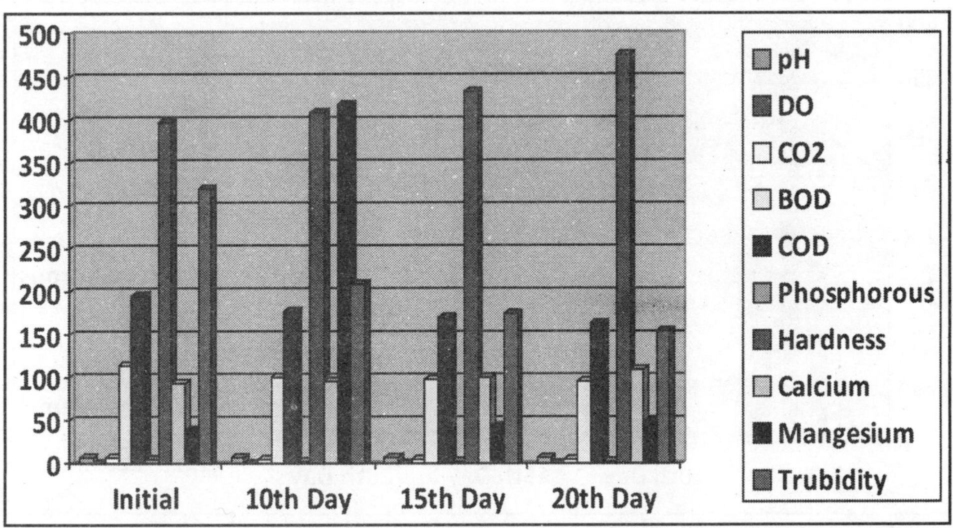


**Fig. 10.4: Changes in Physico-chemical Parameters of Sewage Water (Jagjitpur Sewage Plant) by Water Hyacinth (without Diluted Condition) in Control Experiment**

**Table 10.5: Changes in Physico-chemical Parameters of Sewage Water (Aryanagar Sewage Plant) by Water Hyacinth (with Diluted Condition) in Test Experiment**

| Sample Parameters | Initial Value | Value | | | Percentage of Decrease/Increase | | |
|---|---|---|---|---|---|---|---|
| | | 10th day | 15th day | 20th day | 10th day | 15th day | 20th day |
| Volume (litre) | 3.0 | 5.0 | 5.0 | 5.0 | 0 | 0 | 0 |
| pH | 8.2 | 7.4 | 7.2 | 6.9 | 10 | 14 | 16 |
| DO (mg/l) | 1.3 | 6.8 | 7.6 | 8.9 | 5.2** | 5.8** | 6.8** |
| Free $CO_2$ (mg/l) | 8.3 | 3.9 | 3.1 | 2.2 | 53 | 63 | 74 |
| BOD (mg/l) | 98 | 39.3 | 28.6 | 21.5 | 60 | 72 | 79 |
| COD (mg/l) | 172 | 62.8 | 50.4 | 35.6 | 64 | 71 | 80 |
| Phosphorous (mg/l) | 42.1 | 2.03 | 1.73 | 1.57 | 52 | 59 | 63 |
| Hardness (mg/l) | 370 | 260 | 232 | 214 | 30 | 38 | 42 |
| Calcium (mg/l) | 88.1 | 61.9 | 55.2 | 50.9 | 30 | 38 | 42 |
| Magnesium (mg/l) | 37.1 | 26.1 | 23.5 | 21.5 | 30 | 38 | 42 |
| Turbidity (JTU) | 190 | 70 | 47 | 35 | 63 | 76 | 82 |

** *Enhancement in times*

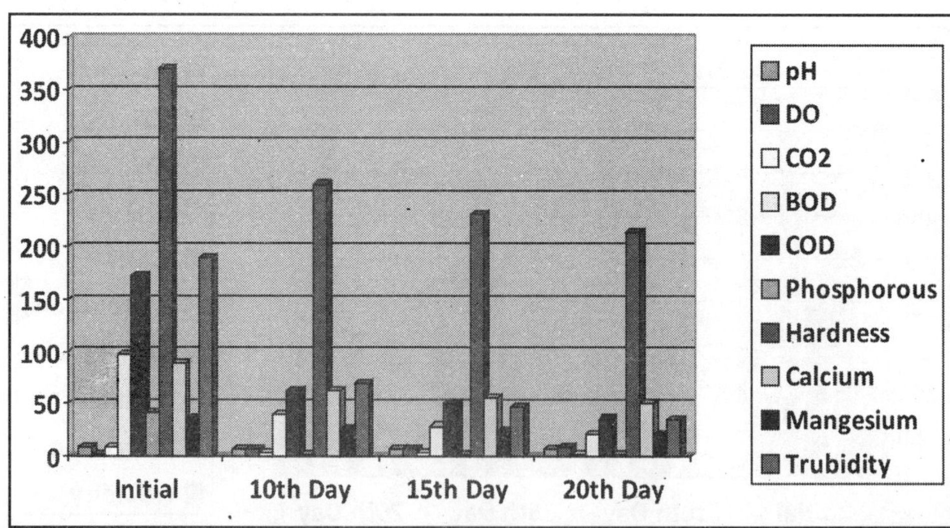


**Fig. 10.5: Showing Changes in Physico-chemical Parameters of Sewage Water (Aryanagar Sewage Plant) by Water Hyacinth (with Diluted Condition) in Test Experiment**

**Table 10.6: Changes in Physico-chemical Parameters of Sewage Water (Aryanagar Sewage Plant) by Water Hyacinth (with Diluted Condition) in Control Experiment**

| Sample Parameters | Initial Value | Value | | | Percentage of Decrease/Increase | | |
|---|---|---|---|---|---|---|---|
| | | 10th day | 15th day | 20th day | 10th day | 15th day | 20th day |
| Volume (litre) | 3.0 | 5.0 | 5.0 | 5.0 | 0 | 0 | 0 |
| PH | 8.2 | 7.6 | 7.5 | 7.3 | 8 | 9 | 11 |
| DO (mg/l) | 1.3 | 3.8 | 5.1 | 6.6 | 2.9** | 3.9** | 5.0** |
| Free $CO_2$ (mg/l) | 8.3 | 5.7 | 4.6 | 3.7 | 32 | 45 | 56 |
| BOD (mg/l) | 98 | 79.3 | 65.0 | 51.0 | 20 | 34 | 48 |
| COD (mg/l) | 172 | 130.4 | 108.8 | 91.2 | 24 | 37 | 47 |
| Phosphorous (mg/l) | 42.1 | 3.43 | 3.12 | 2.93 | 19 | 16 | 31 |
| Hardness (mg/l) | 370 | 344 | 332 | 326 | 8 | 11 | 12 |
| Calcium (mg/l) | 88.1 | 81.9 | 79.0 | 77.6 | 8 | 11 | 12 |
| Magnesium (mg/l) | 37.1 | 34.5 | 33.2 | 32.5 | 8 | 11 | 12 |
| Turbidity (JTU) | 190 | 110 | 87 | 75 | 43 | 55 | 61 |

** *Enhancement in times*

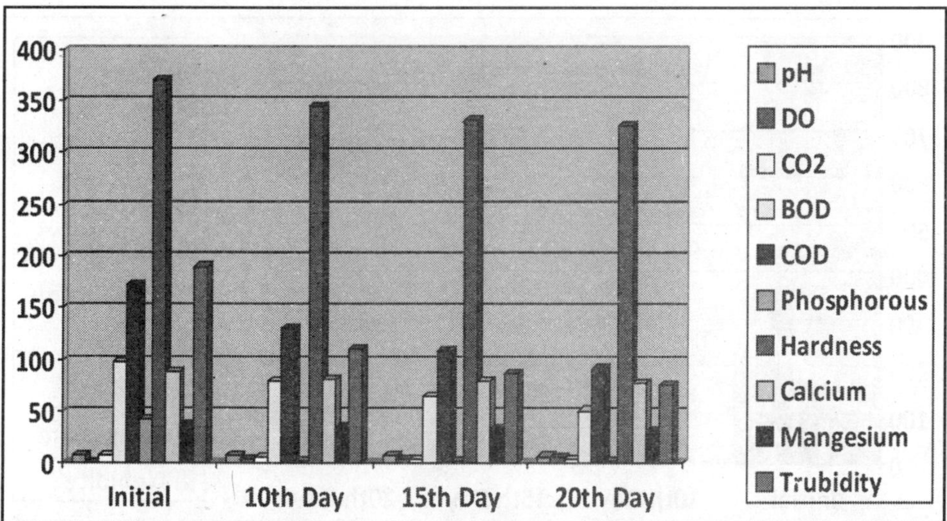


**Fig. 10.6: Showing Changes in Physico-chemical Parameters of Sewage Water (Aryanagar Sewage Plant) by Water Hyacinth (with Diluted Condition) in Control Experiment**

**Table 10.7: Changes in Physico-chemical Parameters of Sewage Water (Aryanagar Sewage Plant) by Water Hyacinth (without Diluted Condition) in Test Experiment**

| Sample Parameters | Initial Value | Value | | | Percentage of Decrease/Increase | | |
|---|---|---|---|---|---|---|---|
| | | 10th day | 15th day | 20th day | 10th day | 15th day | 20th day |
| Volume (litre) | 5.0 | 3.49 | 2.59 | 1.24 | 30 | 49 | 75 |
| pH | 8.2 | 7.8 | 7.6 | 7.6 | 5 | 8 | 8 |
| DO (mg/l) | 1.3 | 5.3 | 6.4 | 7.8 | 4.0** | 4.9** | 6.0** |
| Free $CO_2$ (mg/l) | 8.3 | 5.7 | 4.4 | 3.8 | 31 | 47 | 54 |
| BOD (mg/l) | 98 | 59.5 | 52.3 | 68.5 | 39 | 47 | 30 |
| COD (mg/l) | 172 | 96 | 90.4 | 118.4 | 44 | 48 | 31 |
| Phosphorous (mg/l) | 4.21 | 2.65 | 2.84 | 4.85 | 37 | 32 | 15* |
| Hardness (mg/l) | 370 | 374 | 485 | 815 | 1* | 31* | 120* |
| Calcium (mg/l) | 88.1 | 89.1 | 115.4 | 194.6 | 1* | 31* | 120* |
| Magnesium (mg/l) | 37.1 | 37.4 | 48.3 | 80.9 | 1* | 31* | 120* |
| Turbidity (JTU) | 190 | 90 | 100 | 120 | 53 | 48 | 37 |

* *Percentage of increase*

** *Enhancement in times*

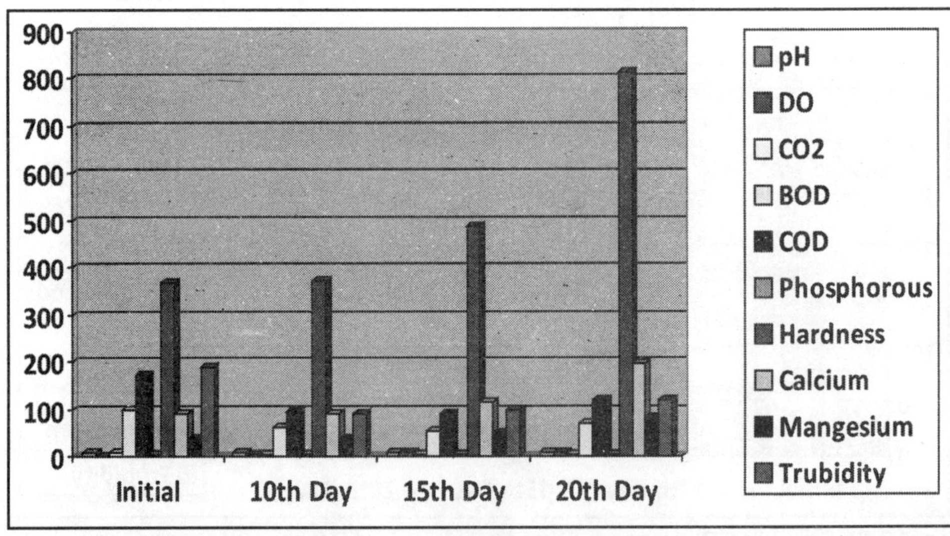


**Fig. 10.7: Changes in Physico-chemical Parameters of Sewage Water (Aryanagar Sewage Plant) by Water Hyacinth (without Diluted Condition) in Test Experiment**

**Table 10.8: Changes in Physico-chemical Parameters of Sewage Water (Aryanagar Sewage Plant) by Water Hyacinth (without Diluted Condition) in Control Experiment**

| Sample Parameters | Initial Value | Value | | | Percentage of Decrease/Increase | | |
|---|---|---|---|---|---|---|---|
| | | 10th day | 15th day | 20th day | 10th day | 15th day | 20th day |
| Volume (litre) | 5.0 | 4.22 | 3.73 | 3.06 | 16 | 28 | 40 |
| pH | 8.2 | 8.0 | 7.9 | 7.8 | 3 | 4 | 5 |
| DO (mg/l) | 1.3 | 3.6 | 4.8 | 5.6 | 2.7** | 3.3** | 4.3** |
| Free $CO_2$ (mg/l) | 8.3 | 6.9 | 6.3 | 5.5 | 17 | 24 | 34 |
| BOD (mg/l) | 98 | 87.5 | 82.3 | 75.6 | 11 | 16 | 23 |
| COD (mg/l) | 172 | 153.6 | 145.6 | 137.6 | 11 | 15 | 20 |
| Phosphorous (mg/l) | 4.21 | 4.01 | 3.87 | 3.78 | 5 | 8 | 11 |
| Hardness (mg/l) | 370 | 407 | 443 | 448 | 10* | 20* | 34* |
| Calcium (mg/l) | 88.1 | 96.9 | 105.4 | 118.5 | 10* | 20* | 34* |
| Magnesium (mg/l) | 37.1 | 41.0 | 44.6 | 49.9 | 10* | 20* | 34* |
| Turbidity (JTU) | 190 | 130 | 115 | 105 | 32 | 40 | 45 |

* *Percentage of increase*

** *Enhancement in times*

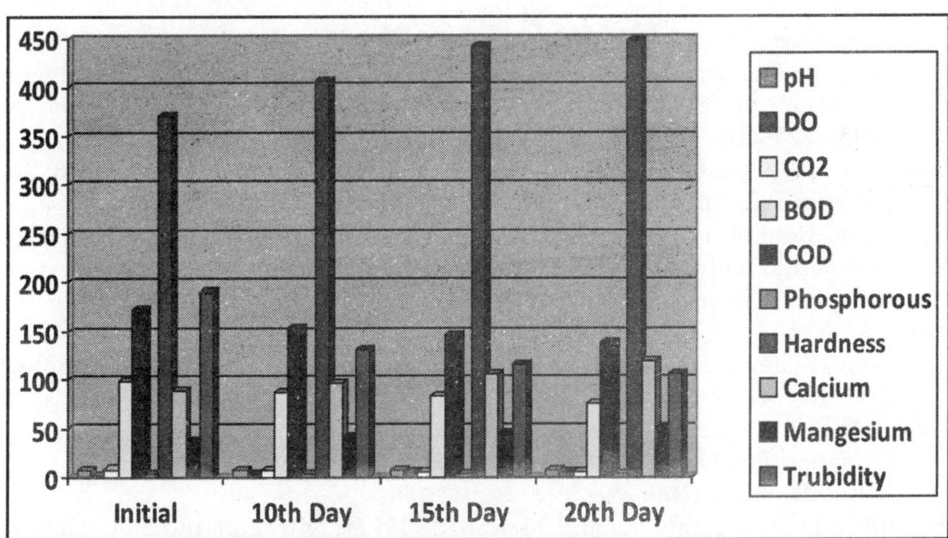


**Fig. 10.8: Showing Changes in Physico-chemical Parameters of Sewage Water (Aryanagar Sewage Plant) by Water Hyacinth (without Diluted Condition) in Control Experiment**

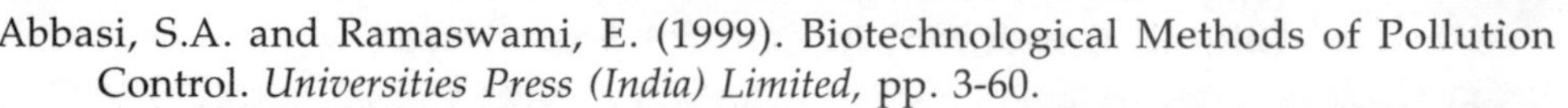

## REFERENCES


Abbasi, S.A. and Ramaswami, E. (1999). Biotechnological Methods of Pollution Control. *Universities Press (India) Limited,* pp. 3-60.

Boys, C.D. (1970). Vascular Plants for Mineral Nutrient Removal from Polluted Water. *Economic Botany,* 24: 95-103.

Dixit. A, Dixit, S. and Goswami, C.S. (2011). Process and Plants for Wastewater Remediation: A Review. *Sci. Revs. Chem. Commun.: 1(1), 71-77.*

Dolan, T.J., Bayley, S.E., Zoltek, J. and Hermann, A. J. (1981). Phosphorous Dynamics of a Florida Freshwater Marsh Receiving Treated Wastewater. *J. Appl. Ecol.* 18: 205-219.

Edwards, R.W. (1972). Pollution, Oxford Biology Readers, 31, Oxford: *Oxford University Press.*

El-Gendy, N. Biswas and J.K.Bewtra (2002). Water Hyacinth System for Municipal Landfill Leachate Treatment. CSCE/EWRI of ASCE Environmental Engineering Conference, Niagara.

Gupta, A. and Sujatha, P. (1996). Treatment of Tannery Wastewater by Water Hyacinth Application. *J. Ecot. Environ. Monitoring,* 6(3), 209-212.

Mehra, A.; Farago, M.E.; Banergee, D.K. and Cordes, K.B. (1999). The Water Hyacinth- an Environment Friend or Pest? A Review Resource and Environmental Biotechnology. 2: 155-281.

Nogales, R.; Benitez, E. and Gutierrez, L. (1994). Nutrient Removal Potential of Water Hyacinth Grown in Static Fe-enriched Sewage Water. *Fresenius Environmental Bulletin.,* 3: 325-330.

Patra, S. Santa, S.C. (1999). Bioremediation of Wastewater from Paper Mill Using Aquatic Macrophytes. Proceeding of *National Conference on Industry and Environment,* Karad, Dec. 28-30, Edited by R.K. Trivedi.

Perdomo, S; Bangueses, C and Fuentes, J. (1999). Potential Use of Aquatic Macrophytes to Enhance the Treatment of Septic Tant Liquids. *Water Science and Technology,* 40 (3): 225-231.

Polprasert, C. (1996). Organic Waste Recycling: Technology and Management: 2nd ed., John Wiley & Sons, Chichester.

Reddy, K.R. and DeBusk, W.F. (1984). Growth Characteristic of Aquatic Macrophytes Cultured in Nutrient Enriched Water, I. Water Hyacinth, Water Lettuce, Water Pennywort. *Economic Botany,* 39: 200.

Divya Singh*, Archana Tiwari and Richa Gupta (2012). Phytoremediation of Lead from Wastewater Using Aquatic Plants. Journal of Agricultural Technology 2012 Vol. 8(1): 1-11.

Sinha, S.N. and Sinha, L.P (1969). Studies on the Uses of Water Hyacinth Culture on Oxidation Ponds Digested Sugar Wastes and Effluents of Septic Tanks. *Ind. J. Env. Hlth. (UK),* 11(3): 297-207.

Tripathi, B.D.; Srivastava, J. and Misra, K. (1991). Nitrogen and Phosphorous Removal- Capacity of Four Chosen Aquatic Macrophytes in Tropical Freshwater Ponds. *J. Environ. Conserv.* 18: 143-147.

Trivedy, R.K. and Pattanshetty, S.N. (2002). Treatment of Dairy Waste by Using Water Hyacinth. *Water Scince and Technology*, 45(12): 329-334.

Trivedy, R.K. and Khomane, B.V. (19840. Water Hyacinth for Removal of Nutrient from Wastewater. *Comp. Physiol. & Ecol.*, 10(3): 123-128.

Warreir, R.R. and Saroja, S. (2008). Historical Studies on Water Hyacinth with Particular Reference to Water Pollution. IJIB, 3(2), 96-99.

# Phenol Toxicity Affecting Hematological Changes in Cat Fish (*Clarius lazera*)

**Mona S. Zaki**, *Egypt*; **Olfat, M. Fawzi**, *Egypt*; **S.I. Shalaby**, *Egypt*

***ABSTRACT***

Phenol and phenolic compounds are xenobiotics stressful environmental factors to which fish and animals are subjected to, and have become environmental problem due to anthropogenic impact on the environment The present study aimed to investigate the effect of phenol pollution on fish with special reference to the hematological, immunological, serum biochemical parameters, where fifty healthy *Clarius lazera* fish were divided into 3 groups. Fish of gp1 served as a control. Fish of gp. 2 & 3 were used for the determination of acute lethal concentration dose and the pathological effect of Phenol on the exposed fish. Blood samples were collected to obtain serum for biochemical studies and heparinized blood for hematological investigations. RBCs, Hb, HCt, and MCHC showed significant elevations, the serum GPT and GOT were increased significantly. L.D.H, glucose and cortisol were elevated, while serum cholesterol concentration was reduced significantly in high temperature 30°C.

*Key words:* Phenol pollution, Tilapia Zilli, Biochemical changes.

## INTRODUCTION

Fish plays an important role, not only in human food diets but also in animal and poultry rations. It is a palatabie and easily digested food which is rich in vitamins, calcium, phosphon.rs and iodine. In Egypt, fish is considered as a cheap food article if compared with other foods of animal origin. The flesh of healthy fish is considered as a marker for the natural aquatic environment[1-7].

Phenol and phenolic compounds are xenobiotics stressful environmental factors to which animals are subjected to serve animia due to phenol and have become environmental problem due to anthropogenic impact on the environment[8]. They also are good research models of wide spread xenobiotics[9]. Also, they are commonly present in industrial wastewaters and in non-specific pesticides, herbicides, bactericides and fungicides[10]. Mukherjee *et al.*[11] reported that they are commonly found in the marine habitat and in fish tissues. Phenol induces toxic effects for fish health.

They induce genotoxic effect[12], carcinogenic effect[13], and immunotoxic effect[14].

Controversy, Stich[15] reported that phenol may act as free radical scavengers and prevent genetic damage caused by other agents. They have a high bioaccumulation rate along the food chain due to its lipophilicity. Thus phenol pollution presents a threat against natural environment and also to human health[8, 16]. When the phenol is present in the aquatic environment, fish food consumption, mean weight and fertility are significantly reduced[17]. For these reasons, phenol intoxication must be taken in consideration in the fish farming systems and also in natural aquatic habitat.

Fish metabolism was adversely affected by phenol[10, 18]. The phenol and its derivatives can alter protein metabolism by altering transamination rate of amino acids by enhancing the activity of aspartate aminotransferase (ASAT, EC 2.6.1.1) and alanine aminotransferase (ALAT, EC 2.6.1.2). Also, the carbohydrate metabolism was affected by phenol by altering the activity of lactate dehydrogenase (LDH, EC 1.1.1.27) thus, affecting the interconversion of lactate into puruvate (8). Gupta *et al* (10) recorded changed ASAT and ALAT activities in different fish tissues induced by phenolic compounds. The enzymes activities (ASAT or GOT and ALAT or GPT) catalyze the interconversion of amino acids and $\alpha$-keto acids by transfer of amino groups. The ASAT catalyzes the transfer of this group from aspartate to $\alpha$-ketoglutarate to form glutamate and oxaloacetate, while ALAT catalyzes the transfer of the amino group from alanine to $\alpha$-ketoglutarate to form glutamate and puruvate[19]. The measurement of transaminase activities in serum is frequently used as a diagnostic tool in human and animals[20, 21]. Damage to the liver, kidney and gills is evident from elevated transaminase activities[20].

The present study aimed to investigate the effect of phenol toxicity on fish with special reference to the haematological, immunological, serum biochemical parameters.

## MATERIAL AND METHODS

### 1. Fish

Fifty healthy fish of both sexes and 150 + 50 gm body weight, were obtained alive and trànsported immediately to the laboratory. They were kept in 5 glass aquaria (100 × 30 × 50 cm) that provided daily with a tap water and continuously with filtered air. The water temperature was adjusted at 15°C along the period of experiment using thermostatic heater. The fish were fed a balanced ration daily using the formula suggested by Ahmed and Matty[22]. Fish were kept under observation for two weeks.

Fish were divided into three groups (gps). Fish of gp1 (10) served as a control with no treatment. Fish of gp. 2 & 3 (20, each) were used for the determination of acute lethal concentration dose ($LD_{50}$ /72 hr, gp2) and to investigate the pathological effect of phenol on the exposed fish (gp3).

### 2. Experiments

### A. *Determination of acute lethal concentration dose*

To determine lethal concentration dose, fish of gp. 2 were subdivided into 5 equal subgroups. Subgroup 1 served as a control. Other 4 subgroups exposed to 35, 75, 150 and 300 mg/L of phenol; respectively. Each dose was dissolved in the distal water of each aquarium. The number of dead fish was recorded within 72 hrs post-exposure and the acute lethal concentration dose was calculated according to the formula of Brown[23].

### B. *Long term exposure*

Fish of gp3 were exposed to 1/100 of $LD_{50}$ /72 hr (1.5 mg/L) of phenol for two weeks according to *Taylor et al*[24]. The excreta were removed regularly and the water was replaced within four days interval. Fish were kept under observation along the 14 days of exposure.

### 3. Sampling

Blood sample were collected from the caudal vein after 3, 7, 14 days of exposure, part of blood was left to clot and then centrifuged at 3000 r.p.m. to obtain serum for biochemical studies, the other part was heparinized for hematological investigations using the methods of Drabkin, 1949[25].

### 4 Haematological examinations

The erythrocytic indices (RBCs, Hb, HCt & MCHC) were estimated according to Schalm et al[26].

### 5. Serum biochemical analysis

Kits Biomericux France were used for the determination of serum glutamic pyruvic transaminase (GPT) and glutamic oxaloacetic transaminase (GOT), lactate dehydragenase (LDH), alkaline phosphatase (AP), serum glucose, serum cholestrol, and total protein. Serum cortisol hormone was analyzed by means of a gemmacoat 125-cortisol radio-imumnassay kit (Diagnostic corporation, USA). Serum Ig M was also measured according to Fuda, et al[27].

### 6. Statistical analysis

The obtained data were statistically analysed according to Snedecor and Cochran[28] by T test.

## RESULTS

### A. Determination of acute lethal concentration dose

Experiment 1 revealed that, the acute lethal concentration dose was 150 mg/L during the 1st 72 hrs post-exposure.

### B. Long term exposure

The effect of phenol exposure on RBC's count, Hb level, HCt and MCHC values of exposed fish were recorded in Table 11.1. Polycythemia was observed on the 14 day ($p<0.01$). Blood Hb, HCt, and MCHC showed a significant elevation by 14 days of experiment.

**Table 11.1: Effect of Phenol on Some Haematological Parameters in *Clarius lazera* Along the Period of Experiment (Mean + S.E.)**

| Parameter | 3 Days | | 7 Days | | 14 Days | |
|---|---|---|---|---|---|---|
| | Control | Exp. | Control | Exp. | Control | Exp. |
| RBCs $10^6/mm^3$ | 3.3 + 0.22 | 3.3 + 0.51 | 3.2 + 0.30 | 4.4 + 0.74 | 3.6 + 0.68 | 4.7 + 0.68* |
| HB g/dl | 7.40 + 0.52 | 8.2 + 0.10 | 7.4 + 0.26 | 8.7 + 0.8 | 7.2 + 0.33 | 8.4 + 0.74** |
| H.Ct% | 18.70 + 1.30 | 21.9 + 1.34 | 18.95 + 0.19 | 26.4 + 1.44 | 22.7 + 2.64 | 28.7 + 1.84** |
| MCHc% | 32.70 + 1.80 | 33.8 + 1.30 | 33.52 + 0.84 | 36.52 + 1.36 | 32.3 + 1.52 | 42.6 + 1.27** |

Exp: experimental

* Significant at $p<0.01$.

** Non-significant

Table 11.2 (*See Table on next page*) revealed the changes of some biochemical constituents in the blood of fish due to phenol exposure. The obtained data revealed that serum GPT activity increased significantly by 14 days of exposure. A significant elevation in serum GOT activity was also observed on the 14th day ($p<0.01$). L.D.H serum activity was elevated along the whole period of experiment especially on the day 14th. Hyperglycemia was constant findings from the beginning of the experiment until the end of the experiment. Serum cholesterol concentration was increased, on the 3rd day and the 7th day and was reduced significantly, on the day 14th day. Cortisol hormone was elevated along the whole period of experiment especially on day 14th.

**Table 11.2: Effect of Phenol on the Serum Biochemical Parameters in Clarius Lazera Along the Period of Experiment (Mean + S.E.)**

| Parameter | 3 Days | | 7 Days | | 14 Days | |
|---|---|---|---|---|---|---|
| | Control | Exp. | Control | Exp. | Control | Exp. |
| SGPT (I.U/L) | 28.2 + 0.3 | 53.3 + 033 | 34.3 + 064 | 45.5 + 1.29 | 35.0 + 1.11 | 48.9 + 2.68* |
| SGOt (I.U/L) | 38.3 + 2.2 | 42.7 + 3.0 | 41.8 + 1.2 | 48.9 + 2.48 | 39.32 + 1.0 | 55.40 + 3.74** |
| L.D.H (I.U/L) | 182 + 4.3 | 192 + 3.94 | 192 + 4.3 | 192 + 5.23 | 195 + 3.40 | 199 + 5.28* |
| A.L.P (U/L) | 3.6 + 2.3 | 3.2 + 1.64 | 3.3 + 1.84 | 4.7 + 1.90 | 2.83 + 1.60 | 5.93 + 2.25** |
| Glucose (mg/dl) | 28.24 + 2.3 | 33.68 + 1.2 | 29.82 + 1.2 | 42.20 + 2.8 | 30.64 + 1.8 | 62.8 + 2.78** |
| Total protein (g/dl) | 246 + 0.43 | 2.43 + 0.14 | 2.50 + 0.64 | 3.1 + 0.29 | 2.5 + 0.55 | 4.70 + 0.94* |
| Cholesterol (ng/dl) | 161.4 + 3.4 | 167.6 + 2.9 | 167 + 3.0 | 163 + 3.23 | 162.9 + 2.4 | 198.4 + 4.3* |
| Ig. M (ng/ml) | 1.8 + 0.13 | 1.60 + 0.24 | 1.80 + 0.42 | 1.43 + 0.92 | 1.75 + 0.12 | 0.3 + 0.065* |
| Cortisol (ng/ml) | 0.87 + 0.24 | 1.53 + 0.06 | 0.98 + 1.24 | 1.86 + 1.21 | 0.84 + 0.73 | 1.95 + 1.63* |

Exp: experimental

* Significant at p<0.01.

** Non-significant

## DISCUSSION

The aquatic environment of the River Nile subjected to many stressful factors, phenol and phenolic derivatives are one of the serious pollutants which cause serve anemia in fish. This observed hepatomegaly may partially reflect the enhancement of the liver size due to destructive changes. Barse *et al.* (21) reported elevated HSI values of *Cyprinus carpio* subjected to 4-*tert*-butylphenol.

Regarding the impact of phenol on the hematological profile of fish polycythemia accompanied by elevated hemoglobin level, HCt value and MCHC were observed. Similar findings were reported by Mckim et al[29], Hilmy et al[30] and Taylor et al (24) recorded polycythemia in *rasy barb*. But in contrary to our finding Hb level and MCHC were reduced in *Clarias lazera* exposed to copper[31]. The increased RBCs count may be due to stimulation of erythropoietin by elevated demands for $O_2$ or $Co_2$ transport as a result of increased metabolic activity or distruction of gill membranes causing faulty gaseous exchange. The increase Hb content could be explained as a process where the body tries to replace the oxidized denatured Hb[32]. The increase of HCt value and MCHC may be attributed to swelling of RBCs due to increased $Co_2$ in blood, hypoxia or stressful procedures[33, 34].

Exposure of fish to sublethal concentration (1.5 mg/L) of phenol for 14 days resulted in a marked increase in the activities of serum GPT, GOT, LDH and ALP. The present findings agree with our microscopic findings, which revealed a marked degeneration and necrosis of hepatocytes as the elevation in transaminases activities may be attributed to the liver injury[35].

Serum cholesterol level, in the present study, showed a significant reduction that could be due to greater level of utilization of cholesterol during corticosteroidogenesis, as it is the precursor for steroid hormones[36]. In addition, they reported a rise in the blood protein resulted in a high density of lipoprotein in the serum and was suggested to be the cause of hypocholesterolemia in exposed fish.

Our results showed similar findings as that of Gill et al,[37] and *Snieszko*[38], who reported that, exposure of fish to phenol had no significant increase on blood glucose of *salmo gairnei*. The blood glucose level reflected the changes in carbohydrate metabolism under hypoxia and stress conditions. Rise of glucose level indicated the presence of stressful stimuli eliciting rapid secretion of both glucocorticoids and catecholamines from the adrenal tissue and accompined by cortisol elevation[39]. Concerning serum protein level, a significant increase was noted 14 days postexposure to phenol. The elevated protein concentration may be due to the induction of protein synthesis in liver.

The serum Ig. M was determined to find out information about fish immune system which was previously investigated in different species by many authors as *Fuda et al,* (27) *O' Neill*[40], in this work, the purified Ig. M was revealed a single perception against specific polyvalent antiserum to fish Ig, similar results was obtained by Bagee et al.[41] who found that, *Coho salmon* Ig was detected by specific anti Ig 14. Our study revealed a significant decrease in Ig. M level in fish exposed to pollution if compared within control groups. *Anderson et al.*[42] found a relation between cortisol and IgM as when cortisol increased IgM decrease. The significant increase in cortisol level in fish exposed to phenol could be attributed to stress factors and the intoxication of fish[43].

We can conclude the fish exposed to phenol cause serve anemia and suppress immunity in exposed fish.

## REFERENCES

1. Dowidar M., Abdel-Magid S. and Salem S. 2001: Biochemical Effect of Lead and Cadmium on Glutathion Peroxidase Superoxide Dismutase Activity, Copper and Selenium Level in Rat. 2nd Int. sc. Conf., Fac. vet. Med., Mansura univ.
2. Tolba K., El-Neklawy G. and Niazi Z. 1994: Lead Residue in Tissue of Slaughtered Cattle Kept at Agricultureal and Industrial Areas. J. Egypt. Vet. Med. Ass., 54 (2) 199.

3. Jarup L. 2003: Hazards of Heavy Metals Contamination. Br. Med. Bull; 68: 167-82
4. El-Nabawi A., Heinzow B. and Kruse H. 1987: Cd, Cu, Pb, Hg and Zn in As Fish from Alexandria Region of Egypt. Bull. Environ. Contam. Toxicol., 39, 889-897.
5. Haneef S., Swarap D. and Dwivedi S. 1998: Effects of Concurrent Exposure to Lead and Cadmium on Renal Function in Goats. Indian·vet. Research, 28, 3, 257-261.
6. Gill S.; Tewari H. and Ponde J. 1991: Effect of Water Born Copper and Lead on the Peripheral Blood in the *rosy barb, barbus*. Bull. Environ. Contan. Toxical., 46, 606-612.
7. Ghalab M. 1997: Clinicopathological Studies on Fish Exposed to Some Environmental Pollution in El-Manzala lake. Ph.D. Thesis, Fac. Vet. Med., Suez Canal Univ.
8. Hori, T.S.F., Avilez, I.M., Inoue, L.K. and Moraes, G. 2006. Metabolical Changes Induced by Chronic Phenol Exposure in Matrinxã *Brycon cephalus* (teleostei).
9. Roche, H. and Boge, G. 2000. *In vivo* Effects of Phenolic Compounds on Blood Parameters of a Marine Fish (*Dicentrarchus labrax*). Comp. Biochem. Physiol., (C) 125: 345-353.
10. Gupta, S., Dalela, R.C. and Saxena, P.K. 1983. Effect of Phenolic Compounds on *in vivo* Activity of Transaminases in Certain Tissues of the Fish of the Fish *Notopterus notopterus*. Environ. Res., 32: 8-13.
11. Mukherjee, D., Bhattacharya, S., Kumar, V. and Moitra, J. 1990. Biological Significance of [14C] phenol accumulation in different organs of a murrel, *Cyprinus carpio*. Biomed. Environ. Sci., 3: 337-342.
12. Jagetia, G.C. and Aruna, R. 1997. Hydroquinone Increases the Frequency of Miconuclei in a Dose-dependent Manner in Mouse Bone Marrow. Toxicol. Lett., 39: 205-213.
13. Tsutsui, T., Hayashi, N., Maizumi, H., Huff, J. and Barret, J.C. 1997. Benzene-catechol-, hydroquinone- and phenol-induced cell-transformation, Gene Mutation, Chromosome Aberrations, Aneuploidy, Sister Chromatid
14. Taysse, L., Troutaud, D., Khan, N.A. and Deschaux, P. 1995. Structure Activity Relationship of Phenolic Compounds (phenole, pyrocatechol and hydroquinone) on Natural Lyphocytotoxicity of carp (*Cyprinus carpio*). Toxicol., 98: 207-214.
15. Stich, H.F. 1991. The Beneficial and Hazardous Effects of Simple Phenolic Compounds. Mut. Res., 259: 307-324.
16. Nassr-Allah H and Abdel-Hameid1 (2007) Physiological and Histopathological Alterations Induced by Phenol Exposure in *Oreochromis aureus* Juveniles. Turkish Journal of Fisheries and Aquatic Sciences 7: 131-138.
17. Saha, N.C., Bhunia, F. and Kaviraj, A. 1999. Toxicity of Phenol to Fish and Aquatic Ecosystem. Bull. Environ. Contam. Toxicol., 63: 195-202.
18. Abdel-Hameid, N.A.H. 1994. Effect of Some Pollutants on Biological Aspects of *Oreochromis niloticus*. MSc. Thesis, Benha Branch: Faculty of Science, Zagazig University.

19. Moss, D.W., Henderson, A.R. and Kochmar, J.F. 1986. Enzymes; Principles of Diagnostic Enzymolgy and the Aminotransferases. In: N.W. Tietz (Ed.), Textbook of Clinical Chemistry. Saunders, Philadelphia: 663-678.
20. Bernet, D., Schmidt, H., Wahli, T. and Burkhardt-Holm, P. 2001. Effluent from a Sewage Treatment Works Causes Changes in Serum Biochemistry of Brown Trout (*Salmo trutta* L.). Ecotoxicol. Environ. Saf., 48: 140-147.
21. Barse, A.V., Chakrabarti, T., Ghosh, T.K., Pal, A.K. and Jadhao, S.B. 2006. One-tenth Dose of LC50 of 4-*tert*butylphenol Causes Endocrine Disruption and Metabolic Changes in *Cyprinus carpio*. Pesticide Biochem. Physiol., 86(3): 172-179.
22. Ahmed T. and Matty A. 1989: The Effect of Feeding Antibiotic on Growth and Body Composition of Carp *(Cyprinus carpio)*. Aquaculture, 77, 211.
23. Brown V. 1980: Acute Toxicity in Theory and Practice with Special Reference to the Toxicology of Pesticides. Wiley in Science Publication. John Willey and Sons, Chichester.
24. Taylor D.; Maddack B. and Murce G. 1985: The Acute Toxicity of Mine Grey List *metalsm* e.g Arsenic, Chromium, Copper, Lead, Nickel Tow, Vanadium, and Zinc Marine Fish Species *lob limanda and grey mullet*. Aqua. Toxicol., 6, 3. 135-145.
25. D. Drabkin 1949: Standardization of Hemoglobin Measurements. Am. J. Med. Sci., 217-710.
26. Schalm O. 1986: Schalm's Veterinary Hematology. $4^{th}$ Edition 524.
27. Fuda H., Sayano K., Yamaji F. and Haraj A. 1991: Serum Immunoglobin M (IgM) during Early Development of *masu salmon* on *corhyrchus masu*. Comp. Biochem. Physiol., 99, 637.
28. Snedecor F. and Cochran S. 1969: Statistical Analysis. Lowa State Univ. Press. Lowa, USA.
29. McKim J.; Christensen G.; Hunt E. 1970: Changes in the Blood of Brook Trout *salsvlinus* after Short Term and Long Term Exposure to Copper. Fish Des Bd Con., 27, 1883-1889.
30. Hilmy M.; Lemke A.; Jaicb P.1979: Haematological Changes in Kuwait Mullet, *liza maeralepis* (Smith Induces by Heavy Metals). Indian Mar. Sci. 8, 278-281.
31. El-Domiaty N. 1987: Stress Response of Juvenile *Clarias lazera* Elicited by Copp. Comp. Bioch. Physiol.,88, 259-262.
32. Cyria P., Antony H., and Nonbisor P. 1989: Haemoglobin and Haematocrit Values in the Fish *Oreochromis mossambicus*, After Short Term Exposure to Copper and Lead. Bull. Environ. Contan. Toxical. 43, 315-320
33. Ellis A. 1981: Stress and the Modulation of Defence Mechanisms in Fish in Pickaring A.D. Stress and Fish Academic Press, New York, 147-169.
34. Nemesok J. and Boross L. 1999: Comparative Studies on the Sensitivity of Different Fish Species to Metal Pollution. Hoto Biol. Hung 33, 27-27.
35. Kristaffevsson R. and Okari P. 1974: Effect of Sublethtal Concentration of Phenol on Plasma Enzyme Activities in *pike* in Brakish Water. Ann. Zool. Fennici, 11, 220-223.
36. Ferranda M. and Andrew M. 1991: Effect of Lindane on the Blood of Fish Water. Bull. Environ. Contan. Toxicol., 47, 465-470.

37. Gill S.; Tewari H. and Ponde J. 1991: Effect of Water Born Copper and Lead on the Peripheral Blood in the *rosy barb, barbus*. Bull. Environ. Contan. Toxical., 46, 606-612.
38. Sniezko S. 1974: The Effect of Environmental Stress on Outbreaks of Infectious Diseases in Fish. Journal of Fish Biol., 6, 197-208.
39. Mareaud M.; Mareaud F.and Donlds E. 1977: Primary and Secondary Effects of Stress in Fish, some New Data with a General Review. Trans. Amer. Fish Sac., 106, 201.
40. O'Neill J. 2001: The Humoral Immune Response of *salmo trutta* Exposed to Heavy Metals. J. Biol. Chem., 201, 706-721.
41. Bagee M.; Fuda H., Hara H.; Kawamura H. and Yamauchi H.1993: Changes in Serum Immunoglobin M. (IgM) Concentrations during Early Development of *chum salmon* as Determined by Sensitive Elisa Technique. Comp. Biochem. Physiol., 106, 69.
42. Anderson D., Roberson B. and Dixon O. 1982: Immuno Suppression Induced by Corticosteriod or an Alkylating Agent in *Rainbow trout*. Dev. Comp. Immunol. Suppl., 2, 197.
43. Aly S.M., Zaki M.S. and El-Genaidy H.M. 2003: Pathologicl, Biochemical, Haematologlcal and Hormonal Changes in Catfish Exposed to Lead Pollution, J. Egypt Vet. Med. Assoc, 63: 331-342.

# 12

# Diversity Indices of a Pond Benthic Community with Reference to Pollution Monitoring

**Habeeba Ahmad Kabir, *India*; Saltanat Parveen, *India***

***ABSTRACT***

In present study benthic organisms diversity were observed in the sequence of Diptera> Hemiptera> Ostracoda> Copepoda> Cladocera> Tricophtera> Ephemeroptera> Rotifera. Species diversity index (*H'*), Evenness index (*J*), index of dominance (λ), Menhinick index and Berger parker index ranged between 2.335–2.461 bits/unit, 0.861–0.976 and 0.871–0.113, 0.095-0.260, 0.110-0.260 respectively. Evenness index (–) was found to increase with increasing diversity.

The maximum density (6018 No/$m^2$) of zoobenthos was recorded in the month of January, 2010. The value of diversity (H= 2.447) indicate that this water body is moderately polluted.

*Key words:* *Benthos, diversity indices, pollution, Pond, physicochemical, water parameters*

## INTRODUCTION

Ponds may have been natural water sources exploited by man at different time to meet different needs, or may have been created for a multitude of different purpose e.g. domestic or agricultural use, for transport, defense, ritual or industrial use, social aggrandizement, swimming, fish farming or the creation of the picturesque (Narayan *et al.*, 2007; Bishnoi and Malik, 2008; Rajagopal *et al.*, 2010). The major problems effecting standing water bodies have been recognized for at least two decades, but their quantification and classification of environmental managers has proved elusive. The Indian environment managers/researchers has recently described the condition of Indian freshwater resources and their management as a prominent environmental problem with nutrition enrichment, acidification and domestic waste, sewage, agricultural and industrial effluents contamination by toxic substances identified as major impacts (Senthilkumar and Sivakumar, 2008, Laskar and Gupta, 2009; Rajagopal *et al.*, 2010).

Biodiversity is one of the most important corner stones of sustainable development and represents the biological wealth of a given nation. The world, today is facing its greatest ever biodiversity crisis. Flora and fauna are becoming extinct because of habitat loss, overexploitation and the threat of global climate changes. Aquatic biodiversity has enormous ecological, economical and aesthetic value and is largely responsible for maintaining and supporting overall environmental health. Water is the basic and primary need of all vital life processes of animals and plants and it is now well established fact that life first arose in aquatic environment.

Thus, conservation strategies to protect and conserve aquatic life are necessary to maintain the balance of nature and support the availability of resources for future generations. The sustaining of the so-called biological diversity is a priority of nature conservation in terrestrial; marine and freshwater environments (Brooks *et al.* 2006). Benthos is an important part of the food chain, especially for fish. The diversity of physiological tolerances, life history strategies, feeding modes, and trophic interactions make sedimentary macrobenthic communities effective estimators of environmental condition (Pearson and Rosenberg, 1978; Boesch and Rosenberg, 1981; Bilyard, 1987; Dauer, 1993; Dauer et al., 2000).

The use of benthic indices to assess the ecological quality status of marine and estuarine environments (Borja et al., 2008). Unlike fish, benthos cannot move around much so they are less able to escape the effects of sediment and other pollutants that diminish water quality. Therefore, benthos can give us reliable information on stream and lake water quality. Their long life cycles allow studies conducted by aquatic ecologists to determine any decline in environmental quality. Chautal pond is a perennial sewage fed, eutrophic pond situated at distance of 1.5 km from department of Zoology in south-west of Aligarh Muslim University campus. The shoreline is somewhat irregular. The depth of the pond varies from 0.5 to 3 meters at different place. The main source of its water supply is sewage water from adjoining colonies in addition to surface run-off from surrounding areas. The water of this pond is used for washing, dumping and other anthropogenic activities. In present study diversity indices and physicochemical parameters have been studied.

## MATERIAL AND METHODS

Collection, separation and identification of benthos: The bottom fauna was collected by bottom mud scrapper with tow line was used to collect the samples from the bottom of the water body for qualitative and quantitative analyses.

After collecting the bottom sample, it was first sieved and then washed from the sediment. For this, transfer preserved macro benthic samples were washed once again on 500 μm sieve in running water, sorted and identified up to genus/species level. Meiobenthic samples were passed through 500 μm and 200 ìm sieves and material retaining on 200 μm sieves was considered as meiobenthos. Further, the meiobenthic organisms were counted and identified up to group level.

Organisms were preserved in 10 per cent formalin and use 70 per cent ethyl alcohol solution, if organisms are having calcareous shells or exoskeleton. The population density was determined per square meter area and result was expressed as Ind/$m^2$. Identification were done with the help of keys given in Edmondson (1959), Needham and Needham (1962), Pennak (1978) and Tonapi (1980).

Dissolved oxygen (D.O.) analysis was performed at the sites by Winkler's modified technique (APHA, 1998).

Transparency, the limit up to which light can penetrate in water body, was measured by using standard Secchi disc having diameter of 20 cm and divided into black and white quadrants at surface. The average of two depth readings at which Secchi disc disappeared and reappeared was noted as transparency.

pH of the water was determined at the sites by using a portable electronic digital pH meter. Water Temperatures were recorded with the help of mercury thermometer graduated up to 100°C between 8.30-9.30 am.

Chloride was estimated by titrating the 50 ml sample with 0.025 N Silver nitrate using 5 per cent potassium chromate as an indicator (APHA, 1998).

Nitrate-nitrogen ($NO_3$-N) was determined following the Phenol-disulfonic method (Triedy and Goel, 1984). Phosphate- phosphorus ($PO_4$-P) was estimated by ammonium molybdate blue method using stannous chloride ($SnCl_2$) as an indicator (Barnes, 1959). Organic carbon was determined by Walkley and Black methods as described by (Trivedy and Goel, 1984).

Benthic species diversity was determined using the following formulae:

**Shannon-Wiener's Index**

H= ($\Sigma$ pi ln pi);

Where,

Pi= n/N

n= No. of individual species,

N=Total density of all organisms.

**Menhinick's Index** (Menhinick, 1964) method using the formula:

$Dmn = S/\sqrt{N}$;

Where;

S= Total number of species

N= total density of all the species

Evenness was calculated using formula:

$E_1 = H^1/ \ln S$ (Pielou, 1975);

Where,

$H^1$= species diversity

S= species richness

**RESULTS AND DISCUSSION**

Monthly variation in physico -chemical parameters has been tabulated in (*See Table 12.1 on next page*). The water temperature varied between 13°C to maximum 34°C. The minimum value of temperature was recorded in the month of January and maximum in the month of June. The value of transparency from 25.0 $\mu Scm^{-1}$ to 47.0 $\mu Scm^{-1}$ the low transparency was recorded in June and extreme high in March. Chloride of sediment was observed to vary between maximum 227 mg/l in the month June of to minimum 135 mg/l in the month of February. D.O. ranged between 3.0 mg/l (July, 2009) to 8.0 mg/l (January, 2010). Free $CO_2$ ranged between 45.0 to 10.0 with higher value in August and lower February. The value of $NO_3$ fluctuate between 0.051 mg/l (January, 2010) to 0.278 mg/l (September, 2009). $PO_4$ content ranged between 0.240 during December, 2009 to 0.950 during May, 2009. The rotifera is one of the most dominating groups among all the other groups; Diptera was recorded to be the second dominating group due to high abundance of *Chironomus sp*. Which serve as most common bioindicator as well as can survive eutrophic condition of water body.

The abundance of benthic (mean count No/$m^2$) in Chautal pond is given in (Table 12.2). A total of 37 species were recorded in this pond. The benthic fauna density showed peak values during winter season, in Chautal Pond (6018 No/$m^2$) during January, 2010 which is due to low predation pressure as well as high dissolved oxygen it making favorable condition for benthic communities whereas it was low during August, (2756 No/$m^2$) and in July, 2009 which is due to high monsoon and subsequent decrease in concentration of dissolved oxygen making unfavorable condition for benthic community. During summer season, the high predation pressure as well as low transparency caused decreases in population of benthic community (*See Table 12.2 on page 180*).

**Table 12.1: Monthly Variation in Different Physicochemical Factors in Chautal Pond from February 2009 to January, 2010**

| Months | Water Temp. (°C) | Transparency (cm) | D.O. (mg/L) | $NO_3^-$ N (mg/L) | $PO_4^-$P (mg/L) | $CO_2$ (mg/L) | Chloride Carbon | Organic |
|---|---|---|---|---|---|---|---|---|
| February, 09 | 19 | 42.50 | 3.4 | 0.081 | 0.584 | 10.0 | 135.0 | 0.636 |
| March | 23 | 47.00 | 3.2 | 0.117 | 0.510 | 20.0 | 142.0 | 1.691 |
| April | 28 | 36.00 | 3.9 | 0.131 | 0.867 | 21.0 | 156.0 | 0.764 |
| May | 28 | 26.00 | 4.8 | 0.151 | 0.950 | 18.0 | 184.0 | 0.669 |
| June | 34 | 25.00 | 4.0 | 0.123 | 0.717 | 19.0 | 227.0 | 1.232 |
| July | 31 | 30.25 | 3.0 | 0.182 | 0.549 | 25.0 | 198.0 | 2.776 |
| August | 30 | 32.50 | 4.2 | 0.202 | 0.586 | 45.0 | 184.6 | 2.918 |
| September | 32 | 26.75 | 3.8 | 0.278 | 0.761 | 35.0 | 156.2 | 2.854 |
| October | 21 | 45.00 | 3.4 | 0.195 | 0.420 | 35.0 | 156.2 | 3.375 |
| November | 19 | 36.00 | 3.6 | 0.122 | 0.510 | 25.0 | 142.0 | 1.883 |
| December | 16 | 41.25 | 7.4 | 0.081 | 0.240 | 32.0 | 149.1 | 1.445 |
| January,10 | 13 | 39.00 | 8.2 | 0.051 | 0.289 | 35.0 | 184.6 | 2.211 |

**Table 12.2: Zoobenthos Population Observed in Chautal Pond from February, 2009 to January, 2010**

| Months | Cladocera | Copepoda | Ostracoda | Rotifera | Diptera | Hemiptera | Coleoptera | Tricophtera | Ephemeroptera | Total Zoobenthos |
|---|---|---|---|---|---|---|---|---|---|---|
| February' 09 | 704 | 162 | 309 | 1541 | 808 | 295 | 333 | 8 | 5 | 4091 |
| March | 438 | 111 | 463 | 1264 | 262 | 81 | 128 | 9 | 2 | 2758 |
| April | 786 | 129 | 355 | 1326 | 248 | 235 | 143 | 5 | 4 | 3232 |
| May | 830 | 171 | 544 | 1239 | 608 | 225 | 203 | 9 | 8 | 3837 |
| June | 715 | 116 | 341 | 1618 | 562 | 284 | 167 | 8 | 5 | 2816 |
| July | 473 | 135 | 318 | 1120 | 349 | 118 | 231 | 8 | 4 | 2756 |
| August | 329 | 162 | 407 | 991 | 400 | 306 | 239 | 7 | 5 | 2846 |
| September | 477 | 148 | 446 | 749 | 461 | 249 | 224 | 4 | 5 | 2763 |
| October | 749 | 247 | 272 | 1106 | 270 | 247 | 215 | 5 | 7 | 3194 |
| November | 582 | 157 | 553 | 1375 | 534 | 228 | 227 | 8 | 9 | 3671 |
| December | 865 | 274 | 618 | 1646 | 1040 | 564 | 320 | 9 | 7 | 5345 |
| January' 10 | 908 | 314 | 722 | 1727 | 1401 | 523 | 403 | 11 | 8 | 6018 |
| Average | 654.6667 | 177.1667 | 445.6667 | 1308.5 | 578.5833 | 279.5833 | 236.0833 | 7.583333 | 5.75 | 3610.5 |
| Percentage | 17.72443 | 4.796607 | 12.06597 | 35.4263 | 15.66455 | 7.569433 | 6.391715 | 0.205311 | 0.155675 | 99.999 |

According to Carr (1965) if benthos occurs in a density of 100-999 individual/$m^2$, the water is unpolluted; 1000-5000 individual/$m^2$ moderately polluted; and more than 5000 individual/$m^2$ shows heavy pollution. As per this data Chautal pond is moderately polluted except for the month of December, 2009 and January, 2010 when more than 5000 individual/$m^2$ showing that it is highly polluted. The overall counts were lower in tricophtera and ephemeroptera when compared to other groups during different seasons. This is due to high pollutants resulting in mortality of sensitive organisms and high abundance of organisms which can tolerate environmental stress and pollution pressure as well as low concentration of dissolved oxygen. The trend of dominance of all these groups of benthic community on basis of per cent composition in these derelict water bodies waterbodies is as follow:

Rotifera (35.4) > Diptera (15.6) > Cladocera (17.7) > Hemiptera (7.5) > Coleoptera (6.3) > Copepoda (4.7) > Tricophtera (0.20) > Ephemeroptera (0.15) (Table 12.2; Fig. 12.1). From the present investigation in Chautal pond revealed the total abundance of more than 1000 pollution indicator of benthic species/$m^2$ irrespective of monthly variation but in some during December and January it is more than 5000 pollution indicator species therefore in these months classification of highly polluted area whereas classification of moderately polluted area in the rest of other months.

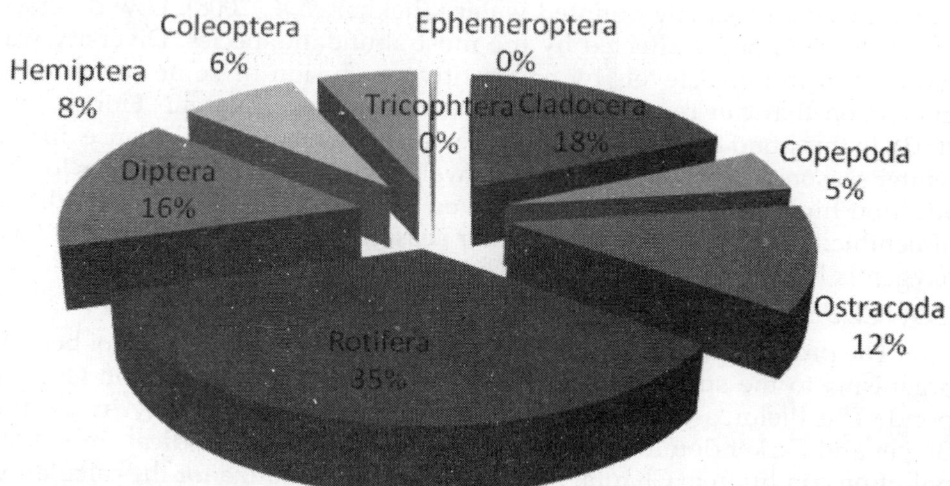


**Fig. 12.1: Pie Digram Showing Per cent Composition of Different Groups of Benthic Community in Chautal Pond**

Statistically water temperature showed negative (r = -0.817) and significant correlation with zoobenthos whereas dissolved oxygen showed positive and significant (P<0.05) correlation with zoobenthos (r = 0.897). $NO_3$ showed negative (r = -0.708) and significant (P<0.05) correlation with zoobenthos. $PO_4$ showed negative (r = -0.561) and significant (P<0.05) correlation with zoobenthos (*SeeTable 12.3 on next page; and Fig. 12.2 on page 184*).

**Table 12.3: Statistical Brief of Various Water Quality Parameters in Chautal Pond**

| Parameters | Parameters | Correlation (r value) | Significant at $P<0.05$ |
|---|---|---|---|
| Zoobenthos | Water temp. | -0.817 | ✓ |
| | Transparency | 0.3141 | – |
| | Dissolved oxygen | 0.897 | ✓ |
| | $NO_3$ | -0.708 | ✓ |
| | $PO_4$ | -0.561 | ✓ |
| | $CO_2$ | 0.085 | – |
| | Chloride | -0.153 | – |
| | Organic carbon | -0.421 | – |

The Pielou's eveness index, Shannon Weaver Diversity index and Berger and Parker dominance index are given in (*See Table 12.4 on next page*). The diversity index is low (2.447) in Chautal Pond. As well as value of eveness is high (0.9632). The resultant value indicates the pollution status of water body under present investigation. ). If the Shannon – Weiner diversity index proposed as diversity index > 4 is clean water; between 3-4 is mildly polluted water and < 2 is heavily polluted water (Shekhar *et al.*, 2008). Low diversity values were strongly affected by the most abundant species. Diversity was reduced to minimal levels by competitive exclusion or some other biotic interaction that can result in steady state assemblage (Naselli- Flores *et al.*, 2003). In this pond the pollution increase during winter season because during winter season decomposition is less as well as predation pressure was low in addition high concentration of dissolved oxygen makes suitable condition of benthic fauna because during winter season the capacity of water to hold oxygen is high.

## CONCLUSION

The present finding revealed that the significance of diversity of benthic organisms to the stressed water body of western region of U.P. in Chuatal pond. The Pielou's eveness index, Shannon Weaver, Diversity index and Berger and Parker dominance index of benthic community indicate moderate pollution condition in Chautal pond. Role of benthic fauna for the calculation of pollution level in water body is very important aspect to compare pollution level between two or more water bodies and monitor the eutrophic condition of different water body as well as with the help of it compare two water bodies and know which water body is more polluted. From my study I have concluded that the value of benthic fauna density was in the range of 1000-5000 individual/m$^2$ and the value of diversity is in the range of 2-3 which shows the mildly polluted condition of this water body but in January the density is greater than 5000 individual/m$^2$ it showed that during this month the water body is more polluted.

**Table 12.4: Monthly Variations in Species Diversity, Species Dominance and Species Evenness of Benthic fauna in a Chautal Pond**

| Indices | Cladocera | Copepoda | Ostracoda | Rotifera | Diptera | Hemiptera | Coleoptera | Tricophtera | Ephemeroptera |
|---|---|---|---|---|---|---|---|---|---|
| Individuals | 7856 | 2126 | 5348 | 15702 | 6943 | 3355 | 2833 | 91 | 69 |
| Dominance_D | 0.08972 | 0.09372 | 0.09079 | 0.08715 | 0.1113 | 0.1025 | 0.09221 | 0.08876 | 0.09305 |
| Shannon_H | 2.444 | 2.428 | 2.441 | 2.461 | 2.335 | 2.374 | 2.433 | 2.45 | 2.423 |
| Evenness_e^H/S | 0.9603 | 0.9443 | 0.9575 | 0.9765 | 0.8612 | 0.8947 | 0.9498 | 0.966 | 0.9401 |
| Menhinick | 0.1354 | 0.2603 | 0.1641 | 0.09576 | 0.144 | 0.2072 | 0.2255 | 1.258 | 1.445 |
| Berger-Parker | 0.1156 | 0.1477 | 0.135 | 0.11 | 0.2018 | 0.1681 | 0.1423 | 0.1209 | 0.1304 |

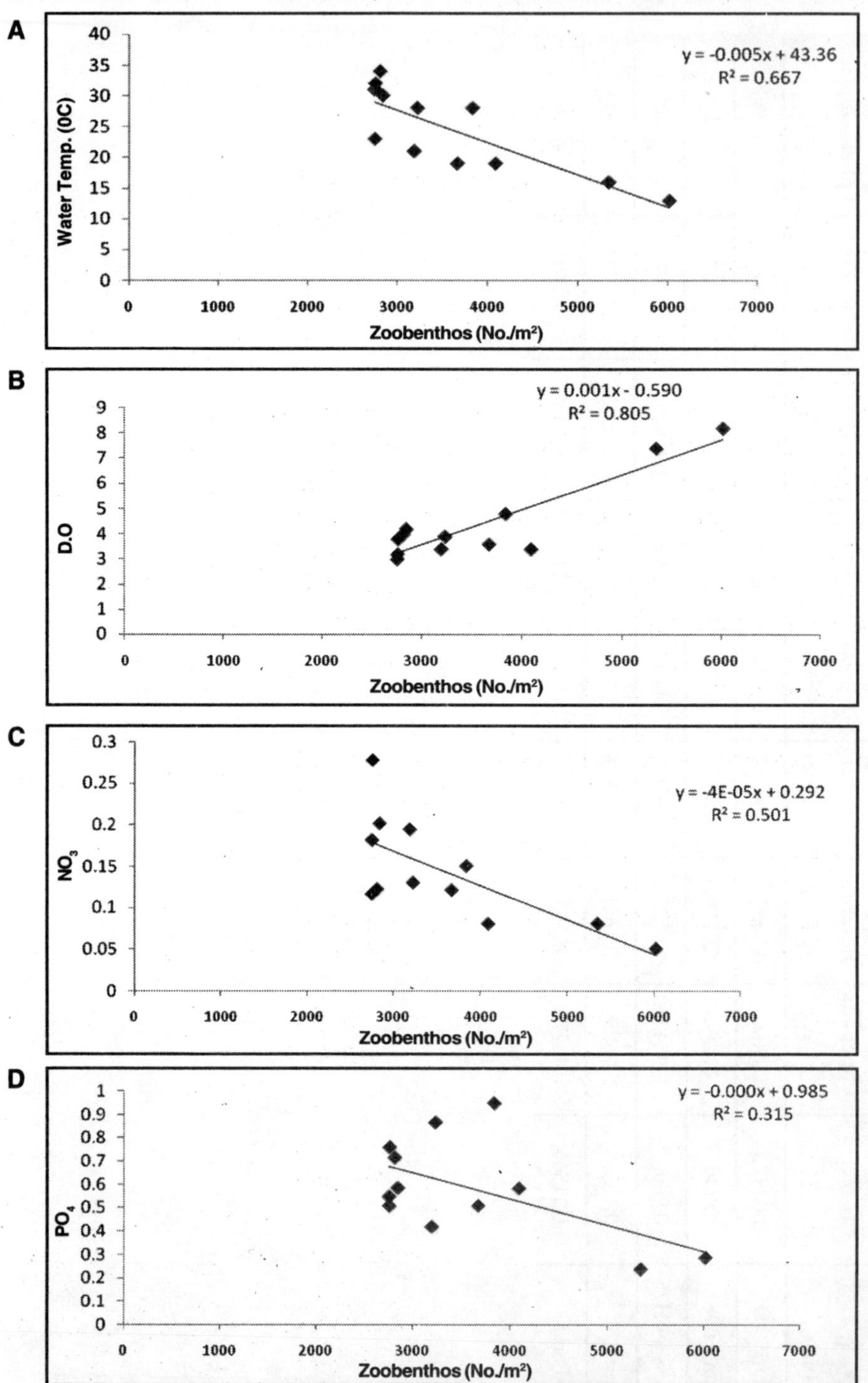


**Fig. 12.2 (A-D): Regression Line Showing Correlation of Benthic community (No/m²) in Relation to Physicochemical in Chautal Pond**

## REFERENCES

APHA 1998. Standard Methods for Examination of Water and Wastewater. American Public Health Association, AWWA, WPCF, Washington, D.C. (U.S.A.), 1193 pp.

Barnes H 1959. Apparatus and Methods of Oceanography. Part I. Chemical. George Allen and Unwin Ltd., 341 pp.

Bilyard GR 1987. The Value of Benthic Infauna in Marine Pollution Monitoring Studies. Mar. Pollut. Bull., 18: 581-585.

Bishnoi M and Malik R 2008. Ground Water Quality in Environmentally Degraded Localities of Panipat City, India. J. Environ. Biol., 29, 881-886.

Boesch DF, Rosenberg R 1981. Response to Stress in Marine Benthic Communities. In: Barret, G.W., Rosenberg, R. (Eds.), Stress Effects on Natural Ecosystems. John Wiley & Sons, New York, pp. 179-200.

Borja A, Dauer D, Diaz R, Llanso RJ, Muxika I, Rodriguez JG, Schaffner L. 2008. Assessing Estuarine Benthic Quality Conditions in Chesapeake Bay: A Comparison of Three Indices. Ecol. Indicators. 8: 395-403.

Brooks TM, Mittermeier RA, Da Fonseca G A B, Gerlach J, Hoffmann M, Lamoreux J F, Mittermeier, C G, Pilgrim J D and Rodrigues, ASL 2006. Global Biodiversity Conservation Priorities. Science, 313 (5783): 58.

Carr JF and Hiltunen JK, 1965. Changes in the Bottom Fauna of Western Lake Erie from 1930-1961. –Limnol.Oceanogr., 10: 551-569.

Dauer DM, Luckenbach MW, Rodi Jr AJ. 1993. Abundance Biomass Comparison (ABC Method): Effects of an Estuarine Gradient, Anoxic/Hypoxic Events and Contaminated Sediments. Mar. Biol., 116: 507-518.

Dauer DM, Ranasinghe JA, Weisberg SB, 2000. Relationships Between Benthic Community Condition, Water Quality, Sediment Quality, Nutrient Loads, and Land Use Patterns in Chesapeake Bay. Estuaries, 23: 80-96.

Edmondson WT, 1959. Ward and Whipple's Freshwater Biology, 2nd Ed. John Wiley & Sons Inc., New York, 1248 pp.

Gauffin AR, Tarzwell CM, 1952. Aquatic Invertebrates as Indicators of Stream Pollution. Pub Health Rep 1952. 67: 57-64.

Laskar HS and Gupta S, 2009. Phytoplankton Diversity and Dynamics of Chatla Floodplain Lake, Barak Valley, Assam, North East India — A Seasonal Study. J. Environ. Biol., 30, 1007-1012.

Menhinick E.F, 1964. A Comparison of Some Species Individuals Diversity Indices in Samples of Field Insects. Ecology, 45: 859-861.

Narayan R, Saxena KK and Chauhan S, 2007. Limnological Investigations of Texi Temple Pond in District Etawah (U.P.). J. Environ. Biol., 28, 155-157.

Naselli- Flores L, Padiask J, Dokulil M. T, and Chorus I, 2003. Equilibrium/Steady State Concept in Phytoplankton Ecology. Hydrobiologia, 502: 395-403.

Needham JG and Needham PR 1962. A Guide to the Study of the Freshwater Biology. Holden-Dey Inc., Francisco, 108 pp.

Pearson TH, Rosenberg R, 1978. Macrobenthic Succession in Relation to Organic Enrichment and Pollution of the Marine Environment. Oceanography and Marine Biology Annual Review 16, 229-311.

Pennak RW, 1978. Freshwater Invertebrates of United States, 2nd Ed. Johan Wiley and Sons Inc., New York, 803 pp.

Pielou EC, 1969. An Introduction to Mathematical Ecology – Wiley Interscience, New York.

Rajagopal T, Thangamani A. and Archunan G, 2010. Comparison of Physico-chemical Parameters and Phytoplankton Species Diversity of Two Perennial Ponds in Sattur Area, Tamil Nadu. J. Environ. Biol., 31 (5) 787-794.

Resh VH, 1995. Fresh Water Macroinvertebrates and Rapid Assessment Procedure for Quality of Water Monitoring in Developing and Newly Industrialized Countries. In Davis WS, Simon TP (eds), Bilogical Assessment and criteria. LewisPublishers, England. 1995; 167-177.

Richards C, Minshall GW 1992. Spatial and Temporal Trends in Stream Macroinvertebrate Species Assemblages: The Influence of Watershed Disturbance. Hydrobiologia 1992; 241: 173-84.

Senthilkumar R. and Sivakumar K 2008. Studies on Phytoplankton Diversity in Response to Abiotic Factors in Veeranam Lake in the Cuddalore district of Tamil Nadu. J. Environ. Biol., 29, 747-752.

Shannon CE and Weaver V 1949. A Mathematical Theory of Communication. Uni. Press, Tllinois. Urban 101-107.

Shekhar STR, Kiran BB, Puttaiah ET, Shivraj Y and Mahadevan KM 2008. Phytoplankton as Index of Water Quality with Reference to Industrial Pollution. Journ. Environ. Biol., 29 (2) – 233-236.

Tonapi GT 1980. Fresh Water Animals of India. Oxford and IBH Publishing Co., New Delhi, 341 pp.

Trivedy RK and Goel PK 1984. Chemical and Biological Methods for Water Pollution Studies. Environmental Publications, Karad, India, 215 pp.

Wilhm JL, Dorris TC 1968. Bilogical Parameters for Quality Criteria. Bioscience 1968, 18: 477-81.

13

# Study on Clinopathological and Biochemical Changes in Some Freshwater Fishes Infected With External Parasites and Subjected to Heavy Metals Pollution in Egypt

**Mahmoud A. El-Seify,** ***Egypt*****; Mona S. Zaki,** ***Egypt***
**Abdel Razek Y. Desouky,** ***Egypt*****; Hossam H. Abbas,** ***Egypt***
**Osman K. Abdel Hady,** ***Egypt*****; Attia A. Abou Zaid,** ***Egypt***

**ABSTRACT**

The present investigation was carried out to study the impact of external parasites and heavy metals pollution on some liver function tests of some freshwater fishes. 470 Fish species (330 *Oreochromis niloticus* and 140 *Clarias gariepinus)* were collected alive from three different ecosystems in Kafr-Elshiekh province, Egypt. The obtained results revealed that aspartate aminotransferase (AST), alanine aminotransferase (ALT) enzymes activities as well as creatinine and urea values were elevated in the external parasites infected fish as well as in the fish exposed pollutants. While fishes exposed to both external parasites infection and heavy metal pollution led to more drastic increase in serum AST and ALT enzymes activities as well as creatinine and urea values. In addition; heavy metals pollution increased the susceptibility of fish to protozoa infection while decrease prevalence of monogenea and crustacean infection. On conclusion; infection with external parasites in fishes exposed to heavy metals had the highest effect on liver and kidney functions in the studied fishes.

*Keywords:* External parasites, Heavy metals, *Oreochromis niloticus, Clarias gariepinus,* AST, ALT.

## INTRODUCTION

Most of fish diseases might be occurred as a result of parasitic infection or environmental pollution (Hussain *et al.*, 2003) Knowledge of fish parasites is of particular interest in relation not only to fish health but also to understand ecological problems (Mahfous, 1997).

Aquatic pollution is still a problem in many freshwater and marine environments; it causes negative effects for the health of the respective organisms (Fent, 2007). The number of studies investigating effects of pollutants and concurrently occurring parasites is still relatively low (Sures, 2007). However the effect of environmental pollutants on fish parasites varies depending on the particular parasite and pollutant that interact (Lafferty and Kuris, 1999). Pollutants may affect the immune system of the fish either directly or by change water quality; that in turn may reduce the fish immunity to parasites (Poulin, 1992) also, water pollution may accelerate the life cycle of the external parasites and promote their spread (Noor El-Din, 1997).

It is well known that certain blood parameters serve as reliable indicators of fish health as many parasites can live in a host, sometimes causing damage to it (Bond, 1979). Therefore, the changes associated with hematological parameters due to various parasites establish a database, which could be used in diseases diagnosis and in guiding the implementation of the treatment or preventive measures. These measures are essential in fish farming and fish industry (Roberts, 1981).

Analysis of blood constituents is considered physiological indicators of the whole body and therefore they are important in diagnosis the structural and functional status of fish exposed to pollutants (Adhikari and Betal, 2004). In this respect; Ranzani-Paiva *et al.*, (2000) demonstrated alterations in blood composition related to parasitism in fish from the Parana River, indicating that, determination of blood parameters of fishes is of great importance in evaluation of disturbance that caused by parasitism. Therefore, this study was aimed to investigate the impact of external parasites on some physiological parameters related to both liver and kidney functions of some freshwater fish *(Oreochromis niloticus* and *Clarias gariepinus)*, as well as to determine the relation between heavy metal pollution and the infection with external parasites.

## MATERIALS AND METHODS FISH SAMPLES

A total number of 470 (330 *Tilapia species* and 140 *Clarias gariepinus* ) freshwater fish were collected a live from three different ecosystems at Kafr El-Shiekh governorate, North Egypt as follow. (River Nile Branch, Drainage canal and Fish farm) by the aid of fisherman and then transported a live to the laboratory where they examined immediately.

## Parasitological Examination

Parasitological examination was carried out for the detection and identification of the external parasites on the skin, gills and the accessory respiratory organs of the samples.

## Collection and Preparation of the Detected Ectoparasites

### *Monogenea*

Monogenea were collected under binocular dissecting microscopic by means of small pipette in small Petri-dish and cleared several times with water to remove the attached mucous and debris. The worms were then left in refrigerator at 4°C till complete relaxation. Then, they were fixed in 5 per cent formalin for permanent preparation, worms were washed carefully in water to get red of formalin traces and stained with Semichon's acetocarmine stain for about 5-10 minutes till reaching staining, the specimens were passed through ascending grades of ethyl alcohol (30, 50, 70, 90% and absolute) for dehydration. Then, cleared in clove oil, xylene and mounted in Canada balsam (Pritchard and kruse, 1982), while the unstained Monogeneas were mounted in glycerin jelly (Abdel-Hady, 1998).

### Protozoa

Some of the positive slides were stained according to Klein's dry silver impregnation method in which the slides were air –dried, covered with 2 per cent aqueous solution of silver nitrate (Ag $NO_3$) for 8 minutes, rinse thoroughly in distilled water and exposed to UV light for 20-30 minutes or to direct sun light for 1-2 hr. The slides were allowed to dry and mounted with neutral Canada balsam. This method is indispensable technique for staining *Trichodina*. Other positive slides were also air-dried, fixed with absolute methanol and stained with 10 per cent Giemsa stain for 20-30 minutes to detect the other protozoa (Ali, 1992).

### Crustacea

The detected crustacean parasites were carefully collected by a fine brush and special needle, and transferred into Petri-dish for cleaning by using preserved and cleared in lacto phenol then mounting with polyvol (Raef *et al.*, 2000).

## Heavy Metals Detection

Three samples of water from the same sources of fish collection were taken in the fore mentioned flask one liter volume capacity after its rinsing several times with distilled water and sterilized in hot air oven at 180°C/ hour. The collected water sample bottles were labeled with the locality, date, and time of collection. Chemical examinations of these samples were done to estimate some heavy metals including (copper, zinc, iron, lead, cadmium, selenium, mercury, manganese and nickel) according to Chapman and pratt, (1978).

## Blood Samples

Fresh blood samples were collected without anticoagulant from the caudal artery. The needle is run, quite deep, as much as possible through a middle line just behind the anal fin in a dorso-cranial direction till striking the vertebrate. By drawing the needle gently backward, blood is usually sucked into the syringe.

The collected blood was centrifuged post collection at 3000 rpm for 10 minutes to separate serum for biochemical analysis.

## Biochemical Analysis

Aspartate aminotransferase (AST) and alanine aminotransferase (ALT) activities in serum were determined according to Reitman and Frankel, (1975). Creatinine value was determined according to Rock *et al.*, (1987). Urea concentration was measured according to Pathson and Nauch, (1977).

All these biochemical analyses were measured calorimetrically using spectrophotometer and purchased kits.

## RESULTS

The effect of heavy metals pollution on the prevalence of ectoparasites on examined fish spp. are shown in Table 13.1 (*See Table on next page*) which indicate that the percentage of ectoparsites infection was 71.8 per cent from the examined *Tilapia spp* in the River Nile branch where the pollution of water with copper (Cu), nickel (Ni), cadmium (Cd), selenium (Se) and mercury (Hg) were higher than the other localities where the degree of pollutants were 2.190, 0.102, 0.260, 3.630 and 1.90 respectively, In this degree of pollution, the present study revealed that ectoprotozoa infection of *Tilapia* spp. were the highest percentage of infection where 65 per cent of examined *Tilapia* fish were infected and it was followed by Monogenea and Crustaceans where they reached 23 per cent and 13.7 per cent respectively.

In Drainage canal, where the heavy metals pollution were lower than that in river Nile branch, 69 per cent of examined *Tilapia* were infected with ectoparasites, where the protozoa parasite decreased than in river Nile branch 48 per cent. While monogenea and Crustaceans increased (41%, 38% respectively).

In Fish farms; the percentage of infection reached 64.9 per cent from the examined fishes. Parasitic protozoa decreased than in River Nile branch 46.9 per cent, while monogenea and Crustaceans increased (38.0%, 34.5% respectively).

In addition; the effect of polluted water on the ectoparasitic infection of *Clarias gariepinus*, it was recorded that, in river Nile branch the fish infected with monogenea (28.7%) and protozoa (36.3%), while in Drainage canal (less polluted with heavy metals) monogenea increased 60 per cent while parasitic protozoa decreased 20 per cent than in River Nile branch. With no infection obtained with Crustacean parasites in the examined areas.

**Table 13.1: Effect of Heavy Metals on Parasitic Infection Among Examined Fish spp. in Different Localities**

| Locality | Parasitic Infection | % of Infection | | Heavy Metal Pollutants in ppm | | | | | | | | |
|---|---|---|---|---|---|---|---|---|---|---|---|---|
| | | Tilapia spp | *C. gariepinus* | Zinc *1 | Lead *_ | Manganes *1.5 | Copper *1 | Nicke *_ | Cadmium *0.01 | Selenium *_ | Mercury *_ | Iron *1 |
| Locality 1 (River Nile Branch) | Monogenea | 23 | 28.7 | 0.2 | 0 | 0.08 | 2.19 | 0.102 | 0.26 | 3.63 | 1.9 | 0.12 |
| | Protozoa | 65 | 36.3 | | | | | | | | | |
| | Crustacea | 13.7 | 0 | | | | | | | | | |
| | Total | 71.8 | 53.7 | | | | | | | | | |
| Locality 2 (Drainage Canal) | Monogenea | 41 | 60 | 0.06 | 0.5 | 0.12 | 0.07 | 0.102 | 0.04 | 0.26 | 0.25 | 0.06 |
| | Protozoa | 48 | 20 | | | | | | | | | |
| | Crustacea | 36 | 0 | | | | | | | | | |
| | Total | 69 | 65 | | | | | | | | | |
| Locality 3 (Fish Farm) | Monogenea | 38 | Not examined | 0.07 | 0.5 | 0.42 | 0.11 | 0.068 | 0.07 | 0.52 | 0.15 | 0.81 |
| | Protozoa | 46.9 | | | | | | | | | | |
| | Crustacea | 34.5 | | | | | | | | | | |
| | Total | 64.6 | | | | | | | | | | |

- * Permissible limits of trace elements detected in ppm. According to Egyptian Law
- No available guide line

As shown in Table 13.2; (*See Table on page 193)* Alanine aminotransferase (ALT), Aspartate aminotransferase (AST), Urea and Creatinene were higher in infected *O. niloticus* taken from River Nile branch than infected *O. niloticus* taken from other localities as they were (78.6 U/l), (115 U/l), (52 mg/dl) and (1.9 mg/dl) respectively while in non infected *O. niloticus* were (69 U/l), (101.5 U/l), (41 mg/dl) and (1.54 mg/d/) respectively. In Drainage canal, Alanine aminotransferase (ALT), Aspartate aminotransferase (AST), Urea and Creatinene were (61.3 U/l), (96.7U/l), (37.3 mg/dl) and (1.4 mg/dl) respectively in the infected *O. niloticus* while in non infected were (51.5 U/ l), (85U/l), (26.5 mg/dl) and (1.18 mg/dl) respectively. In Fish farm, Alanine aminotransferase (ALT), Aspartate aminotransferase (AST), Urea and Creatinene were (67 U/l), (97.3 U /l), (36.3 mg/dl) and (1.6 mg/dl) respectively in the infected *O. niloticus* while in non-infected were (55 U/l), (81 U/l), (31.5 mg/dl) and (1.3 mg/dl) respectively.

Table 13.3 (*See Table on page 193*) showed that in River Nile Branch, Alanine aminotransferase (ALT), Aspartate aminotransferase (AST), Urea and Creatinene were higher in infected *Clarias garipinus* (101.7 u/l), (177.7 u/l), (69 mg/dl) and (2.17 mg/dl) respectively . Than non infected *Clarias garipinus* as they were (85 u/l), (130 u/l), (50mg/dl) and (1.6 mg/d/) respectively. While in Drainage canal, Alanine aminotransferase (ALT), Aspartate aminotransferase (AST), Urea and Creatinene were (73.3 u/l), (94u/l), (38.7 mg/dl) and (1.63 mg/dl) respectively in the infected *Clarias garipinus* while in non-infected were (54 u/l), (76u/l), (28.5 mg/dl) and (1. mg/dl) respectively.

## DISCUSSION

A negative relationship was detected between heavy metals pollution and prevalence of monogenic infection in River Nile drainage canal branch as well as fish farm during this study. This result agreed with Blanar *et al.*, (2009) which may be attributed to the toxic effect of the heavy metal on the parasite itself Gheorghiu *et al.*, (2006).

The present study denoted that the incidence of external protozoa among examined fish was higher percentage in River Nile Branch which it is more polluted with heavy metals than other localities this may be attributed to that the heavy metals decrease the immune system of the exposed fish which become more susceptible to protozoa infection Khan and Thulin, (1991). The lowest rate of infection with parasitic crustacean was recorded in River Nile Branch, where the heavy metals pollution increased, this result agree with Galli *et al.*, (2001) who recorded that the distribution of *Lamproglena pulchella* was limited to the unpolluted and slightly polluted river sectors. This negative relation may be attributed to the toxic effect of the heavy metals on the crustaceans which may cut its life cycle Ruben *et al., (*2006).

**Table 13.2: Liver and Kidney Function Tests of *O. niloticus* Infected with Ecto-parasites in Different Localities**

| Locality / Parameter | River Nile Branch | | Drainage Canal | | Fish Farm | |
|---|---|---|---|---|---|---|
| | Non-infected | Infected | Non-infected | Infected | Non-infected | Infected |
| ALT (U/L) | 69 | 78.6 | 51.5 | 61.3 | 55 | 67 |
| AST (U/L) | 101.5 | 115 | 85 | 96.7 | 81 | 97.3 |
| (Mg/dl) | 41 | 52 | 26.5 | 37.3 | 31.5 | 36.3 |
| Creatinene (Mg/dl) | 1.54 | 1.9 | 1.18 | 1.4 | 1.3 | 1.6 |

**Table 13.3: Mean Liver and Kidney Function Tests of *Clarias gariepinus* Infected with Ecto-parasites in Different Localities**

| Locality / Parameter | River Nile Branch | | Drainage Canal | |
|---|---|---|---|---|
| | Non-Infected | Infected | Non-infected | Infected |
| ALT (U/L) | 85 | 101.7 | 54 | 73.3 |
| AST (U/L) | 130 | 177.7 | 76 | 94 |
| Urea (Mg/dl) | 50 | 69 | 28.5 | 38.7 |
| Creatinene (Mg/dl) | 1.6 | 2.17 | 1.1 | 1.63 |

**Table 13.4: Mean Liver and Kidney Function Tests of Fish spp. Infected with Ectoparasites in Different Localities**

| Locality / Parameter | River Nile Branch | | | | Drainage Canal | | | | Fish Farm | |
|---|---|---|---|---|---|---|---|---|---|---|
| | *O.niloticus* | | *C. gariepinus* | | *O. niloticus* | | *C. gariepinus* | | *O. niloticus* | |
| | Non-infected | Infected | Non-infected | Infected | Non-infected | Infected | Non-infected | Infected | Non-infected | Infected |
| ALT (U/L) | 69 | 78.6 | 85 | 101.7 | 51.5 | 61.3 | 54 | 73.3 | 55 | 67 |
| AST (U/L) | 101.5 | 115 | 13O | 177.7 | 85 | 96.7 | 76 | 94 | 81 | 97.3 |
| Urea (Mg/dl) | 41 | 52 | 50 | 69 | 26.5 | 37.3 | 28.5 | 38.7 | 31.5 | 36.3 |
| Creatinene (Mg/dl) | 1.54 | 1.9 | 1.6 | 2.17 | 1.18 | 1.4 | 1.1 | 1.63 | 1.3 | 1.6 |

The blood serum Aspartate aminotransferase (AST), Alanine aminotransferase (ALT) enzymes activities, Creatinine and Urea values were elevated in the infected fish species (*Oreochromus niloticus* and *Clarias gariepinus*) with external parasites than the non infected fishes in different localities, this indicate that the external parasites stimulated the activities of ALT and AST enzymes as well as both Urea and Creatinine. This result was agreed with Younis, (1999) recorded that aspartate aminotransferase (AST), alanine aminotransferase (ALT) and urea showed significant increase in *O. niloticus* infected with external protozoa and monogenetic trematodes. Osman *et al.*, (2009) reported that blood serum Aspartate aminotransferase (AST), Alanine aminotransferase (ALT) enzymes activities, Creatinine and Urea values were increased in Trichodina infected *Clarias gariepinus*.

Concerning the effect of parasitic infection on biochemical parameters of examined fish in the presence of heavy metal pollution, the present study indicated that the blood serum Aspartate aminotransferase (AST), Alanine aminotransferase (ALT) enzymes activities, Creatinine and Urea values were more higher in both *Oreochromis niloticus* and *Clarias gariepinus* that examined from river Nile branch (more polluted locality with heavy metals ) than infected fish spp. taken from drainage canal and fish farm (less polluted with heavy metals). This indicated that exposure of fish to parasitic infection in the presence of heavy metals is more powerful in stimulating the activities of ALT and AST enzymes (Adams, 2002). This may be due to hepatic cells injury or increased synthesis of the enzymes by the liver (Yang and Chen, 2003). The elevation in the urea level in the infected fish may be due to gill dysfunctions as the urea excreted mainly through the gills (Murray *et al.*, 1990). Also these findings may be attributed to the inflammatory reactions and intoxications produced by the parasite in the affected fish.

## REFERENCES

Abd EL- Hady. O.K (1998): Comparative Studies on Some Parasitic Infection of Fishes in Fresh and Polluted Water Sources. Ph.D. Thesis (Parasitalogy), Fac. Vet. Med., Cairo Univ.

Adham, K.G. (2002): Sub Lethal Effects of Aquatic Pollution in Lake Maryût on the African Sharptooth Catfish, *Clarias gariepinus* (Burchell, 1822). Journal of Applied Ichthyology, 18: 87-94.

Adhikari, S. and Betal, S. (2004): Effects of Cypermehrin and Carbofuran on Certain Haematological Parameters and Prediction of Their Recovery in Fresh Water Teleost, *Labeo rohita* (Ham). Ecotoxicol. Environ. Safety 58: 220-226.

Ali, M.A. (1992): Biological and Ecological Studies on Protozoan Parasites Infecting Cultured *Tilapia* in Serow Fish Farm. M.Sc. Thesis, Fac. Science, Cairo Univ., Egypt.

Blanar, A.C.; Munkittrick, R.K.; Houlahan, G.; Maclatchy, L.D. and Bond, C.E. (1979): Biology of Fishes. Saunders College Publishing, Philadelphia, Pennsylvania, USA.

Chapman, H.D. and Pratt, P.F. (1978): Methods of Analysis for Soils, Plants and Waters. Univ. California Div. Agric. Sci. Priced. 4034.

Fent, K. (2007): Ökotoxikologie. Georg Thieme Verlag, Stuttgart, 2007.

Galli, P.G.; Crosa, G.; Mariniello. L.M.; Ortis, M. and D'Amelio, S. (2001): Water Quality as a Determinant of the Composition of Fish Parasite Communities. Journal of Hydrobiologia, 452: 173-179.

Gheorghiu, C.; Cable, J.; Marcogliese, D.J and Scott, M.E. (2006): Effects of Waterborne Zinc on Reproduction, Survival and Morphometrics of *Gyrodactylus turnbulli* (Monogenea) on Guppies (*Poecilia reticulate)*. Int. J. Parasitology, 37:375-381.

Hussain, S.; Hassan, M.Z.; Mukhtar, Y. and Saddiqui, B.N. (2003): Impact of Environmental Pollution in Human Behaviour and Up-left of Awareness Level Through Mass Media Among the People of Faisalabad city. Int. J. Agric.Biol., 5: 660-661.

Khan R.A., Thulin J. (1991): Influence of Pollution on Parasites of Aquatic Animals. Advances in Parasitology, 30: 201-238.

Lafferty, K.D. and Kuris, A.M. (1999): How Environmental Stress Affects the Impacts of Parasites. Limnol. Oceanogr., 44: 925-931.

Mahfouz, N.B.M. (1997). Effect of Parasitism on Immunity of Cultured Freshwater Fish. Ph D. Thesis, Faculty of Veterinary Medicine, Tanta University, Egypt.

Murray, R.K.D.K.; Rranne, P.A.M. and Rodwell, V.W. (1990): Harper's Biochemistry Publisher, Norwalk, Connecticut/ Los Altos, California.

Noor El-Din, A.N. (1997): Studies on the Effect of Water Pollution Along Different Sites of the River Nile on the Survival and Production of Some Freshwater Fishes. Ph.D. Thesis, Zoology Dep, Fac. Science, Cairo Univ., Egypt.

Osman H.A.M.; Ismaiel, M.M.; Abbas, T.W and Ibrahim, T.B. (2009): An Approach to the Interaction Between Trichodiniasis and Pollution with Benzo-a- pyrene in Catfish (*Clarias gariepinus*). World Journal of Fish and Marine Sciences 1(4): 283-289.

Pathson, C.J. and Nauch, S. R. (1977): Determination of Serum Urea. Anal. Chem., 49: 464-469.

Poulin, R. (1992): Toxic Pollution and Parasitism of Freshwater Fish.

Pritchard, M.H. and Kruse, G.O.W. (1982): The Collection and Preservation of Animal Parasites. Univ. Nebraska, Lincoln, London, 141 pp.

Raef, A.M.; El-Ashram, A.M. and El-Sayed, N.M. (2000): Crustacean Parasites of Some Cultured Freshwater Fish and Their Control in Sharkia. Egypt. Vet. J., 28(2): 180-191.

Ranzani-paviva, M.J.T.; Silva-souza, A.T.; Pavanelli, G.C. and Takemoto, R.M. (2000): Hematological Characteristics and Relative Condition Factor (Kn) Associated with Parasitism in *Schizodon borellii* (Osteichthyes, Anostomidae) and *Prochilodus lineatus* (Osteichthyes, Prochilodontidae) of the Paraná River, Porto Rico region, Paraná, Brazil. Acta Scientiarum, Maringá, 22(2): 515-521.

Reitman, S. and Frankel, S. (1957): Colorimetric Composition of Glutamic Oxaloacetic and Glutamic Pyruvic Transaminases, Am. J. Clin. Pathol., 28: 53-56.

Roberts, R.S.(1981) Patologia de los peces. Madrid, Mundi-prensa, pp: 336.

Rock, R.C.; Walker, W.G. and Jennings, C.D. (1987): Nitrogen Metabolites and Renal Function. In: Tietz, N.W., ed. Fundamentals of Clinical Chemistry, 3rd Ed Philadelphia: W.B. Saunders, pp: 669-704.

Ruben, A.P.; Asbjorn, L.V.; Lars, E.W.F. and Antonio, B.S.P (2006): Effects of Aqueous Aluminum on Four Fish Ectoparasites. Biology Journal of the Linnean Society 90(3): 525-538

SURES, B. (2007): Host-parasite Interactions from an Ecotoxicological Perspective. *Parassitologia, 49,* 173-176.

Yang, J. and Chen, H. (2003): Serum Metabolic Enzyme Activities and Hepatocyte Ultra Structure of Common Carp after Gallium Exposure. Zoological Studies, 42(3): 455-461.

Younis, A.A.E. (1999): Effect of Some Ectoparasites on the Blood and Serum Constituents of *Oreochromis niloticus* Fish with Referring to Treatment. Beni Suif. Vet. Med. J., 9(3): 341-351.

# Index